Teaching Children through the Environment

Pamela Mays

HODDER AND STOUGHTON
LONDON SYDNEY AUCKLAND TORONTO

British Library Cataloguing in Publication Data

Mays, Pamela
  Teaching children through the environment.
  1. Environmental education – England
  2. Human ecology – Study and teaching
  (Elementary) – England
  I. Title
  372.8'3   GF28.E/

  ISBN 0 340 35902 1

First published 1985
Copyright © 1985 Pamela Mays

Printed and bound in Great Britain for
Hodder and Stoughton Educational,
a division of Hodder and Stoughton Ltd,
Mill Road, Dunton Green, Sevenoaks, Kent,
by Page Bros (Norwich) Ltd.

Set in 11/12 pt Linotron Plantin by
Rowland Phototypesetting Ltd, Bury St Edmunds, Suffolk

Contents

1

What is the Environment?

The scene is in a small, happy nursery school. Ben, who is nearly five years old, makes incessant journeys up and down the room, sometimes running or hopping, sometimes on a scooter, but always humming as he goes. Kate, aged four years and one month, is a great holder of conversations, tempting others by means of imaginative little overtures into talking with her. Diddy, who is just over five, is a quiet boy, spending a lot of his time sitting on a big cushion reading or fitting things together. All these children are very young, all are markedly different from each other, and all are exploring their environment.

Ben, Kate and Diddy were three of twelve children between the ages of three and five studied by a group of students and myself. Our aim was to examine the ways in which the children dealt with their environment and, if we could, to gain some insight into how they saw themselves in it. We were inspired in our undertaking by a sense of unease. 'Environmental studies' had been written into the timetable. We felt an urgent obligation to hurry out and count the buses in the High Street or draw the wild flowers growing by the river, but these ideas filled us with gloom. On talking it over with each other, we realised that this was because we were not sure what we were supposed to be doing. Moreover, we felt that beginning in this way was putting the cart before the horse. We knew too little about how young children cope with their environment to be sure of the impact of such experiences. We decided to begin by finding out.

The nursery we used gave the children as much freedom of activity as possible. The teacher and her assistant helped and encouraged the children to do whatever they wished, only intervening in cases of tears or fighting, which were rare. In short, the children were, as nearly as possible, free to behave in a way natural to them. This is an important point, for there is no such thing as a completely free environment; the environment itself acts as a constraining influence on the individual. In this school, there were sand and water, plentiful toys, books, puzzles and a climbing-frame and also paint and clay; the children were as free as they could be.

Our method was for each student to observe one child for one hour at the same time on a Friday of each week. Everything the child did or said during the hour was recorded so that at the end of the observation periods we had a series of information charts.

We learnt a great deal. We found that it was impossible to study the children's environments without studying the children themselves. What emerged was a series of portraits of twelve vivid, intensely different, personalities. These personalities had contrasting strategies for dealing with their world, but they also showed much in common. Most striking was the way in which the children took the initiative in coping with their environment. Equally so was the breathtaking speed at which events took place. Let us take, for example, Cassy, a little girl of four years and six months. At 11 a.m. Cassy started a jigsaw, at the same time helping a boy with his jigsaw and carrying on an argument with another girl. At 11.05 a.m. she jumbled up the jigsaw and went to hold a little boy's hand. Then she had a conversation with the helper. At 11.10 a.m. she was pretending to be a police lady. At 11.11 a.m. she threatened another girl for pushing her and then busied herself arranging pegs in the peg-board and putting them away in the cupboard. Then, at 11.15 a.m., Cassy took a little boy by the hand in order to show him the hyacinths. She had only been in the room fifteen minutes. In the rest of the hour, Cassy played with her friends in the Wendy house, not at families, incidentally, but at pretending to be cats; then she changed the game into cooking and housework and had numerous conversations both with other children and the teacher. By twelve noon, not surprisingly, she was tired out and sucking her thumb.

We learnt from these and other similar observations that children act *in* the environment, taking the initiative. One cannot therefore separate the environment from the person acting in it.

We tried to explain another connected feature, that the environment of these children was packed with rapidly occurring and absorbing events. Of course it resulted from the nature of the children because it was they who created the events. It appeared primarily to arise from their intense responsiveness, a responsiveness typical of early childhood and one which becomes modified later by the older child's greater powers of abstraction. The inability of these young children to concentrate on any one activity for any length of time also played its part, though this did not mean that their concentration was shallow. On the contrary, they were completely absorbed in whatever they happened to be doing. We might note, though, the importance of these events. Adults may well think of the outside world as comprised of trees, buildings and hills, but to children, what is interesting in the world is what is happening in it.

Their world is also full of people. In this nursery school, the teacher and her helper were clearly seen as 'parent' figures: calm, strong and kindly. Their authority was never questioned and there was not a single incident recorded of violent behaviour towards either of them. This, of course, is how fortunate, loved young children do see the adults in their world. A different situation existed between the children. During the hour, there would be many occasions when one child would be helpful to another. Sometimes a child would comfort a friend in a moment of intense grief, or show a companion something of interest, like the gerbil, or the spring flowers growing in a pot. Many a pleasant conversation was carried on. Almost as frequently arose violent quarrels, shouting matches and short-lived fights. We counted these. One child engaged in fourteen co-operative incidents and seven quarrels during the hour. The real war, however, was being fought not between the children, but actually within each child. It was the battle between the desire to be good and loved on the one hand, and strong egocentricity on the other. The incidents reflected the growing social dimension of the children's personalities and showed us something else about young children's environment, that it is the place where they come to terms with other people.

It is a popular view that young people are extremely active physically and this we found to be true. In fact, the many kinds of physical activity engaged in by the children, and the reasons we surmised for their doing so, would have made a study in themselves. A great deal of time was taken up playing on the climbing-frame, scooting up and down, or simply running about. Outside in the play area, the children crawled up the grassy banks, climbed the fence or kicked a ball. Every child engaged in physical activity at least once during the hour, but some engaged in it ten, seventeen or twenty times. One activity was surprising in its great popularity: it was making a journey. Some children seemed to spend most of their time travelling backwards and forwards. Chris and Susy, for one reason or another, made as many as twenty journeys during the hour and the average was over eleven. Why was physical activity so popular? Some of it must have stemmed from the sheer need of young, growing bodies to exercise themselves, and so activities like climbing and rolling about were engaged in for their own sakes. There seemed to be more to it than that, however, because there was something compulsive about the children's need to travel round the room; moreover, journeys were often undertaken with surprising regularity, one every two or three minutes on the part of the most active children, and the younger children, those under four, were on the whole more eager travellers than the older ones. We concluded that moving through their physical environment is one way in which young children come to know it. It is as if they are using their own bodies as measuring instruments.

All the children used speech. Sometimes words were used to express their feelings, as when Lee, who was four years old and one month, exclaimed suddenly and without apparent cause, 'I've been annoyed.' At other times words were used to give definition to what was occurring in the environment, or to a child's activity. Lee, for example, explained to herself as she heaped sand into a container, 'I'm making jellies.' Such a statement of course approaches hypothesis-making, valuable because all the resulting activities then fall into a pattern. Just over half the children talked to themselves in these kinds of ways during the hour in which they were observed. They used language in order to define, control and explore their environment.

Holding a conversation was an extremely popular occupation. Several children were great talkers, often walking away while doing something else. Only one child did not talk at all during the hour; most spoke to someone else on between two and fifteen occasions. These conversations rarely followed the rules of adult encounters. Kate, for example, asked another little girl, 'Are you my friend?' The little girl responded by reprimanding Kate for tasting the water with which she was playing, to which Kate replied, 'It's not dirt.' She asked again, 'Are you my friend?' Her companion replied, 'Yes, but I won't be in a minute.' Kate then said, 'Your supper's going to be cooked in a minute,' but her friend ran off. A conversation implies the inclusion and an awareness of someone else in one's environment; it involves reaching out and exploring the reality of the other person's existence; it means compromise; it is an exploration of the environment in human terms.

If we define an intellectual activity as one which enables a child to learn about the world, then it is clear that these young children were intensely intellectual, often using the equipment provided for them in the school. In one way or another, they were thinking and experimenting all the time. Much of it took place during their so-called 'play'. They built out of bricks and Lego, put together jigsaw puzzles, drew pictures and practised writing, but sometimes they worked in unconventional ways. Chris, who was four years and two months and a thoughtful little boy, spent a long time slotting plastic bricks together, making various shapes. Then he became absorbed in a book, not incidentally reading it, but turning it round this way and that, so that he could see how it looked from various angles. Only two children did not attempt any kind of intellectual activity during the hour in which they were observed; most worked in this way at least twice. Once again, far from being passive inhabitants of the environment, they were the explorers, the initiators.

Max was one of the youngest of the children observed. He was three years and two months. The following extract covers his activities over a period of six minutes.

11.14 a.m. Crawls with another boy on all fours making growling noises; hides under a table. Picks up a toy and uses it as a gun to shoot a girl. Moves to the pictures, points the gun at them and says, 'Kill you!'
11.16 a.m. Runs to helper and says, 'Kill you!' Sits on a carpet with another boy and girl, then follows the helper and says, 'Got big gun.'
11.20 a.m. Follows teacher with a gun and says, 'I'm shooting you. I'm going to help you and kill you!'

Most people who have anything to do with young children will recognise this kind of episode. It is fantasy; that is, when the individual acts from within his (her) own mental world, a world which is not bound by the logic and reasoning that we associate with maturity. In the mature adult, fantasy is at the root of much creativity; in the very young it has a more complex significance. Max was experimenting with different roles in life, first as a fierce animal and then as a powerful, dangerous person with a gun. He was trying them out, as well as the effects of his own aggression, in the safety of the nursery school. He may also have been attempting to resolve conflicting attitudes towards his teacher; after all, he assured her that he was both going to help *and* kill her. Although fantasies of this kind have a deeply personal significance, they also serve as a bridge between the child's own world and the one beyond it. That is, they too have an environmental significance. On many occasions they are a kind of hypothesis-making, a 'what happens if I do this?' experiment; on other occasions they are ways of looking at the world from another point of view, on all fours as a cat or a dog perhaps, or as those much favoured 'pretend' figures of young children: doctors, parents and nurses. It's nice to be these important and powerful people in society as well, instead of being little and helpless and in a nursery school.

Max broke off his fantasy and went off and did something else, but he returned to it continually throughout the hour. This, too, is typical of young children. Most of these we observed worked on two or three fantasies during the time we were with them; often they coloured whatever else went on. Mental life, this told us, is carried on at various levels at the same time, and a single action can have relevance to them all.

Considering this, we were led to realise that what is perceived by the individual in the outer world takes on a many-coloured significance in his, or her, inner mental life. We could not come to this by observation, of course, because one cannot see what is going on within another person's head; we did it by recalling our own memories of childhood. Nearly everybody had memories of quite simple objects, like a swing, a gate and even an old pair of curtains, that held a meaning for the individual far beyond that of its immediate use. These objects were associated with comfort, love and also a sense of adventure. It is not too far-fetched to assume that the same was true of the children in the nursery school. There is then a two-way traffic between the individual and his environment. Fantasy is one bridge.

Fantasy is part of the young child's strategy in handling his environment. So also, we found, was the children's awareness of their own bodies. It has already been mentioned how we suspected that their fondness for journeys and travelling up and down was a means of measuring up their environment by means of their own pace-making. As well as this they all sucked their thumbs, tugged their hair, held an ear or curled up their legs. Their own bodies were real to them. They were part of the environment.

When the observations were complete, we drew up an activity profile for each child. Seven activities emerged as particularly relevant, namely, physical activity of various kinds, fantasy, creative activity, intellectual work, talking to oneself, handling oneself and holding a conversation. Each activity was represented by a block three centimetres wide, and three millimetres were drawn downward for each occasion when a child engaged in a particular occupation. A dotted line was used to indicate when a child did not participate at all. The profiles of three of the children,

Activity profiles of nursery school children

Chris: 4 years 2 months, boy

Physical activities

Fantasy

Creative

Intellectual

Talking to self

Handling self

Conversations

Cassy: 4 years 6 months, girl

Physical activities

Fantasy

Creative

Intellectual

Talking to self

Handling self

Conversations

Diddy: 5 years 2 months, boy

Physical activities

Fantasy

Creative

Intellectual

Talking to self

Handling self

Conversation

Chris, a boy of four years and two months, Cassy, a girl of four years and six months, and Diddy, a boy of five years and two months, are reproduced opposite. They represent both the children as personalities and the ways in which they interacted in their environment. The two canot be separated.

The children were clearly very different from each other. Cassy was one of the world's great talkers; Chris did not talk a great deal but explored his world physically; Diddy was the intellectual of the group. These differences indicate an important implication for the teacher; the environment of young children needs to be as rich and as varied as possible, with opportunities for many kinds of activity, so that every child can work out his or her own strategy.

Some years ago, I went down to the park with my own children and the two-year-old son of a neighbour. There we found a huge, old oak tree. The two-year-old was fascinated by it and I was pleased, preparing in my own mind a little explanation as to how the tree grew, what the leaves were for, and so on. Then I realised that what he was asking, which he did by means of a mixture of speech and gesture, was whether the jagged pieces of bark on the tree were teeth, and whether they would bite him. Most people will have experienced the sudden sweeping away of the ground beneath one's feet by someone whose sense of reality is, quite simply, different from one's own. It raises a profound question. At what age do children see the world as we do? Quite clearly, environmental studies, and indeed teaching of any sort, are not going to be very meaningful if teachers and taught have vastly dissimilar perceptions of reality.

Many people have given thought to this. An interesting and thorough piece of research has been carried out by Aggernaus and Haugsted in Copenhagen.[1] They asked at what point the world becomes real to children in the same sense that it is real to adults. They postulated that an object is 'real' with reference to several categories. For example, a lamp can be seen as real in the sense that it can be switched on, that is, with regard to its behavioural relevance. A lamp can be real when it is recognised as being experienced in at least two modalities, in that it can be both seen and touched. Again, it is seen as real when its independent existence has been accepted, when it is realised that it exists even when nobody is looking at it, or reading by it, or thinking about it. Aggernaus and Haugsted, working with three- to six-year-olds, investigated at what age children understood objects as real in the senses defined above. They suggest that while a normal three-year-old tends to confuse imaginary and real objects, this tendency is declining by the fourth year and, by the sixth, has disappeared altogether. They suggest also that, from the age of about four, normal children can differentiate positive from negative qualities of sensation, that is, they know that 'seeing with the eyes' is different from 'seeing with the thoughts'. In normal three-year-olds there is a tendency to magical thinking, which again disappears by the time the children are six. Lastly, some time between the ages of three and five children come to

7

realise that they cannot change the world simply by their thoughts. In other words, the general conclusion of Aggernaus and Haugsted is that, by about the age of six, the child's view of his (her) environment, his sense of reality, approaches that of the adult. Careful studies along these lines would be appreciated showing how older children, too, see the world.

So far in this chapter, we have tacitly implied that the environment is that which is outside the child. Many teachers of environmental studies would, however, define it as that which exists outside the school. There is a validity in this distinction between life in school and what goes on outside it, but the implications have not been examined closely enough and have actually weakened the development of environmental studies as a discipline. We should remember that, to the child, there is only one environment – his, or her, own. The real mystery lies in why the world outside school was ever excluded from the classroom. Many of the reasons are historical and become clearer when we consider the circumstances that underlay the movement towards universal education in the nineteenth century. Much of the impetus came from the need to rescue children from the increasingly harsh environment that came with the industrial revolution. One way of doing this was to put them into school. In a sense, schools were actually refuges from the world outside, so that it is not surprising that there was seen to be little joy in sallying out there once more. This isolation of children in school was reinforced by the popular view of them at the time as easily distracted, basically naughty, creatures for whom education had to be a kind of strait-jacket. The windows of many schools built in the nineteenth century, and indeed of those built in the early years of this, had windows placed well above eye-level, presumably so that the captives inside could not look out. In some ways nowadays the emphasis has changed, but in others it remains the same. The emphasis in education is increasingly to help children towards an understanding of their own society, not to shy away from it, and children in school are no longer seen as prisoners. Child-centred education has done away with the view that knowledge has to be poured into children like liquid into empty vessels and has emphasised their need to be allowed to explore naturally, reaching understanding in their own way. The environment outside school, with all its richness and variety, is seen as life's laboratory.

Nevertheless, in spite of these changes, schools remain apart from what goes on outside them, simply because their underlying ethos is unique. They are places of learning, and much of this learning has to take place in school; it would never be discovered by children on their own; it has to be taught.

With these considerations in mind, we should ask ourselves in what respects the school environment and that outside differ, and better still, how each can contribute to the other.

One characteristic they have in common, is that the learning that goes on in both, whether inside school or outside it, is of the same kind. It is intellectual, and its raw material consists ultimately of concepts and ideas.

Frequently it is assumed that an environmental study is conc
the physical and the material, and with science subjects rathei
the arts. It means a lot of counting of things like buses and du
rarely deciding which local community is leading a better life.
no study can be concerned merely with the physical and the ....rial,
simply because these do not exist by themselves. Even counting buses and
dustbins implies some understanding of the concepts which underlie
them, concepts incidentally which might not exist in other societies. On
the level of simple perception, each act transforms the object perceived
and makes it unique to the individual.

The sheer exuberance and variety of life outside school act as
tremendous stimuli to learning. There are to be found, moreover, people,
animals and a complexity and magnitude of events that cannot be matched
in the classroom. Yet the skills learnt in the classroom help children to
order and refine what they have experienced outside it. They are given the
opportunity and the time to reflect, to test the knowledge gained and to
carry it further. If they learn, for example, about a town in America, that
in itself will tell them something about their local town, because towns the
world over have a lot in common; if they learn about the lives in factories of
the children of the early nineteenth century, they will be finding out about
their own lives. One process complements the other.

The environment outside school differs from that within it along the
human dimension. Within school there is a simplified social structure.
The young child will meet the head, the teachers and other children. Most
of his (her) waking day will be spent in the company of children of his own
age. The relationships he forms will be working relationships of a particular kind. Outside, the situation is very different. Not only are there many
more people, but they range in age from babies to old age pensioners, they
do not necessarily agree in outlook, in the work they do or in what they
want out of life. The relationships the child experiences will be complex
and subtle, from the close bond that binds him to his parents, to the
commercially-based but cheery one he has with the lady who sells him
sweets in the corner-shop. Moreover, it is the human experience to be
found outside school that illuminates the academic disciplines. Our ears
have continually reverberated in recent years to complaints by various
investigators that school learning, particularly in mathematics, is dis-
gracefully poor because it is 'unreal'. School-leavers, even responsible
adults, are unable to solve even the simplest mathematical problem; we are
told, in fact, that some even run away rather than face their interrogator.
Yet outside school walls, thousands of mathematical problems are happily
solved every day, and the very people who run away from the tests can be
found wallpapering the front room, buying seed for the budgie and doing
the football pools. The truth is that many apparently abstract problems are
really human ones when set in the context of everyday life. Once removed
from this context and put into a form like, 'If X is two-thirds the age of Y
and Y is thirty, how old is X?' – something one would never be asked in

real life – they become boring, frightening and insoluble. The environmental study, based as it can be on relevant human experiences, can do a lot to put things right.

The world at large is also the world of events, the place where things happen. The kind of things that can happen and the scale on which events take place are much more diverse, exciting and instructive than anything that can happen inside school. Events can range from the miniscule to the earth-shaking, from the discovery of a strange cat sitting in one's garden to a violent thunder-storm, or the news that inflation is up again. Events in the world at large can be very exciting, but their significance goes deeper than that, for they instruct us in the laws by which our lives are ordered. These laws may be human and controlled by society, or physical and quite beyond our influence. The thunder-storm is an example of the latter kind, while inflation has to do with human society. As for the cat sitting in the garden, well, that is the result of all kinds of things, including a human life-style that entails building homes and which, in England certainly, values friendship with animals, not to say the curiosity of the cat. Events teach children to understand these laws and conventions; they also teach them to distinguish between the various kinds of laws that govern our existence. One distinction which children generally can make by the age of about eight is that between social conventions, which are changeable, and physical laws, which are not. Young children are well aware of the significance of events, even if they cannot put their feelings into words. That is why they will often question adults so closely when something seemingly quite everyday and unimportant occurs. Why do the dustmen come on Wednesday, a little girl might ask, why not on another day? Suppose they *don't* come on a Wednesday one week, will they come on another day? Suppose you are ill and don't put your dustbin out, what happens then and will they be cross? The questions are endless, and so is the learning.

The environment outside school helps young children to develop intellectual and cognitive skills of many kinds. Because of the great variety of phenomena there, all kinds of hypotheses can be formulated and tried out. They may be scientific, like finding out whether it rains more during the night or during the day, or they may be aimed at illuminating human nature, like seeing whether the lollipop lady is nicer when you smile at her. Problems have to be solved as well, and this means that the individual has to be resourceful and able to weigh up evidence, the pros and cons. If a bicycle tyre is flat, several possible explanations have to be explored and eliminated before it can be mended, and usually they quickly are. The consequences of a flaw in reasoning cannot be avoided as they sometimes can in school, or at least be embodied in an ineffectual form like a cross instead of a tick. The tyre remains flat. These are the very skills that children need in school, of bold hypothesis-forming, balanced judgement and reasoning. Added to this, in the out-of-school environment, young children can be active, creative and learn in ways natural to themselves.

Years ago, Piaget demonstrated that the young child inhabits a different mental world from that of the adult, and that he/she travels through several stages before his/her thinking is mature. Recently there has been a great deal of investigation into how this journey is completed. One question is crucial: whether cognitive development is step-by-step, inevitable and single-line, or whether, and to what degree, it is influenced by environmental factors. From our point of view, this resolves itself into a reassessment of the importance of the environment in education. Recent research has made a considerable contribution to the discussion, which can be illustrated here by its application to one field of knowledge, that of geography. Geography teachers are well aware that it takes young children some time before they can truly understand a map. Yet it has been shown that sheer familiarity with an area is a factor in the ability to master complexity, differentiation and abstraction in a map. In other words, familiarity with the material can push a child, in Piagetian terms, from the pre-operational to the operational stage.[88] The significance of the environmental study hardly needs emphasising, for it would appear that in allowing young children free and ample contact with that which they know well, their own environment, we are stimulating their intellectual development.

Demonstrably, the out-of-school environment enhances those skills which children need in the classroom. Equally, children need what they are taught in the classroom in order to interpret their environment. One can argue that the academic disciplines are themselves ways of interpreting life, originating in men's and women's attempts to make sense of the world in which they find themselves. The disciplines differ from each other in the kind of questions they ask, the terminology of their language and the conceptualisation of the answers given, but they all embody a basic perspective.

Geography is rooted in man's view of his environment as a source of food and survival; history looks at the evolution of that environment through time, while biology inquires how living organisms function and survive.

The core material of these disciplines is far from a static affair; on the contrary, it is constantly changing, as new questions are asked, new concepts are formed, and the body of knowledge develops.

This perspective is not all there is to the subjects taught in school, however; they represent no one man's or woman's thinking but are the combination of hundreds of years of intellectual exploration, each building on what has gone before. They are part of a shared cultural heritage. It is not possible for any individual, child or adult, to come to an understanding of them unaided; Shakespeare could not have written his plays without the English language, which had evolved many years before his time; Einstein would not have evolved the theory of relativity had he not understood the mathematical thinking of previous centuries. On the humbler scale, the five-year-old working away at his coloured bricks in the infant school is trying to master ideas and concepts that he might never arrive at by himself because they are the products of other people's thinking. The academic disciplines represent the cultural dimension of the environment, when that term is used in its fullest possible sense. It is this cultural dimension that sets school apart from the world outside, making it a place of concentrated intellectual effort. It is why teaching has to take place in school, for nobody arrives at an understanding of botany by skipping gaily into the fields and looking at the buttercups, though the interest may begin there. There is no dichotomy though between a child's learning inside school and what he (she) learns outside it. It is within traditional modes of thinking that he explores his own world and lives in his own society. He does not fully appreciate his own locality until he knows what a town, a factory and a farm are; he cannot really understand the buttercup he has noticed in the field until he realises the importance of roots, stems and flowers. Child-centred ultimately means subject-centred.

Considering the popularity of environmental studies and the part these can play in education, surprisingly few questions are asked about children's lives out of school. Do most of our children live in towns or rural areas, in homes of their own or on housing estates? What do they do in their spare time? How far do they travel? We need to know exactly what the out-of-school environment is. Government publications provide information of a general kind. In Greater London, 29 per cent of children between the ages of two and nine live in flats, many of them above the second floor. In the rest of Britain, 7 per cent live in similar circumstances, with the exception of Wales, where the proportion is 1½ per cent. There are striking class differences – 96 per cent of the children of professional parents live in a conventional house and none at all, apparently, in high-rise flats. Far fewer of the children of manual workers have parents who own a house. This means that the teacher in a school drawing its children from a poor, working-class area will not profitably be able to refer to gardens. The children will, however, be well acquainted with streets, shops, gangs and television.[2]

The students and I gained a picture of the out-of-school lives of the children we observed in the nursery school by getting to know their parents and talking to them. These very young children had only a restricted area of action, spending a lot of time in their own homes. The streets they knew were those leading from home to school, from home to the local shops and to a nearby park or playing-space. All of them went shopping with their mothers, usually on the way home, and that was also when they dropped in at the park for a turn on the swings. On Saturdays, nearly all the children went off to the local supermarket with both parents to do the weekly shopping. They used the car if they had one. On Sundays, they often went off in the car again, frequently on surprisingly long journeys, in order to visit other members of the family. Aunts and grannies were popular! Rather surprisingly, for these were not well-off parents, there seemed quite a compulsion to take the children on a special excursion at the weekend, if not to granny, then to the local fair, or to the seaside, or to a place of historical interest. The lives of the children then, centred on their own homes and their immediate vicinity. Nevertheless, every child watched television, often for several hours a day, which meant that they were aware, albeit dimly, of the existence of people outside their everyday lives, like the weather-man, the newscaster and the introducers of children's programme. For people under five they led quite sophisticated lives. Children in other parts of the country may live in similar environments; on the other hand, they may not.

Even when areas are geographically close together, the environments in which children live may be vastly dissimilar. The following three studies were made in localities not twenty miles away from each other. One investigated the outdoor leisure activities of forty children aged between eight and twelve, living on a council estate in inner London in Putney.[3] The estate consisted of eight-story tower blocks, with some maisonettes. Council rules prohibited games on the grass areas; cycling and tree-climbing were also forbidden. No pets could be kept. Near the estate was a large wild common, with foxes, rabbits, streams and many wild flowers. However, parents discouraged their children from going there because of the danger of child assault. There was also a park in the area, again with a wild area and a lake. Here, once more, tree-climbing, the lighting of fires and tunnelling were forbidden by the local by-laws and guard-dogs were used during the school holidays in order to prevent damage to council property. All of this, of course, presents the familiar picture of children living in superficially pleasant but actually restrictive and intensely hostile surroundings. It is a picture familiar to many teachers. What, then, did these children do when they were out of school? What was their true environment? Mainly, they played in the immediate area of the flats. The girls liked dressing up, hopscotch and roller-skating and they often went shopping. The boys went in for ball games and chasing round the buildings. Many of the children, but the boys particularly, formed into gangs, fighting with billiard cues and bottles. These activities went on far into the evening and, in the summer, even very young children under five played outside until 9.30 p.m.

In spite of the restrictions in the park, the groundsman complained of signs of camps and dams being built in the wild area, as well as tunnelling going on. There were traces also of a cycle track.

Hillingdon, the subject of another investigation, lies a few miles away from the first area studied. The leisure pursuits of a similar group of children were investigated.[4] Hillingdon has remained comparatively undeveloped until fairly recently, so that it still possesses some naturally wild areas. Nevertheless, the children were found to remain closely within the area of their own homes because of the high accident rate on the busy main roads that run through the borough, and because of the dangers hidden in unused land, like gravel-pits. The Hillingdon children spent their time in much the same way as those in Putney, but this study went further, in that it asked the children what they would like to do if they had the chance.

Unanimously, boys and girls alike said they wanted more adventure and more intensely physical activities. All asked for horse-riding, judo, swimming and camping. Girls as well as boys wanted to play football; girls, but not boys, requested cookery and needlework. Organised clubs were not wanted at all. When asked why, the children explained that they were bossed about too much.

The third study took place in the Great London area of Waltham Forest, where 220 boys and 253 girls from six schools answered a questionnaire.[5] They were between ten and eleven years old. Unlike those of Putney and Hillingdon, many of these children lived in houses and had gardens; 395 lived in a house and 434 had a garden. Most of their families had two or three children; 40 had more than five. Asked to write down the five occupations they most enoyed out of school, football was overwhelmingly the most popular with the boys, then watching television, reading and playing with friends. The girls liked playing with friends most of all, then watching television, reading and listening to records. The girls also enjoyed looking after their pets, helping at home and swimming.

The Waltham Forest children wrote down how they spent their time during the previous evening, from 5 p.m. onwards. Of the girls, 181 watched television some of the time, 38 helped in the house, 18 played in a park or street, three took the dog out; others went shopping or visited friends. Of the boys, 192 watched television some of the time, 70 played in a park or the street, 24 read, 18 followed a hobby and two (with whom one has some sympathy) did nothing. The same pattern emerged at the weekend. Like the children in the other areas, nobody wanted more clubs and nearly everybody disliked organised activities.

Investigations like these tell us a good deal, both about the out-of-school environment and about the children themselves. It would seem that most young children, for one reason or another, do not stray far from home, so that is the area they know best. In the physical sense, their environment is restricted. Although, geographically speaking, children may live fairly close to each other, their environments may be quite dissimilar. Reading the studies, it is clear that the Waltham Forest children lead different lives from those in Putney; in fact they came through as different children. Yet, in the ways in which they long to explore their environments, all the children have much in common. It is true that the Hillingdon girls have a yearning for football which does not haunt those of Putney and Waltham Forest, but the children of all three areas are crying out for physical activity and, above all, for freedom. There is an obvious lesson here for teachers, an obvious way, too, in which the environmental study can contribute to education, in that it can be so designed as to allow children opportunities for adventure and exploration in their own way.

Nearly all the children had active hobbies. Hobbies, too, are a means to children of exploring the environment, not just in the physical sense, but in the social and cultural sense as well. Following their hobbies, young children often display staggering discipline and dedication. This area of their lives has been aptly described by Kevin McGrath as constituting 'an underground curriculum' of their own.[6] Often these interests can be used in schools and in pursuit of them the children will work individually. In fact they usually prefer to carry out their explorations by themselves, provided the opportunity is given to them. McGrath, amusingly, quotes one twelve-year-old girl, whose hobby was playing the organ, as saying, 'I would prefer less help from my father as I'm better than him so his information is useless.'

We should always look at the environments of children, and their lives, sensitively. If we do not, we miss a lot and we also run the risk of distorting their view of life. I once read an account describing the existence of children in an inner city area and the work the author was doing with the deprived boys and girls who live there. She described the dreariness of the run-down streets, the council flats, the absence of trees or of any natural life. This shocked me, as I happen to know the area very well. The young children I knew there did not see their lives as dreary, nor themselves as deprived. There is a thriving street market, with colour, lights and people; so popular was this with the five-year-olds whom I was looking after that we used to wander down there as a treat, listening to the busy hum of voices and looking at all the cheap toys. One stall used to sell scraps of material for a few pence and you could likewise pick up glass beads, odd cups and saucers and bits of wood. A couple of minutes away is a wonderful railway station and another favourite occupation was to stand on the bridge and watch the express trains roaring through, or study the people hurrying on and off the platforms. Nature wasn't far away. The father of one of the children worked on the Thames, and after a short bus ride, the children could see tiny, glittering silver fish swimming in the water. This father also showed us where a great eel lived, apparently trapped behind a stone. Further, in this down-at-heel inner city borough, there exists an exceptionally fine public library, with a staff who are always eager to cater for the needs of young children, and who lay on special courses and talks for them in the school holidays. Life was exciting, and while not discounting the stresses under which many people are forced to live in the inner cities, true deprivation is a much deeper and subtler affair than that of physical surroundings.

The discussion so far in this chapter has centred on the question, 'What is the environment?' We can summarise by saying that the environment is everything that is outside ourselves, including, in a subtle way, individuals themselves. It includes not only physical phenomena but people, culture, and ideas as well. Even this is a simplification, for some aspects of the environment fall into no particular category, being the result of interactions that are not necessarily constant. Television programmes, for example, are part of nearly every child's life today, although this would not have been the case thirty years ago. They are the result of art, culture, technology and the outlook and power structure of the many people involved in making them. They are complex.

The environment changes as the individual grows older; it is not constant and it is not a stable entity. The two-year-old lives in a different world from that of the nine-year-old, whose world is, in turn, not the same place as that of a fifteen-year-old.

When we ask how the young child comes to conceptualise the environment and to devise strategies for dealing with it, we are in difficulty. Only part of the answer is known, having been meticulously provided by careful research; much is only partially known, being still sought in the exciting but nebulous areas of intuition and the long experience of those who work with children; a great deal of the answer is completely unknown. All of it needs to be shaped by a coherent body of concepts.

A further difficulty is that there are no commonly agreed ways of analysing the environment. There are no environmental facts in the same sense as there are historical or scientific facts. All we can do is to describe the environment in the terms we have available and to accept that, for the moment, the environmental study represents an intellectual perspective rather than a body of subject matter. We may have to rethink the established academic disciplines if a true science of the environment is to be made possible. They may have to be seen in terms of strategies and interactions rather than in terms of static concepts. The strategies would be those of the individual as he (she) struggles to make sense of, and to use, his environment; the interactions would be those occurring between the individual and the objects and phenomena in the world outside himself. Biology, for example, is concerned with the structure of organisms, but even structures can be seen in terms of interactions. From the moment of conception until the moment of death, an organism can be conceptualised as an unending series of interactions modifying an ever-changing structure. History is full of events, and these may be seen as the culmination of a whole series of human responses to an environmental situation.

We will need also, if we are to build environmental studies in schools into a subject of any real depth, to rethink, or rather to put into a new perspective, what we know about young children. It is possible, even popular at the present time, to compile taxonomies of children's skills as they develop their understanding of the traditional school subjects. We know that, at the age of five, they should be able to count up to ten and that they know what 'long ago' means in history. No such taxonomy of skills and concepts has been compiled for environmental studies. We will, however, attempt to make some generalisations as to what should be considered.

Sheer physical growth and the development of sensory perception must be important to young children as they evolve their environmental strategies. The nine-year-old, being bigger and stronger than the three-year-old, can travel much further, so that his (her) environment is more extensive in the physical sense. The world must, quite literally, look different to the under-fives, because research indicates that young children do not perceive all the colours of the spectrum with equal clarity.

Objects will not be seen in the same perspective as that perceived by an adult, for the very reason that young children are much lower on the ground. Anyone doubting this should try going round the room on his or her knees and seeing how everything looks.

As children grow, so they come to know more people. The children who were observed in the nursery school probably only knew the members of their immediate families well, their mothers and fathers, brothers and sisters. A nine-year-old will also have friends and know all sorts of people outside the family. Moreover, the kind of relationships he (she) forms with people will differ from those formed by the four-year-old; as he grows older they are likely to be less egocentric, more able to take into account another person's needs and his own sense of reality. In other words, the human environment changes. This is what an eight-year-old thought about grandmothers: the description was quoted by the Archbishop of Canterbury in the House of Lords during 'The Family in Britain Today' debate on 16 July, 1976.

> Grandmothers don't have to do anything but be there. They should never say, 'Hurry up'. Usually they are fat, but not too fat to tie children's shoes. They wear glasses and funny underwear, and they can take their teeth and gums off. They don't have to be smart, only answer questions like why dogs hate cats and why God isn't married. They don't talk baby-talk like visitors. When they read to us, they don't skip bits or mind if it is the same story over again. Everybody should have one, especially if you don't have television, because grandmothers are the only grown-ups who have time.

Detailed comment would spoil this description, speaking as it does so clearly and so delightfully with the voice of childhood. Suffice it to say that this boy will not see his grandmother in that way when he is ten years older, that he shows in his writing that he already possesses considerable social skills, and that the development of these skills modifies his environment.

Mental motivation is equally important. One aspect of children's developing intellectual powers is their increasing ability to make and handle concepts. Leaving aside the immense and fruitful controversy as to how this is achieved, it is clear that the ability to conceptualise the environment must change it. Once the concept of something simple like a leaf has been grasped (though not so simple when we think about it), or of something difficult like the laws underlying physical change, the environment can be thought about. This, of course brings about the possibility of being able to modify and manipulate, giving the child a powerful environmental strategy.

The converse is true, and this is often overlooked. When a concept is applied to that which is perceived, it does indeed open up new frontiers of thought and control, but it also acts as a kind of strait-jacket, excluding anything that falls outside its own boundaries. In this way, the environment becomes limited. The growing powers of young children's concept-making both expand and contract their world.

It is vital not to underestimate the importance of language. Not only are most concepts expressed in words, but language reaches out into the environment. Even the nursery school children of under five used it to reach each other, to stake out hypotheses and to modify their own and others' perception of reality.

Other mental abilities may seem less dramatic but they are equally significant. One is the ability to remember. Once a child can remember what happened yesterday or the day before, once he (she) can carry in his mind the images of people, animals and objects, he is no longer chained to the immediate; he can think about ideas. His environment correspondingly contains less of the material and physical and more of that which is not immediately perceived. He is removed from the tyranny of the concrete.

A skill which has only recently received attention from psychologists and educationists is the facility the young child develops of classifying information. In these and other skills, like recognising what is like and unlike and in perceiving what is relevant, the human mind acts as a computer. It is probably our growing knowledge of computers that has encouraged us to look at human mental powers in this way. These abilities form part of our strategies for handling the environment, being particularly important in problem-solving. A young child can only solve the problem of why his bicycle tyre is flat, for example, if he can hold in his mind all the possibilities and eliminate them one by one. Once he can apply this kind of thinking, the environment changes from being a place in which he exists, and becomes a many-faceted area to be explored, investigated and acted upon.

The child's strategy in his environment is immensely complex. It does not remain the same for long, but continually develops. It is the product of many factors: physical, mental, social and cultural. Some aspects of it may be due to inheritance and genetic endowment, others to learning and maturation. There is, as yet, no coherent body of theory or terminology which enables us to describe it. The teacher of environmental studies, though, must always be aware of it, and aim to understand it. It knows no boundaries.

2
Perception and the Environment

Long before they are born, the sensory perception of babies is sensitive, complex and discriminating. Babies are rounded personalities, interacting with the environment in a way that is at once basic and subtle. A great deal of research in the last twenty years has shown that these sensitive individuals are highly aware of what is going on around them. They have a particularly acute sense of hearing and some of them have quite sophisticated tastes in music being, apparently, very much taken with flute music, especially if it is in the key of G. It is not unknown for a pregnant woman to have to leave a conert hall because of the kicking of her unborn baby in response to the lively tempo. Babies are soothed by their mother's heartbeats and this response continues even after they are born, so much so that fractious young babies can be quietened by playing a record to them of all the sounds they must have listened to while still in the womb. It has been shown that excessively loud noise can harm unborn babies; as a result, in countries like Japan, pregnant women are not allowed to work in noisy factories. In other experiments scientists have recorded on ultra-fine equipment the movement the mother's blood makes through the placenta that connects her to her child. Apparently the sounds are rather like those of the waves of the sea as they break endlessly on the shore. Certainly this is an auditory image that remains attractive and nostalgic to many adults throughout their lives.

New-born babies are equally sensitive. One interesting change occurs though in that, while before birth the most acute sense seems to be that of hearing, after birth it rapidly switches to that of sight. Sight is the most vivid form of perception that human beings possess, being very much connected with our mental processes. In general, this reliance on sight distinguishes us from other animals.

To quote from one study undertaken fifteen years ago, the reactions of eighteen new-born Negro babies, or neonates as they are called, to various kinds of visual stimuli were studied. Every week, for eight weeks, the babies were shown their mother's face, a non-live female face (a manikin), and an abstract form (a colander).[7] Their responses were carefully chronicled. These infants, by the second month, could discriminate perfectly between the three forms. Far from what was expected, they paid least attention to their mother's face. The authors concluded that this was because they knew their mothers well already and were anxious to move on to more interesting things. The babies' ability to concentrate improved rapidly during the period of observation, the maximum improvement occurring between the fifth and eighth week. Amusingly, they also developed a mature and sophisticated repertoire of behaviour. If they did not wish to look, they refused to do so. Being only a few weeks old, they were unable to move away, but they rolled their heads, gave just a quick look and looked away or peeped sideways. If all else failed, they closed their eyes. Even in the dry pages of research, these children emerge as vivid characters, reminding us that both perception and behaviour have to be seen in the context of the whole personality. The authors concluded that these new-born babies rapidly became adept not just at distinguishing visual images but at responding to them and controlling them by means of their own behaviour. Helpless and physically vulnerable as they were, these babies were setting out to control their environment.

Young babies are equally aware of sounds, and are able to tell one sound from another. Even at two and three days old they are aware of complex auditory stimuli.[8] Those of between three and eight days react differentially to various kinds of noise. Low continuous tones soothe them, while intermittent sound has less effect.[9] Significantly, it emerges in this area, as in that of visual perception, that a baby's response to sensory experience cannot be considered apart from its development in all aspects as an individual. One investigator, presenting babies of three, six and nine months respectively with recordings of their mothers' voices, found that those of six months became very upset.[10] This was because, by that stage, they had not only formed a very strong attachment to their mothers, but knew that if they could hear them, they should be able to see them as well. Perception is rapidly modified, even at this age, by experience, memory and reasoning.

Simple recognition of the sounds and sights of the environment is not enough. The skills involved would only result in a very simplified representation of the world in which we live. An important ability is that of being able to recognise the representation of an object. This makes possible an infinite variety of ways to learn about the environment. To take a simple example, once we can accept that the picture of a horse represents a horse, we can learn all sorts of things about it, by means of pictures perhaps and later through words, which are a more complex representation, without having to have a horse actually in front of us. Further, an individual who can recognise representation is on the way to grasping the nature of a symbol, which is a kind of shorthand for conveying information and which forms the basis of both language and mathematics.

It would seem that at five months old infants can recognise photographs of live people.[11] At twenty-four months, they are able to transfer from an object to a picture and from a picture to an object; that is, they understand equivalence.[12] The authors of this research suggest that these young children had already formed concepts of the objects shown to them.

Another crucial ability is that of being able to translate information gained from one sense into that of another. When can a child connect the bark of a dog with the image of a dog and know that it is not a cat that is making the noise, or a rattle? In a broad sense, this skill is a basic one to build up the reality of the world, to enable the child to picture life and all its variety in much the same way as an adult does. In a narrow sense it is vital for the formation of concepts and the development of reasoning. We cannot form a concept of anything until we understand the modes of its existence, and we cannot reason or form hypotheses about an object until we have the concept.

It has been shown that infants of 15 to 16 weeks realise when toys have been mismatched with their sounds. They expect a rattle to rattle and are not pleased if it does something else.[13] In the last few years it has been demonstrated that one-year-old children are skilled in cross-model transfer. They are able to gain information about the shape of objects by feeling them with their mouths and can then recognise the object they have just felt.[14] Very young children, then, are able to understand the 'wholeness' of an object.

Babies and young children are often portrayed as egocentric, unable to look at life from any point of view other than their own, locked up in their own private needs, limited memories and misapprehensions. Yet the bulk of research suggests that, as soon as they are born, they start finding ways through their egocentricity, and that many of these ways are based on sensory perception. Even babies of a few months old are capable of following the gaze of an adult.

In this chapter, we are considering the importance of sensory perception to children in helping them to build up a strategy for learning from their environment, so at this point we might draw some conclusions.

The first conclusion is that very young children have extremely sensitive, refined and sophisticated sensory abilities. It is surprising that this has taken so long to be recognised in certain academic circles. Almost every day one can read in the popular press yet another investigation purporting to be new, and always the findings are greeted with surprise. Yet this kind of research has been going on for years. It may be that we are reluctant to accept the full implications of such investigations because they clearly involve some painful rethinking about children. Certainly the research illustrates a lack of communication between those who carry it out and those who have a lot to do with babies and young children in the unforced, natural circumstances of everyday life. The revelations about their abilities cause surprise to very few teachers, and to no mothers.

We can also conclude that sensory perception is bound up with the development of cognitive skills. As the research quoted indicates, the babies used their perceptual abilities in order to form concepts, to draw conclusions and to learn about the laws governing their environment. They were not passive, either; even at a few weeks they set out to explore and to control.

The connection between perception and the building up of a concept can be illustrated, on a simple level, by considering the efforts of a four-year-old in learning about steam and smoke, two phenomena which she will often observe in everyday life. In the early days, she might well conclude that smoke and steam are the same, as they look alike. However, this little girl might notice that they originate in a different way, the smoke coming from a bonfire and the steam from a kettle; they don't feel the same, either, because steam is wet, whereas smoke is dry and leaves dirt on your skin. Neither do they smell the same. Using all these sensory cues, the four-year-old will evolve concepts of both steam and smoke. She will come to understand how they come into being, how they behave, how she can use them. Her concepts are not static affairs, she will go on adding to them, making them more and more complex, for the rest of her life. Language is important in this process; not only does speech enable this little girl to hypothesise and to reason, ultimately it gives her a separate word for each phenomenon, 'steam' and 'smoke'. This is not the end of the story, though. Once the little girl has formed her concepts of steam and smoke, they can be used to recreate the sensory experience. It may be that the word 'steam' will always bring back to her the sound and sight of a bubbling saucepan with the lid angrily bouncing up and down. The word 'smoke' might well remind her, many years on, as it does most of us, of the pungent smell of burning leaves on a sunny Autumn day. The relationship between sensory and cognitive processes is not a simple, one-way matter. They stimulate each other.

Some of the most significant ways in which perception and sensory experience contribute to a child's relationship with his (her) environment are not demonstrable by means of research. This is because they are so pervasive and subtle. A continuous stream of sensory experience is vital for emotional well-being and mental health. In adults, sensory deprivation is the cruellest form of torture. Within a few hours of being blind-folded or hooded and cut off from all outside sensation, the victim will suffer hallucinations and great mental distress. If he (she) is deprived for any length of time the damage can be permanent. His mind has gone. The most dreaded prisons, and those with the highest attempted suicide rate, are those which are clean, modern, and boring. Even children leading lives that pass as normal can suffer from sensory deprivation. Teachers can testify how silent and fearful children can become as a result of living conditions which deny their need for a variety of shape, colour and sound. The senses are our interpreters of the outside world and the balance is delicate. One is reminded of the little girl of three, who burst into tears when she stood outside her back door and saw the vast, empty night sky. 'Why are you crying?' asked her father comfortingly, 'there's nothing there.' She replied, 'But that's what I'm afraid of.' One knows exactly what she meant.

Apart from giving us our terms of reference in the world and providing our bearings in it, it is through our perceptions that we see beauty. Beauty cannot be quantified and the perception of it can rarely be demonstrated, but its significance should never be denied. To some people it is all that makes life worth living. It is order and symmetry and radiance, and young children are very sensitive to it. They respond to beautiful colours and shapes. They respond to beautiful people, too, as anyone who has seen a young child reaching out to touch soft skin or a piece of shining hair will accept.

Perception is at the inner core of the personality. It provides the route out of egocentricity and the strategies by which children reach out into the environment.

It is impossible even to take a walk outside unless one can see, or hear, or both. Further, although we all possess the same senses to a greater or lesser degree, the ways in which the information they provide is used remains a highly individual matter. Psychologists have demonstrated this by asking people to explain what is happening in a simple picture. They always give widely varying interpretations. One might describe a bright, sunny scene; another will see the same picture as eerie and full of hidden menace; to a third it will depict just an everyday happening.

If sensory experience is basic to the development of motor skills and thinking processes, it also underlies the working of the imagination. It is not easy to define imagination, but the word itself gives a clue. It is based on the word 'image' and many images cannot be formed without sensory experience, so that, in yet another sense, perception is behind that creative reaching-out of the personality that transforms the world around it.

We would like to know how the perception of a young child develops. Is there, for example, a steady progression towards improved perception, whether it be in vision, hearing or touch? Does this development follow the conventional learning pattern of progress in leaps and bounds followed by static periods, of upward curves followed by plateaux? How do the various forms of perception become integrated with each other and what is the exact relationship between the cognitive and the perceptual processes? It may be that the integration is only ever partial and that we continue, to a large extent, with two existences on the mental level all our lives, the cognitive and the perceptual, each continually sending messages to the other. Above all, as teachers, we would like to understand the role of experience in the development of these abilities and how such experience can be provided.

We have at present only some of the answers. This is partly due to the kind of research that has been carried out. In order to throw light on two great questions, that of the development of perceptual skills as the child grows older and that of the integration of these abilities with mental and cognitive processes, we need a series of longitudinal studies. These entail making detailed studies of children, at various points in their lives, until patterns emerge. As it is, observations are made on a group of children, all of the same age, in order to elucidate one particular point. At best, the findings can be compared with those obtained from another group of children, this time older. Another shortcoming is that there is a great deal of interest in very young children, especially those under five years of age, but very little work has been done on the perception of older children up to the age of sixteen. Individual differences between children have received hardly any attention. The greatest difficulty is even more fundamental, in that there is no accepted theory of child development into which to fit what findings we have. There is no universally accepted theory of cognition, no theory of perception, but many theories of personality. The fragmented state of research denies us a clear perspective.

In this situation we have to piece together what we do know and use it to the children's advantage. For example, it would be a mistake to assume that children's perception progresses steadily from being imperfect and imprecise in childhood to being complete and efficient in adulthood. This may be the case with some forms of perception, as with that of shades of colour, but in other ways young children are more efficient than adults. They are better at locating particular areas on their skin. One piece of research found that pre-school children of four years old were better than adults at applying spatial analogies, provided that the analogies given them to use were related to their own bodies.[15] They were good at providing the correct answer to the question, 'If this (pictured) mountain had a knee, where would it be?' One would guess also that a child's sense of smell is acute and more sensitive than that of adults, a little researched area. A great deal of research, some of it quoted in this chapter, has proved how discriminating children's perception of sight and sound is.

This leads us to ask a question, essential to try to answer. We have seen that children possess considerable environmental skills. Young babies are well able to integrate the information they obtain from their senses, from their eyes, ears and sense of touch. They have powers of abstraction and can recognise the representation of an object. They make hypotheses about their environment and are well on the way to understanding the laws that govern it and how it works. Further, they are not passive inhabitants, but are inquisitive, explorative and out to control. They do not see the environment solely from their own point of view, but are capable of looking at it from someone else's, as well. If young children are so skilled, what, then, is left for them to do? What makes them, in other words, 'non-adult'? Here we must remember the work of Piaget and researchers like Aggnernaus and Haugsted which demonstrates clearly that children really do think differently in some respects from adults.

Such a question is, of course, immensely complex but it is possible to put forward a few suggestions to answer it. In the first place, the very fact that children are physically different from adults (not necessarily inferior) means that they will think differently. If we take the comparatively simple matter of the ability to recognise colour, for example, it has been suggested that young children acquire colour recognition in the following order; firstly, black as opposed to white, then red, green-yellow, blue, brown, purple-pink-orange, and lastly, grey.[16] Between the ages of two and a half and four years, children improve steadily at naming colours, girls finding it easier than boys, due either to a differential development, or to their superior acquisition of vocabulary. It also appears, from a study of children aged between two and 12, that young children find it easier to perceive the longer wavelengths in conditions of low illumination than they do the shorter wavelengths.[17] That is, they see red and yellow more clearly than they see blue or green. Acuity improved steadily with age, and again girls tend to perceive better with low illumination than do boys.

This is interesting to teachers because it explains why red and yellow are such favourite colours with the under-fives. It so happens that red and yellow are the colours they can see. On this quite simple level, therefore, children will not be thinking along the same lines as adults because they are not receiving the same sensory information.

Another source of disparity is a more complex matter. Young children, we are told, think magically and animistically. A two-year-old boy thinks a tree has teeth and might bite him; a four-year-old girl is grief-stricken because her father has had an accident and she thinks she may have caused it by her own hate feelings; a five-year-old assumes that when he cannot see a table lamp it isn't there. One can see what is missing in the thinking of these children; they have not yet recognised the limitations of their own thoughts and wishes; they have not yet understood the conditions which govern the existence of other objects, and other people. Much of this must be due to sheer lack of experience. The two-year-old concerned with the tree is quite right to think it might bite. After all, he himself has teeth and probably bites. What he is doing, because he doesn't yet know about trees, is using his knowledge of himself to make an analogy and find out more. The four-year-old who is worried about the effects of her negative feelings on the well-being of her father is not being illogical either. How could she know, how do any of us know, that our thoughts are limited in their influence until we find this out by unlimited, slowly acquired and oft-repeated experience? As for the table lamp, until we have gleaned more information about its behaviour, it may well disppear when we can't see it, or may dance around the room singing pop songs for all we know.

The differences between the way in which children think about the world and the way in which we do may simply be due in part to a lack of experience.

Children also lack a social and cultural dimension to their thinking. The implications of this are so subtle and far-reaching that they are not easy to demonstrate. A general way of putting it would be to say that everything we perceive is influenced by the perception of other people. Even on an intellectual level this is true. In the chapter on mathematics, an account is given of the attempts of a Western lecturer to teach a concept like area to students in Papua.[18] They found this concept impossible to grasp, as they did the related areas of width and length, because these ideas were irrelevant in their culture. It is hard for us not to perceive them, even when we are very young. Much of our conversation with others, and especially that between adults and children, is directed towards shaping children's perception so that they perceive what we hold to be important and repress everything else. When a mother remarks to her child, 'The sun is hot,' she is also saying that the heat of the sun is its important characteristic and that its other attributes do not matter so much. Young children have not received the years of cultural conditioning that adults have; they still retain their originality and can surprise us by thinking that it would be nice if the sun were pink, or if a candle threw out flower petals from its flame instead of heat.

The research on young babies quoted in this chapter showed how discriminating they were. However, it is significant that, in these experiments, they were only asked to deal with one thing at a time. They had to distinguish their mother's face from others or fit a sound to an object. One might say that the problems they had to solve were single-faceted; they were only required to hold on to one criterion and to apply it. Mature logical thinking, however, of the kind that solves problems and elucidates the answers, requires a computer-like ability to hold several possibilities in the mind at once and to examine criteria in an orderly fashion one by one. This computer-like ability develops in children slowly, over a long period of time. The beginnings are there, and there is no difference in kind between the thinking of children and that of adults, but the reasoning capacity of children cannot be so wide ranging or so accurate. Mature thinking involves the sorting and using of many criteria of varying kinds and so, by its very nature, it needs time to evolve.

Time is crucial to another process, that of the integration of all information, whether this is gleaned from sensory cues, from reasoning or hypothesising, or from inherited patterns of behaviour. We can take a simple illustration, that of a young boy of four, who, because his colour recognition is not fully developed, sees red and yellow clearly, but not pink or brown. His thinking will be based on this. He might choose to have red wellingtons, red and yellow flowers in his little patch of garden and he might hate his brown raincoat. He might trip over the grey step in front of his house, especially at dusk, because his eyes may not be able to register this colour and he will assume it is not there. However, as this little boy grows up and he is able to perceive more and more colours in all their subtle hues, his thinking will inevitably change because he will have more and increasingly accurate information. When we add to this all the information that comes from experimenting, reasoning and concept-formation, it is clear that such integration must take a very long time. It is a process that continues throughout life and one which divides the child from the adult. It may be that new light would be thrown on children's thinking if we thought about it less esoterically and more in terms of the maturation of processes.

The great question to answer is how far, and in what ways, the environmental study can contribute to the development of sensory perception in young children. It is of help if teachers remember the following. Sensory perception is vital to the building up of an environmental strategy in the young child; in fact other more abstract and cognitive skills are based on it. A continuous stream of sensory experience is necessary for mental and emotional health, and for the growth of the personality. Sensory perception is a function of the whole personality, experience, memory and reasoning contributing to it. There are individual differences in perceptual skills, not only in the varying degrees of ability but in the ways in which these are applied. The processes involved are long-term and cannot be hurried, development being a matter of both maturation and learning.

It is clear that the paramount need of children is for a continuous and varied stream of experience. Everything matters. Some of this experience can be provided in the classroom, but even more can be gained from outside, where there is so much variety and stimulus. Every trip taken round the park or the shops, every painting done in the classroom, every bit of coloured cellophane peered through and exclaimed upon, all are worth while. Every aspect of teaching is important, not just conscientious-ness in providing the children with a wealth of materials, but also in helping them to use language and to think. Good number work aids perception. Because children differ in their perceptual skills, and because perception is at the core of personality, children need freedom to experi-ment. The school day, and the classroom, should be organised to allow this. Endless time is necessary; perception is not a subject that can be placed on the school timetable and taught, rather does it pervade all activities, in and out of school.

Apart from being sensitive to these broad needs, it is possible to help children more specifically and most teachers are aware of this. Some forms of perception are of greater significance to the higher mental function than others, and most significant of all is probably sight. This may be, in part, a reflection of the kind of society in which we live and the kind of thinking it values. Were ours a hunting society, in which the ability to track and identify by means of smell was paramount, we might place the emphasis elsewhere. Be that as it may, intellectual skills in our culture are rooted in the perceptual. We can see this by considering a child of five learning to read and by bearing in mind the constant interplay between his experience of his environment, his facility in handling sensory cues coming from more than one source, and the concept he is forming. Our little boy is reading the sentence, 'Henry saw the cat climb up the tree.' Long before he has reached this confrontation with the printed word he has built up a wealth of experience. He knows that Henry is another boy, he knows what a cat is and he is acquainted with trees. Had he not built up this experience the sentence would be meaningless; as it is he is content to accept that the words indicate reality. Thus he has accepted that a word is a symbol, a kind of shorthand for real experience. In order even to concentrate on reading the printed sentence, this little boy has to bring into play mental abilities that frequently accompany the exercise of perception; he has to focus his attention and he has to use his memory.

When he comes to look at the actual words in the sentence, he must be able to see the letters, the words and the sentence, all at once. He recognises these both as individual symbols and as parts of a whole. C, A and T are the letters making up the word 'cat', and 'cat' is also part of the sentence. The whole sentence must be seen at a glance for the reader to make sense of it and read it properly. It is easy to convince oneself of this by reading a sentence one word at a time, with the others covered up. It conveys very little. In this way, a fluent reader has to take in the end of the sentence before he can understand the beginning.

If the five-year-old is reading the sentence aloud, he will use all the skills associated with speaking. At the same time as reading, he will be listening to his own speech as a kind of check on his visual perception. Later this speech will become internalised and he will be able to read silently. Research has shown, however, that most adults listen to this inner silent voice while they are reading. Very delicate and complex sensory abilities are involved, then, in learning to read.

Visual perception has many aspects, among them those of colour, shape, space and depth. In schools, studies of colours and shapes in the environment are great favourites, but helping children to order space and to perceive depth are rarely considered, even though it is obvious that these forms of perception are of great importance to children personally. Getting lost, in school, on the way home or anywhere else, is one of the great worries of childhood and none of us would survive long were we unable to perceive that we might fall off a ladder or down a deep hole. Possibly the reason for this kind of omission is that environmental studies is still seen in terms of bringing inside the environment outside school, and less in terms of helping children form their own environmental strategies, which is what we are concerned with here.

The world sparkles with colour. Just to appreciate this adds meaning to life. The environmental study can help children to perceive colour and can also encourage a finer discrimination. There is much more variety and subtlety of colour outside school than inside it, so this is where trips outside the classroom can help. To give just two examples, a visit to the green grocer can be exciting for young children. There is the bright orange of the carrots and the oranges, although if one looks closely, the shades of orange vary; there is the earthy, pinky brown of the potatoes and the milky white of the cauliflowers. Even an apple is not merely green, its skin is red and brown as well, and inside it is pale and fresh. In the summer there are the flowers to look at; even a single flower is full of delicate colours shading into each other.

It is not always possible to take children outside school but several of the television programmes specially produced for pre-school children can be of great help. The BBC programme, *Playschool*, always takes its viewers on a short journey round the streets, or on to a farm or into someone's house and garden. Often the programme will be devoted to a theme, like spring-time or water or people's work, and this theme is developed throughout the half-hour with little songs, games and a story. Teachers, of course, could use the material presented in various ways for the children, encouraging the perception of colour among them. *Playschool* is at present (1984) broadcast in the afternoon on BBC 1, so that it is possible to watch it in school, and repeated a week later in the middle of the morning. This programme has a further value in that it does not confine itself to any one environment, so that children living in the heart of the city can get a glimpse of the country, and those from the country can see the lively bustle of town life. *Playschool* is a model of how to present material to young children and any teacher can glean countless ideas from it.

The experience the children gain can be followed up and refined in the classroom, providing an object lesson in how learning outside school can be reinforced by what goes on inside it. The teacher in the classroom is able to pin-point the children's attention to one issue at a time, and this holding of attention is an important aspect of perception. Teachers have various ways of doing this. Some classrooms have a 'blue' table for a week or two, on which the children place anything blue they can find. It is followed by a 'red' table, then a 'green' one and then a 'yellow' one. Language is a great aid to discrimination; it has been suggested that the superior language development of young girls as opposed to boys gives them a more accurate perception of colours. This means that plenty of discussion and, in particular, the naming of the various colours and their shades will be very helpful to children. What is the word used to describe the colour of a pillar-box? How exactly can one describe the colour of a carrot? The discussions will be long-winded, meandering but very fruitful. Research has shown that young children find difficulty in discriminating certain colours, such as the blues and the purples; they also need help in learning to distinguish various shades from each other, for example, crimson and scarlet in the case of red. Colour cards are useful here. Several firms produce them; some addresses are given in the Appendix (page 233). There is one last point to remember. Maturation processes play a large part in the development of the perception of colour, so that children should never be hurried and there will be no breathtaking sudden results. As rich and varied an experience as possible, often repeated and frequently discussed, is what helps children most.

We live in a world of forms and shapes just as much as we live in a world of colour. Learning to appreciate these is a basic environmental skill, as many a four-year-old who has run into the sharp corner of a table or tripped over the doorstep already knows. At the same time, an appreciation of form and shape is the foundation on which more abstract mental skills are built. Such is the case in reading, mathematics and engineering. Form and shape are also part of the beauty of the world. Young children have their own characteristic ways of exploring them, learning primarily by doing. Further, they learn about form before they learn about shapes, because shape is really an abstraction, being a form with one dimension missing. The first priority is to allow the under-fives plenty of interesting

Teaching Children through the Environment

Handprints of a class of seven-year-olds
(Isleworth Blue School and Maria Grey Nursery School)

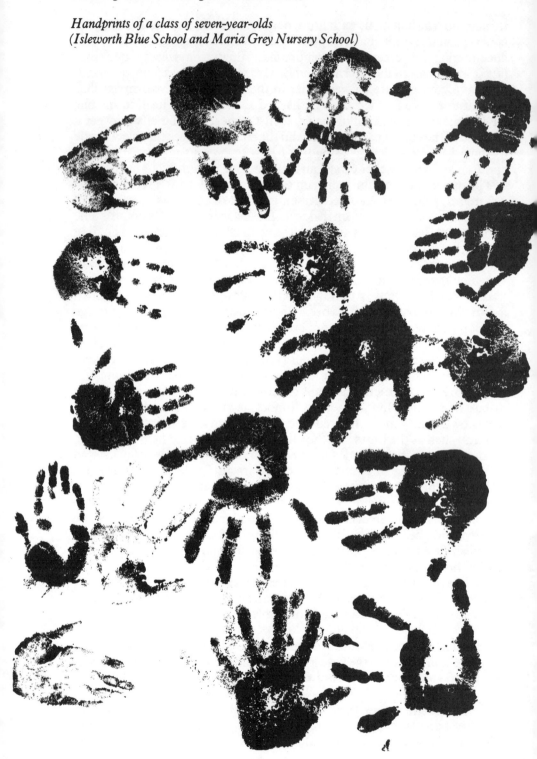

materials, and plenty of time in which to play with them. The materials do not have to be expensive, it is actually better if they are not, because young children are usually more at home with the simple things that can be found anywhere. They like cardboard boxes, empty bottles, particularly scent and talcum powder containers which smell nice as well. They are themselves enthusiastic collectors and will bring in sticks from the park and sea shells from a day at the seaside. They love digging up stones, posting letters, and poking plasticine into cracks. All these activities teach them about forms and shapes, and about what can be done with forms and shapes as well; that is, about area and volume and engineering. They learn, too, from their own bodies, which after all, they know best of all, and they learn from their own activities. The children who were observed in the nursery school, running up and down, must have been absorbing a great deal of knowledge about the area and shape of their classroom.

Opposite is a reproduction of the handprints of a class of seven-year-old boys and girls. Each child put his or her hand into a flat tray of poster paint and then pressed out a handprint on to a large sheet of plain paper. The result is attractive but there is more to it than this. Hands are functional, as are all parts of the human body. The fingers are of varying length; the thumb can move freely and is very strong. These features enable us to use our hands – we can grasp objects. We would not be able to use them nearly so well if all the fingers were the same length, or if they had no joints and did not bend. It is interesting for children to investigate shapes and forms in this way; they not only enjoy it, it gives real meaning to an important aspect of the environment. There are many more fascinating illustrations of the functional importance of shape. If the children examine their own teeth, they will see that these, too, vary in shape. The front teeth are flat and are ideal for biting; the big molars at the back are the grinders, while the pointed eye teeth were probably used, in the past, for tearing at raw meat.

A class of four-year-olds in an infants' school collected leaves on a walk with their teacher in the park near the school, then each leaf was painted in poster paint and pressed on to a large sheet of paper. Leaves, like hands and teeth, have a purpose. It is not beyond a four-year-old to notice that the leaves of trees and plants are invariably narrowed at one end; this enables excessive rain to run off and prevents the plant becoming waterlogged. Nature has many examples of how shapes and forms are bound up with the way in which living creatures survive. Most children have at some time a boiled egg for breakfast or tea. If they try to roll a (hard-boiled!) egg off the flat surface of a table, they will find it almost impossible to do, because one end of the egg is more pointed than the other. Because of this feature, the seagull and many other birds can keep their eggs safely on a cliff-top.

The children's investigations can go further in that they can explore the ways in which shapes and forms are used in all sorts of ways in our society. Although teachers are very willing, as part of an environmental study, to

Shapes that work for us
(A hand, two cog-wheels, a hen's egg, and a leaf. Photos by Wendy Mays.)

encourage children to notice abstract shapes in the environment, like the rectangles of bricks and blocks of flats and the circular shapes of coal-holes, they very rarely carry this further and encourage the children to ask *why* these things are the shape they are. Some of the reasons are complicated and rooted in history, it being part of western culture, from the ancient Greeks onwards, to see 'thinking' as more dignified than 'doing', or to put it more accurately, not to realise that doing *is* thinking. Thus we are happy to ask children to look at circles and squares, as a way of introducing them to geometry, but not so happy to introduce them to the cog-wheel, as a means of helping them make a clock. Not only is this socially harmful, creating unpleasant forms of snobbery, it ignores the fact that young children are natural mechanics and learn by doing.

Even very simple man-made objects are beautifully designed for the work they have to do. Little children are well able to appreciate them. There is the cork, for example, and the cork-screw, also an aeroplane wing and a cup and saucer. Children need time to collect and to consider interesting objects, and also to make their own. Boxes, wheels from a discarded scooter and prams, odd lengths of wood, are all useful and so is the abundance of educational materials, like pegs and peg-boards, cog-wheels and jigsaws, produced for schools by educational suppliers.

Children of seven years of age onwards often show amazing ingenuity and they need correspondingly more complex materials and greater freedom to experiment. They are well able to build simple bridges, huts and go-karts, as well as being adept at taking old clocks and radios to pieces. A few precautions have to be taken. It should be impossible for them to plug a radio, or any electrical equipment, into the mains supply, and they should never be allowed near a television set. Television sets are always volatile even when not plugged in, and should only be examined by experts.

Teachers are well aware of the need to introduce children to the concepts of circle, triangle and square because they form the basis of more advanced studies later. Giving children the opportunity to observe these shapes in the environment helps them. In particular, because of the great variety it is possible to find especially outside school, children come to understand the essential nature of the concepts. After all, a wheel, a halfpenny, a saucer and a pillar-box may differ in colour, size and purpose, but they are all circular in shape. On a walk outside school, they can note all the different shapes they see. Back in the classroom, their observations should be carefully classified and thoroughly discussed before being displayed.

Visual perception is, as we know, not carried out in isolation. Children see with their ears, their sense of touch and their memories as well as their eyes. This co-ordination is vital for the development of the higher thinking processes. Many games with children of all ages can be played to encourage this kind of multiple, integrated perception. One favourite is to place a variety of objects, such as a brush, a rubber, a bottle and a card-board square, in a drawstring bag and ask the children, one by one, to put a hand in the bag, feel an object, describe it and guess what it is. Then they pull out the object and see if they have guessed correctly.

Accurate visual perception also plays a crucial part in motor ability. The two combined enable us to move about and to develop skills essential both to survival and to learning. Together, they are basic to anyone's environmental strategy. Yet young children often find themselves in difficulty here. They are clumsy; they can't tie their shoe-laces or do their buttons up; they don't find writing easy. Many a five-year-old finds school a nightmare because he (she) takes ages to put on his wellingtons or can't turn a door handle. Children need the opportunity to develop these skills in a tranquil, unstressed atmosphere. In the play area and in the Wendy house should be plenty of dolls and bears all wearing brightly coloured felt shoes that tie up or buckle, and coats that zip or button up. Gaily painted pieces of cardboard can be laced and unlaced. There should be attractive bootles with tops waiting to be screwed on and unscrewed. Special attention can be paid to those aspects of motor skill and hand-eye co-ordination that are essential to reading and writing. In our culture, moving the eyes from left to right is vital to reading. This can be encouraged by allowing the children to solve maze or dot-to-dot puzzles, always working from left to right. Often young children are unable to focus their eyes on a particular point on a page for any length of time, which is why, when they are reading aloud, even at seven or eight years of age they will break off in the middle of a line and continue on a sentence much further down the page, their eyes having slipped. Video games might help them here. Practising the recognition of shape-outlines will help the under-fives to recognise words when they come to read. They can either fit the shape to the picture or word, or draw round it, as below. As can be seen, the shape of the cat is quite different from that of the house; so is the shape of *have* from that of *take*.

Research has centred emphatically on the development of young children, so that there is much less known about the needs of the five- to nine-year-old. This omission may be partly due to the fact that, once a

Shape outlines

a cat-shape   a house-shape

two word-shapes

have   take

child leaves the nursery school, the school day is more structured and subject-based, so that there is little place for the broad approach implied in sensory education. Almost certainly though we can assume that older children too need opportunities for visual exploration. They can take the study of shape and form even further. They can consider shapelessness, or rather those shapes and forms that have apparently come about by chance, like those of rocks, rivers and the contours of land. They can reach beyond the limitations of their own senses by using the microscope. A snow-flake appears to the naked eyes as a white blob; under the microscope it is seen as a structure of infinite variety and delicate regularity. The leg of a wasp, a hair-like strand at first sight, is revealed as beautifully designed for its purpose. On considerations such as these rest science and geography.

The perception of beauty in the environment is as much a part of our strategy for survival as is the ability to see danger. In the last resort, it is probably what many people value most, and it comes largely from the gift of vision. There can be no lessons on it, and here again what children need is the freedom and time to look at the world in their own way.

Being able to see provides children with a way of ordering the environment; being able to hear provides them with another. Recent research has shown that very young children possess an acute sense of hearing. They can discriminate soft from loud tones, intermittent from continuous sound; even at four months old they can match a sound to a corresponding object; they like music. There is a great deal, however, that we still do not know. We do not know exactly how the information gained from hearing is processed by the individual, or, in detail, what the patterns of learning are. Still less have we an understanding of the environmental influences that may influence this learning. Research has concentrated very much more on the visual perception of young children than it has on their auditory perception, possibly because visual imagery is the more highly significant for mental processes. Consequently, we are left with many unanswered questions, particularly when we consider the ways in which children may interact with their environment by means of their sense of hearing. For example, we know that children build up visual maps of their environment. Do they also build up auditory ones? Are they guided through the day, or through a geographical space, by means of various key sounds? It is possible.

The importance of being able to perceive and discriminate sounds is unchallenged. This ability gives children a way of ordering, not only their environment, but themselves too. Hearing provides one system of reference for thoughts and actions, another dimension to the world. Without it, the mental concepts formed about phenomena would be incomplete, as would be the case if we were unable to match the visual image of a thrush with its song. Because they are human beings, the ability to hear has a unique significance for children, as on it is based speech. Speech enables children to explore the environment in the fullest possible sense, enabling them to interact with other people, and underlies the cumulative culture on which society is based. It is no exaggeration to say that, without a sense of hearing, there would be no society as we know it today. Yet, far-reaching in significance though it is, speech is firmly rooted in the individual perception of sound, in the ability to hear the rhythm, tone and shape of a sentence.

In the absence of unequivocal guidance, teachers of young children have to rely on their own intuitive understanding and experience. While working in or out of the classroom it is possible to bear in mind several characteristics of auditory perception. Like other forms, auditory perception operates within certain mechanisms and acknowledges a system of rules. The ability of the individual to focus attention on what he or she is hearing and to censor whatever is irrelevant is of particular importance. The reason is simple: we cannot shut out sounds by physical means. We can shut our eyes against an unwelcome sight and eliminate it altogether, but the ears have nothing equivalent to eyelids. Mental abilities must therefore play a correspondingly great part in enabling the mind to order the environment through auditory perception. To the teacher, this means that, when young children are required to listen, it helps to give them a strategy to draw them into concentration, getting them to sit in a certain position or perhaps to close their eyes.

Stating what is probably obvious, all young children need the opportunity to hear tones, rhythms and sounds in abundance, and to think and talk about them. One of the best ways of becoming aware of the sounds around them is for the children to listen in silence. The world in which we live has been a noisy place for millions of years, ever since the first creatures grunted their way over the earth, or flapped through the air on leathery wings. The classroom, likewise, is full of sound and, with their eyes shut, children can discriminate these sounds. They may hear the little nestling noises of the gerbil or guinea-pig; someone might move slightly, or cough; sounds will filter through from outside, like the slow drone of an aeroplane or the cheep of a sparrow. Two minutes of such listening is long enough for most children. After this, the sounds that have been recognised should be discussed. How exactly can one describe the noise a little animal makes? Some sounds can be classified; some will be loud, some so tiny that they can hardly be heard; some will be pleasant, others won't be. Words, it must be remembered, encapsulate and analyse sensory experience, as well as enabling it to be recalled.

Outside school there will be many more sounds of a different kind. A walk will prove this. There are cars, lorries, the sounds of people working, and lots of voices. The sea makes all kinds of sounds, and so does the wind. Even if it is not possible for the children to go out of school, the sounds outside can be brought to them. A class can watch a television programme, such as *Playschool* or *Watch with Mother*, and concentrate on discriminating the sounds, rather than the images. A popular game is for a teacher to record sounds on a tape recorder and ask the children to guess what they are listening to. These could be footsteps, bacon sizzling, a door closing.

Older children, many of whom have tape recorders these days, enjoy making their own recordings of various sounds and getting the rest of the class to guess what they are.

Another suggestion, and one that is fun, is to encourage the older children to construct an auditory map. What are the sounds that guide them through the day? If they stood with their eyes closed, in an empty street, or a field, or the local market, how would they know where they were?

Creating sounds and rhythms of their own helps to refine the perception of children. This is easily done, using materials that come readily to hand. When they go out for a walk, the children can bring back all the things they love to pick up, like stones, twigs and dead leaves. When these are put in empty yoghurt or cream cartons and shaken up and down, they produce many sounds of great variety. Dead leaves will not sound the same as stones. It is a short step from this to making music.

The importance of auditory perception to speech has already been stressed. It is not just a matter of perceiving sounds and tones, but also rhythms and periodicity. All children should be given constant opportunities of hearing various patterns of speech. If there are Welsh girls and boys in the class, or Irish, or Scots, among others, the children should listen to them carefully and discern the varying (and musical) patterns they make with the words they use. The children's own names produce varying patterns when strung together. 'John, Jennifer, Jean and Nicholas', spoken aloud, have a different pattern from, 'Kevin, Sandra, Paul and Sarah'. It is fun to string together the names of pets as well, like 'Tabby, Tan, Snowflake and Joey'.

There are forms of perception which operate on a limited unitary and specialised scale, such as sight, hearing, taste and touch. Then there are forms which have a broader field of activity, which are more concerned with abstractions and which are more complex. Such are the perceptions of time and space. They are complex firstly because they operate on several scales at once. The perception of space can involve the ordering of a large area like the school playground; it can equally well be involved in recognising the shape of a word, for all shape is space defined on a small scale. The perception of time can either mean being able to estimate the intervals between the drips of a tap, or it can mean having a historical time sense and knowing that the Tudors did not wear top hats.

The perceptions of space and time are complex secondly because they imply the use of most of the other senses, and the utilisation of a variety of environmental cues. When young children come to order their own street in terms of space, for example, they will probably use their senses of hearing, touch and smell, as well as their sense of sight.

The significance of a child's ability to develop a sense of space and a sense of time as part of an environmental strategy hardly needs emphasising. Her or she would be lost, literally, without them.

Piaget has suggested that, when a child is very young, its temporal and spiritual concepts are basically undifferentiated. One is frequently judged in terms of the other; for example, a child will assume, ignoring all other considerations, that the greater the distance an object has to travel, the longer time it will take. Recent research, however, indicates that young children are rather more sophisticated than has been suspected. Children of between three and five years of age were tested to see how far they were able to understand that words like, 'before', 'after', 'first', 'last', 'behind', and 'together' have both spatial and temporal meanings.[19] The younger children, the three-year-olds, could understand the words in either their temporal or their spatial contexts, but rarely in both. The five-year-olds, however, could apply the terms flexibly in either context, showing that they were, in fact, able to differentiate. We can note two things about these obervations: firstly, that the difficulty experienced by the three-year-olds arose from single words having more than one meaning, and, secondly, that the authors, Friedman and Seely, suggest that it was the children's repeated experience in the environment that enabled them to build up accurately the concepts involved two years later.

There has been a great deal of interesting and valuable research into the spatial perception of young children. Some of it can be quoted here with an eye to the implications for an understanding as to how young children develop their strategies for ordering the environment in terms of space, and the significance this has for the teacher.

In the study,[20] which will interest all teachers, children ranging in age from four to six years were asked to construct models of their classroom, in an attempt to assess what internal representations they were able to form of large-scale space. The authors found that the children's accuracy in constructing their models increased in accordance with their familiarity with their classroom. It was also helped by the provision of significant landmarks. Environmental cues were held to be important in enabling the children to form representations of space, but they were not all that mattered. Maturation played a part: in other words, the children improved simply because they grew older. From these observations, it would seem that the ability to form spatial representation is a complex affair, helped partly by the utilisation of sensory cues, but also resulting from processes which are beyond external control. Where the teacher can help is by paying attention to the layout of the classroom. Young children need to make their home in one room for a considerable length of time. It will not help them if they are continually marching round the school. Their classroom should have a clear shape, with certain well-marked focal points, like the blackboard in one corner and the Wendy house in another.

The cues that children use in order to systematise space are many and varied. It takes years to sort them all out and sometimes the children become confused. In another study,[21] when groups of children of nine and ten years of age were asked to travel over a route along which there were various obstacles, it was found that they tended to judge distance according to ease of travel. A journey that involved climbing a hill or turning a corner was perceived as longer than a straightforward one, even if, in terms of actual distance, it was not. It is interesting that the cues involved here are not necessarily physical; any kind of stress can influence the perception of distance. We have probably all shared an experience like going to the dentist, when the journey there seems endless, while we trip back miraculously fast, even though both journeys cover the same distance and take a similar time. A control group of adults was used in this experiment; their reactions, and their misjudgements, were the same as the children's. Amusement at this should not be allowed to mask its significance; what mattered was familiarity with the environment, allowing everyone, both children and adults, to pick out the significant cues.

It is possible to conceptualise an area in several different ways, whether this is a room in our own home or the local park. We can see it as a flat surface, plane-like, on which we weave our comings and goings, unaware of what lies beneath or above or to the side of us. Alternatively, we might conceive of this space as being composed of a series of small spaces linked together, the identity of each part being recognised by the objects in it, such as furniture, trees or street signs. Lastly, we might perceive our space as a three-dimensional whole, with depth and more space above and to the sides. We would then be able to stand in any part of it and visualise correctly what is in the rest.

Various studies, carried out in the last ten years, suggest that young children progress from a simple to a complex concept of space.[22] It is suggested that, when they are only two and three years old, children perceive their environment as consisting of fragmented, thread-like routes. They find their way about by learning to recognise certain cues, visual cues being the most important. They also learn by recalling what action on their part is called for along the route, like climbing a hill or jumping a stream or tripping over a chair leg. Probably many of us can remember the creaky stair that tells us we are half-way up the stairs, or the door on the landing that has to be pushed hard before it will open. All of this is certainly in keeping with the behaviour of the under-fives who travelled ceaselessly (described in Chapter One), the journey itself being the vital undertaking.

Between the ages of eight and ten it is suggested that children perceive the landmarks along the routes through space as being connected in small clusters. They think of an area as being composed of several smaller areas. Round about the age of ten, however, children make a significant leap forward, for they learn to form a *Gestalt*-like representation of the environment. They can perceive the inter-relationships of all the parts of a given space; they know that space is three-dimensional. In practical terms, this means that if they are standing in the centre of their town they know that there are several ways of getting home; if they are standing in the kitchen of their home, they are aware that the ceiling is the floor of the bathroom.

This is borne out by research into the behaviour of both young and older children.[22] Children of between tree and six, taken along a specified route and given various tasks to do afterwards (travelling the route in reverse, naming the sequence of landmarks along the reverse route, inferring the relationship between parts of the environment not directly travelled between and constructing a model of the environment) found, of all the tasks, relating parts of the environment to each other by far the most difficult.

The all-important questions we have to ask are how young children come to order their environment spatially and what the implications are for teaching. It is suggested here that they progress by using their own bodies as analogies, by utilising many complex environmental cues, by maturation, and by gaining experience. Experience, and by this we mean not just being passive but being active in the environment, is vital. This is because it takes time and much thinking to assimilate all the evidence presenting itself. Take the examples of a little boy watching two trains and a young girl watching two horses. In the case of the trains, one has big wheels that revolve slowly, while the other has small wheels which go round very fast. In the case of the horses, one has long legs and takes slow strides of great length, while the other is a pony whose legs tumble along very quickly. Nine times out of ten, a five-year-old will insist that the small-wheeled engine and the short-legged pony are going faster than their companions and will cover a greater distance irrespective of whether they reach their destinations together or not. The reason is that they overestimate the significance of one set of cues at the expense of others, simply because these are eye-catching. The fast-moving legs and the quickly revolving wheels *look* faster, and so other elements in the situation, like the length of stride and the size of the wheel, are not taken into account. In time they will be though because eventually it will dawn on the children that the engines keep together in spite of appearances; so do the horses. The children will then return to the situation and seek out further cues; more than this, they will be forced to estimate their relative importance.

In like fashion, the children studied by Cohen, Sherman and Baldwin[21] who thought that the more difficult route must be the longer one, will eventually, through familiarity, come to utilise all the cues in the environment and in themselves, and arrive at a more accurate estimate of distance. They might note a keypoint on the routes, a tree or a roof-top; they might realise that they are not actually taking many more steps, or feeling much more tired when they travelled the more complex route than when they travelled the simple one. They might even decide to time themselves.

It was experience, too, that enabled the five-year-olds described by Friedman and Seeley[19] to come to realise that words like 'before' and 'behind' can apply to both time and space. From living, working and perceiving in the environment, young children build up absolute, objective standards. Sheer lack of experience and of familiarity with what they are perceiving causes the spatial perception of children to differ from that of adults. This is shown by the behaviour of adults when research into children includes them too. Unfortunately, not much research does. When adults are included as a control group, they react in the same way as the children provided they are in a novel situation. They, too, perceive a journey as longer if they have to climb over an obstacle or go round a corner; they, too, are not certain whether the ceiling of the kitchen is the floor of the bathroom or is part of the cupboard at the top of the stairs.

Experience, however, is not everything. Maturation plays its part in the evolution of the child's strategy. One can see that this would be true, for all forms of perception must be based on the maturation of the nervous system.

Children utilise many cues from the environment in order to arrive at an accurate spatial representation. Hazen, Lockman and Pick[22] have suggested that visual cues are valuable to them. It can be added that children probably use sounds and smells also. The actions required of them in travelling through a space are important as well. If they jump over the sand-pit when running across the playground, that will help them to measure the latter. This kind of action enables young children to use their own bodies and their own movements in order to build up their concepts of space. They use their pace and also their own bodies as interpreters. Gentner[15] has demonstrated how good four- to seven-year-olds are at using spatial analogies relating to their own bodies. Actually, when the mappings were made more difficult by the inclusion of more objects and misleading detail, the children's grasp of the situation proved firmer than that of the adults. The adults became confused, but the children did not.

How can the teacher help young children in the spatial ordering of their environment? Of paramount importance is the provision of experience and the repetition of that experience. Children need plenty of opportunities to be active, to run about, to traverse a space at varying speeds, because that is how they learn. Familiarity with the environment has been shown to be significant, so that a walk through the park or round the village should be repeated several times, sometimes varying the route slightly, so that the children can build up their *Gestalt* of space. Landmarks help them, both in and outside the classroom. These can be pointed out and discussed. The children should be given the opportunity of finding their own landmarks, because what is eye-catching to an adult may not matter to them. The chair with the splinter, or the hot-water pipe that makes a cosy little area round it, may make a deeper impression on them than the educational picture pinned up on the wall. Building models of their own homes or the classroom assists young children in ordering space. It helps them realise that there are parts to a space that can be related to each other and that every space has an up and a down, a sideways and a lengthways, that space has several dimensions. In all these ways, young children can be helped to make the environment their own.

Space and time are both dimensions of the environment; frequently one dimension is judged in terms of the other. If a long distance has been travelled, it seems reasonable to assume that the journey has taken a long time; if we have spent a long time getting to one place from another, it feels as though we have covered a vast distance. Space and time are, however, separate concepts, implying different means of ordering the environment, and the evidence is that quite early on in life young children realise this.

Of all forms of perception, the perception of time is the most complex, the hardest one to grasp and the most delicately balanced. The way in which it orders the environment is quite different from the kind of ordering that takes place by means of the other senses, such as those of vision and hearing. In seeing and hearing we have firmly in front of us concrete phenomena; in contrast, the perception of time is not directly dependent on anything immediate in the environment. Rather does it call for the learning of standards of comparison; the comparing of what an object was yesterday to what it is today and may be tomorrow. The perception of time also depends on the ability to recognise the occurrence of events. Some of these events may be simple and easy to understand, like having cornflakes in the morning for breakfast and coming home to tea at night, but other events are culturally determined and have to be learnt through experience. Societies adopt various ways of ordering time and have evolved a variety of methods of assessing it. In our own society in medieval England, few people possessed a clock, so that telling the beads of a rosary was one means of telling the time. In Madagascar the frying of a locust used to be a time unit; the Andamar Indians mark the seasons of the year according to their scents.

The spacing we give to our day, the week, the year and even our lifetime, does not arise from our biological needs: it is an artefact, imposed on us by circumstances that are artificial and external to ourselves. Many of these circumstances are determined by the kind of society in which we live.[23] We do not have to get up at seven o'clock, start work at nine and go to bed at night. What evidence there is suggests that human beings are very much more flexible. Observations of people living under various conditions indicate that some are more efficient when they divide the twenty-four hours of the day into smaller stretches of time, say six or eight hours instead of twelve. These people are happiest working six hours, resting six, and so on. When human beings are kept without an artificial means of counting the hours, they quickly lose their sense of time. Our favourite adventure stories are full of hardy characters, marooned in out-of-the-way foreign parts, who only keep track of the passing of the weeks and the months by notching up the days on a piece of wood.

Because the sense of time is less innate than other forms of perception with a higher cultural content, because it is at once abstract and artificially imposed, because it has to be learnt, it is also the most sensitive and easily distorted. We are always losing our sense of time. Under great stress or emotion it can go completely. It is also much affected by other personal factors. A little girl of six asked me why time goes so slowly when you're bored and so quickly when you're interested in what you are doing. I could not think of an adequate answer.

To these characteristics we must add another, that time-perception is a broad term implying the ability to discriminate a whole range of phenomena, rhythms and events. Some are simple, like the changes in the size of one's feet as one grows older. Others are abstract and cultural in nature, like the differences between Tudor people and ourselves. These are harder to perceive.

Although the ordering of the environment in terms of time is no easy task for young children, it is essential to their well-being. It has a social significance because ours is a technological society which demands of its members an accurate assessment of the passing of time and the ability to organise activities within it. Being able to arrive at school on time, catching buses and trains, are cases in point. Learning to perceive time-scales in the environment also helps young children to order themselves. Not only do they learn more about themselves when they see that they are growing bigger or that they will be going on holiday in the summer, they are helped to put their own emotions in perspective. One reason for the almost uncontrollable emotions of young children, their intense rages and deeply felt griefs, is because they have not yet learnt that time passes and things change. If the teacher is cross today, she (he) may not be tomorrow; if your mother won't let you watch television on Monday, she might be persuaded next time. Learning to perceive this adds to a child's self-control. It also allows him to order his own actions. This affects his behaviour. Even in everyday occurrences, such as going on a journey by bus, we order our reactions in accordance with our knowledge of its time-span. If we know it will be a long journey, we arrange ourselves mentally, settling down and investing the passage of time with a kind of pattern.

The accurate perception of time is an essential part of the child's environmental strategy. How does the time-sense of a young child develop? Evidence suggests that quite early on in life a child understands that time and space are separate dimensions of the environment. One piece of research involving nursery school children demonstrates that the children's concepts of time are basically temporal, but they are continually vulnerable to counter-suggestions from other factors, like those of speed and pace.[24] This would be so in the case of the little girl (page 40) who believed that, because a pony's legs were moving faster, he must have been covering the ground faster than a horse. It has already been mentioned that three- to six-year-olds can grasp the spatial and temporal meanings of words.[19]

The development of time-sense implies the ability to perceive time-patterns in the environment. It takes a very long time to see these in all their immense variety and, in order to do so, children have to utilise many environmental cues. They also come to learn which cues, coming both from within themselves and from the world outside, are the vital ones, and which are mere distractions. Very young children will probably be most aware of these changes occurring in themselves. They will realise that they are hungry when they wake up in the morning and that they are tired by the time it is dark. They will come to recognise, even when they are only a few weeks old, that the changes in themselves are linked to what is going on outside. They will be subconsciously aware that when they waken, as well as feeling hungry, daylight has come; they can hear the birds, the hum of traffic in the distance and the merry clinking of cups and saucers in the kitchen. One day, those sights and sounds, by a process of conditioning, may make them feel hungry even when they are not, particularly. They are now part of a time rhythm. In this way, using sensory cues from the environment, children form time schema, simple at first, but more complex and extensive as they grow older. Round about the age of four, they can grasp the pattern of a whole day; before then, as people with experience of young children are well aware, they will often get morning and afternoon mixed up. Then children come to see the pattern of a week, a month and, much later, longer, historical periods of time. Two things have to be noted. Firstly, this process, involving the amassing of as much information as possible, is not a simple one. The information used has to be assessed according to its usefulness and this means using the higher mental processes of reasoning and thinking. The little girl who is confused over the pony's legs will only find the answer when she sees that her conclusion does not match what actually transpires and she thinks it out more. Further, a kind of censorship is involved. Not everything can be remembered; forgetting is an essential part of remembering. As the time-spans become greater, so only the key events stand out. It is rather like rising higher and higher above the ground in an aeroplane, until, slowly, all the people and houses disappear and only the big landmarks are left.

The second point to note is that, as the time-schemata become more complex, so cues of varying nature are utilised. They may be biological in the early stages, but historical time-sense implies an understanding of the nature of social and cultural cues, which demand quite a sophisticated experience of life.

Young children become aware of the stream of time, and of time patterns in the environment, long before they see that time can be measured and that this measurement provides an objective standard for all to use. I remember a little girl who, when asked how many hours there were in a day, replied that it depended on what time she got up. I myself have been heard to enquire of a friend what time the two o'clock film was due to start. In their early days children do perceive rhythms in time but it is their time and it is not shared by everybody else.

Although maturational factors must be significant in this kind of perception, young children can be helped by good teaching. The teacher can ensure that various patterns in time are presented to them for examination and discussion. The easiest patterns for them to recognise are those which involve themselves, because there they have the evidence in front of them all the time. They will all get up in the morning, eat meals at regular intervals, and go to bed at night. They can chart their days and hang the charts up in the classroom. There should be a great deal of discussion. A broad pattern will emerge, and, within this, many variations. Everybody will get up in the morning but not exactly at the same time and they will probably have different things for beakfast. If the children are under five and go home at about twelve noon, Henry might go off to the shops with his mother, while Jane might hurry home to watch the midday television programmes. The variations in the pattern are just as significant as its broad outline for, by considering these, the children will slowly come to an understanding of the tacit conventions, the mutual agreements and also the pressures that underlie the ways in which we organise time.

Even the under-fives will be aware of time passing in their own lives. They will all probably have at home photographs of themselves as tiny babies, then perhaps as toddlers on a family holiday, and, finally, more recent pictures of themselves as school children. If the photographs are displayed in the classroom, the children can see for themselves the ways in which they have changed. They need plenty of time for discussion and the opportunity to make their own commentaries. The babies in the early photographs may not have any teeth, and not much hair; someone will be holding them because they are unable to support themselves. The pictures of the four-year-olds will be very different. They will have teeth, hair, strong arms and legs and grown-up expressions. Time has passed and, by discussing all these changes, the children will come to recognise the signs which tell us it has done so.

All children love to talk about their pets. Their lives too illustrate patterns in time. They are instructive because their life-spans are shorter than ours and because children usually know their pets very well indeed. On page 46 three photographs show the development of a puppy called Baloo. In the space of three years, he progressed from being a tiny puppy, through the silly lolloping stage of adolescence to becoming a fully-grown dog. He changed not only in appearance but in character, habits and intelligence as well. At two years he is not as playful as he used to be, and much more conscious of territory. Even if the children are unable to bring several photographs showing the time sequence in the life of their cat, dog, budgie, gerbil or guinea-pig, they will probably possess one photograph, or they can draw a picture. They will enjoy comparing notes.

The children can create their own evidence as to how time passes by growing seeds. Mustard and cress seeds are ideal. If they are sown on Monday, on moist lint, they will send out roots and leaves within a day or two and be mature by Friday. A favourite way is for each child to grow the seeds in the shape of the initial of his or her first name; this can be done by making stencils of the initials. All the stages in the progression should be carefully noted: how, for example, two thick 'leaves' (the cotyledons) come first. The children can be led from this to consider the life-spans of other plants and living creatures. An oak tree takes a very long time to grow; some are hundreds of years old. Some creatures, like hamsters, only

Time-sequence in the life of a family pet

Baloo is three months old. He needs someone to look after him.

At three years, Baloo is fully grown.

Baloo is nine months old. He is interested in the world around him.

live a couple of years; on the other hand, tortoises can live longer than we do. The elephant has a life span similar to our own.

The ability to recognise sequence is essential to the perception of time. Children can practise this kind of recognition by using pictures. The educational suppliers whose addresses are given in the Appendix (page 233) produce sets for this purpose. Teachers can also build up their own supplies from colour supplements and magazines. Using these materials, young children place a baby first, then the child, then the adult, demonstrating the pattern for themselves. Alternatively, they may order the pictures of an oak tree, showing how it grows through the stages of acorn and sapling.

Being able to perceive the many ways in which the environment is ordered in time is one thing and is essential to the environmental strategy of the young child; being able to organise his own activities in accordance with the rhythms of the day, the month and the year, is quite another matter, being much more difficult and is, consequently, a longer process. Many people never achieve it, being, like half the members of my family, always late, or, like the other half, rather anxious about being on time and as a result always early. Both are equally irritating to other people. Young children do not find it easy to order their activities within time, but they can be helped. Their day should be given a strong, clear framework, as indeed it is in most schools. Within the classroom also, it pays to punctuate the day with various key events, like news-time first thing in the morning, milk at playtime and a story just before going home.

Until children can perceive the patterns of time in their environment, and respond to them, they are not properly attuned to life. These rhythms are all around them, in the whirring of bicycle wheels, in the clackety-clack of trains, in the songs the children sing, and in their own lives.

Children are able to perceive time long before they are able to tell the time.

In fact, children gather experience of sequences and patterns while they are coming to grips with the mysteries of the clock. Learning to tell the time means learning a technique. There are no logical reasons why the day is divided into hours, minutes and seconds, nor do we have to use clocks. As we have seen, other societies do not possess them. Because telling the time involves mastering a technique, good teaching has a great part to play, and it should be made fun. The essence of time-keeping, whether this be by means of clocks, sun-dials or noting when the locusts come, is that it gives us a way of measuring time, and that it imposes an objective standard on all of us. Even very young children can imagine and be amused by the chaos that would ensue if everyone went his or her own way and nobody knew what time of day it was.

At about the age of six or seven, many children become intrigued by clocks and ways of telling the time. Often they will be quite obsessed with timing their own and other people's activities. I remember feeling terribly irritated at my own young son once when he met me at the front door, stop-watch in hand, to tell me that I had taken one hour, two minutes and thirty-two seconds to do the shopping and he was now going to time me peeling the potatoes. This, then, is a good age at which to introduce children to the clock.

First the teacher has to decide on what terminology to use. When the hour hand points to eleven and the minute hand to three, is this to be referred to as 'a quarter past eleven' or 'fifteen minutes past eleven'? When the hour hand points to eight and the minute hand to seven, is this 'eight thirty-five' or 'five and twenty to nine'? It does not really matter which terms are used, so long as the children are familiar with them and so long as they remain the same.

As with every learning task, telling the time should be carefully structured. This means breaking it down into stages. The children should begin by taking a good look at the clock-face, noting how it is designed to have two hands, the long minute hand and the short hour hand. Then they can learn to tell the time on the hour, when it is one o'clock, two o'clock and so on.

Once the hours have been mastered, the children can learn to tell the time at half-past, a quarter past and a quarter to the hour. If they can do this by the time they are eight, they will have done well. The technique of the twenty-four hour clock can be left until later.

It helps if children each have a clock-face in front of them. These can be bought from educational suppliers, or can be easily made by the children. Each child needs a circle of cardboard or stiff paper on which the hours are marked. The younger children need help in getting the hours evenly spaced. The hour hand and the minute hand should be clearly differentiated, preferably in contrasting shape and colour. The stiff silver foil of take-away containers is ideal for the hour hands. The two hands are fixed on to the centre of the clock face by driving them through with a spiked paper-clip.

It is useful for the teacher to make a big clock-face, so that he or she can use this with the children, placing the hands at various times and asking the children to follow suit. Children enjoy games involving actions and learning to tell the time can be made fun if games are devised round the activity. For example, they can all decide on certain actions to be performed when the clock-face denotes a given time. If the hands say two o'clock, everyone has to raise their right hand; at eight o'clock they stand on one foot; at twelve o'clock they all bend down and look between their knees. Alternatively, the games can be played in reverse, with one child performing the action and the other children adjusting their own clockfaces.

Older children, from the age of about seven, can arrive at a far deeper understanding of the whole concept of time. To begin with, they can relive the experiences our ancestors must have had before they worked out ways of telling the time by means of clocks. Before our ancestors had this truly brilliant idea, they must have used many cues in order to estimate time. If the children all remove their watches for a morning they will find themselves doing the same. How do they know when an hour has passed? How do they know it's time for milk? They will judge by taking into account all kinds of changes, some of them very small. They might notice that the sun is shining on a different point in the classroom, or at any rate that the light is brighter; they will hear the clatter of knives as the dinner-ladies start to prepare school dinner; later, their own bodies will tell them that they are hungry and thirsty. By a careful but often subconscious noting of cues, they will know that time has passed.

However, it is not enough merely to be aware that time has passed. In any but the simplest of societies time has to be measured. It is a tribute to the early thinkers that they used these sensory cues in order to invent ways of telling the time, in other words, to forge an objective standard. This is not an easy thing to do. Can the children then devise a method of measuring the passing of time, without, that is, using their own watches as checks?

What our ancestors did was to note that some natural forces never vary. The sun always moves across the sky in a certain way every day, and in fact we still frequently use it as a means of telling the time. Parents often say to their children, 'Be home by sunset.' Gravity likewise exerts a uniform pull. With great ingenuity, the people of long ago used these natural forces to make time measuring devices, or clocks. Here are some examples which the children will enjoy making for themselves.

A shadow-clock

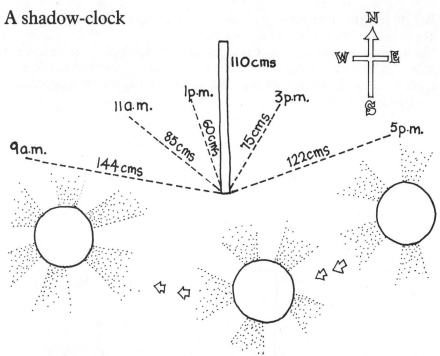

Even young children can make a shadow-clock. The time of day is estimated according to the length of a shadow on the ground. The diagram below shows how the shadows cast by the sun varied during a summer's day in June (British Summer Time).

A float-clock

This has been used for telling the time in ancient civilisations. A basin with a small hole in the bottom is floated in water. Slowly it sinks. Plasticine can be used to adjust the width of the hole.

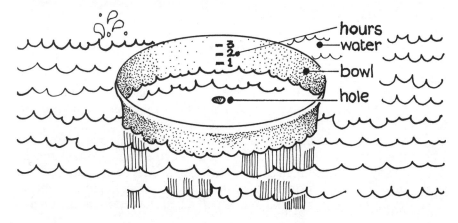

49

An hour-glass

The action of gravity can help us to judge the passing of time. This is the principle behind the egg-timer where the sand trickles through a tiny aperture. The children could use clear plastic containers, with dry sharp, not builder's, sand.

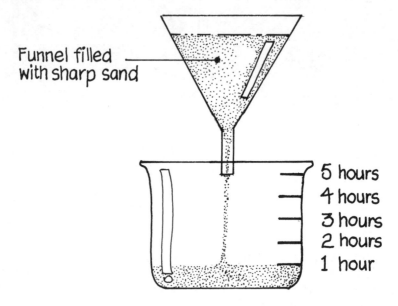

Funnel filled with sharp sand

5 hours
4 hours
3 hours
2 hours
1 hour

A candle-clock

Provided they are shielded from draughts, candles burn at a steady rate. The Anglo-Saxons used this as a method of telling the time. Slow-burning candles are best.

A mechanical clock

Many of our modern clocks involve linking the turning of cog-wheels to the swing of the pendulum. Grandfather clocks are the best examples. Our smaller clocks do not have pendulums and, though they are too intricate for young children to build out of their own raw materials, some big toy shops and educational suppliers produce brightly coloured plastic kits from which a child can construct a simple working model.

Children have immense ingenuity and they might well have other ideas. There was once, for instance, a clock that rolled down a gentle slope all day. Can anyone build an alarm into their clock? Maybe the candle-flame could burn through a string at playtime and release a (small!) weight, or the water in the floating basin could set off a bell at a certain hour. Digital watches are popular now and many children have them, but do they know how they work?

Perception remains the basis on which the environmental strategies of the young child are built. We have engaged in a preliminary discussion of some of its forms in this chapter. This, however, is by no means the end of the story. There are some forms of perception which have only recently been thought about, and others which, as yet, have not been adequately described. The social perception of children is an important area, playing a vital part in their dealings with people, who constitute what some might argue is the most significant environmental dimension of all. Then there is that kind of total awareness that children develop, of themselves as entities interacting with the world outside. It is a kind of self-image. Its physical manifestation can be seen in young children as they come whirling, hopping, jumping and shouting out of school.

We are not yet near a true understanding of the role of perception, though we can be certain that, without it, there is no environment.

3
Language and the Environment

'John, what are you doing?'
'Nothing, Mum.'
'Stop it, then.'
'All right.'

The participants in this short exchange show a sophisticated grasp of the use of language. Words are used with accuracy; there is no mistaking their meaning; further, John and his Mum are both using their conversation in order to control the other. Mum won. Significantly, what probably matters most in this conversation is the way in which both of them understood the reality of the situation behind the words; language is based on such sensibilities.

It takes a long time before a young child reaches this stage. Spoken language is not the only means of communication and does not become so, for, long before they can speak, young babies communicate by means of gesture, expression and manoeuvre. If everything else fails, they cry, indeed crying could be described as the language of early childhood. All forms of communication have their roots in need and the needs of a baby are desperate because he (she) cannot satisfy them by himself (herself). Crying is a very potent means of communication, its efficiency being demonstrated by the speed with which a new mother learns to interpret her baby's cry, and the urgency with which she responds. Many women, having had children of their own, remain, for the rest of their lives, quite unable to be at ease if they can hear a child crying, even if it is far away and has nothing to do with them.

There is far more to this than the mere expression of need. Through his unspoken language the baby not only makes his needs known but also expresses his own feelings, and, incidentally, binds the people he needs close to him. There are other aspects of language, those of self-expression and the desire for human contact. Actually, to refer to the desire for human contact is to put the matter too loosely; language plays a vital part in the bonding between mother and child, so that the environment of language is the environment of human relationships. By understanding the significance of the unspoken communication between parent and baby, we can see the spoken word in a new perspective. When the baby is very young, the bond between himself and his parents is cemented by close physical proximity, by gesture, smiling and, a little later, by eye-to-eye contact. As the baby grows older and physically more independent, he has to relinquish much of this contact, for he cannot remain near his father and mother for ever. The spoken word becomes a substitute. Spoken language takes over in part the task of bonding.

Spoken language enables children, as they grow older, to draw more and more people into their orbit, not merely just to have them there, but also to explore their personalities and to exercise a degree of control over them, to enter into their view of reality. There is an interesting illustration of this in a piece of research carried out in Indiana, in which the spontaneous conversations of groups of three- to five-year-olds were analysed.[25] Not only do we see the children's increasing grasp of the rules of language, we see their development as narrators and listeners. The three-year-old speaker telling a story spoke briefly and gave his listener little information that might enable him to orientate himself, such as when and where an event took place or who were the people involved. The three-year-old listener, likewise, did not bother to ask for additional information and did not display great interest in what she was hearing. She was not, in other words, the kind of person to whom you or I would enjoy telling a funny story.

The four-year-old speaker, on the other hand, took rather more care of the person he was talking to, often including an introduction to his story so that it could be understood more easily. The four-year-old listener reached out in similar fashion to the narrator, frequently asking for more information and responding verbally for over half the time.

The five-year-olds were the true sophisticates. The five-year-old speaker made real attempts to influence his listener's interpretations by underscoring meanings he thought important. The typical listener of five made many comments on the narrative she was hearing and was responsive, interested and encouraging. The five-year-olds were exchanging meanings in a truly interpersonal way.

Another trend reveals itself in this study of the way in which young children talk to each other. By means of language, they are growing through egocentricity and are learning to share other people's experience. This relinquishing of an idiosyncratic viewpoint has been shown to be greatly assisted, not only by contact with other children, but also by contact with adults, particularly those close to the child. This comes about by ordinary, everyday interchange. It has a social and a cultural significance, being one means by which the social culture decrees for the individual what he shall perceive. For example, it is a common sight to see a mother wheeling her baby along in a pram though the streets or the park. The baby will often point to things that interest her and, in response the mother might say, 'That's a bus', or 'There's a dog'. She is naming what the baby sees, shaping the baby's perception by means of the spoken word. She is doing more than this, for she is implicitly drawing the baby's attention to those features of the environment that are considered important in our culture, even if she is not herself aware of the fact.

Parents and family are of great value to children in continuing this education. In a careful study[26] of three children between the ages of one and three years, it has been suggested that through the kind of naming that takes place within the context of parent-child verbal exchange, the young child takes a great step forward in the development of his (her) communicative abilities. The author, Maris Rodgon, remarks, 'The importance of naming in focusing shared parent-child attention on relevant features of the world probably cannot be overestimated.' Moreover, the responses of the children to questions put to them were greatly influenced by the models provided by the parent. The spoken word is invested with meaning through human and social relationships.

Jerome Bruner and his colleague Nancy Ratner have pointed out another way in which, by means of language in the home, the young child is helped through egocentricity.[27] Bruner and Ratner observed two young children of five months and nine months respectively until they were nearly two years old, noting the games they played with their mothers. They concluded that a valuable characteristic of many of the games played was that they allowed reversible role relationships between speaker and hearer. Role-reversing, of course, is an excellent way of compelling a participant to assess a situation from another's point of view.

Spoken language, evolving in part from unspoken communication, is a powerful means of ordering the environment. It forms the basis of relationships with other people and it brings about socialisation. Nevertheless, part of the function of language is to enable the individual to be a-social, to guard his individuality, to express his secret thoughts and feelings. No individual is ever completely socialised. The spoken word enables us both to be drawn into the social stream and to remain private. Young children are adept at preserving what is precious to them in the face of the onslaught of adult language and logic. They often force adult ideas to fit what they see as real. One small boy of five reported to his mother that religious instruction was his favourite lesson at school because he was learning all about a bear. His mother could not recall a bear figuring in the Bible or the Prayer Book and asked to be told more. Her son explained that the bear couldn't see very well and that they sang about him. His mother, still puzzled, enquired as to the bear's name and was told it was 'Gladly, the cross-eyed bear'.

Apart from being the guardian of the integrity of the personality, language constitutes a cognitive tool of great power. It truly transforms the environment. It encapsulates experience, thus relieving the individual of the need to see, hear or feel everything at first hand and enormously expanding his field of thought. It defines what is perceived, allowing some attributes and excluding others. In this way, language enables hypotheses to be formed and explorative thinking to take place. Finally, it makes it possible for the individual to preserve and to recall experience. It makes him a richer person altogether.

By what means do young children come to order their environment through language? It is a long and complicated process but it is clear that even young babies possess sophisticated abilities in perceiving speech; observations of infants of six months have shown that they are able to discriminate between a variety of consonants and vowels.[28] Where we are in difficulties is in conceptualising the development of language in children. It is vital not to dwell too much on the technicalities of the process, to be over-concerned with the order children acquire the abilities to use nouns, verbs, and to speak whole sentences, but to put these developments in the broadest possible perspective. The language of children is embedded in experience and situation; to see it as the acquisition of a succession of single skills is like trying to examine a sea shell without visualising the sea-shore, or looking at the petals of a daisy without realising that the plant grows in the earth. People who know children are aware of the ways in which language is related to their lives. As Margaret Donaldson has put it in her clear, sensitive book,[29] the child, 'interprets situations. He is more concerned to make sense of what people do when they talk and act than to decide what the words mean.' This may well be the reason why children of obvious intelligence 'fail' tests. They are simply not interested in them. The linguistic environment is, then, highly complex; it consists of the child himself, his needs and his growing ability to explore. It consists of other people. It consists of all that is rooted in society and it may be personal or impersonal, like ways of thinking and the events that occur during the child's day. The linguistic environment is never static, but ever-changing, growing with the child himself.

A whole volume of ongoing research suggests that personal relationships are of paramount importance in influencing the linguistic development of the young child. The greatest single influence has been found to be that of the mother. In a study of children under five,[30] in which a variety of variables were assessed, the education of the mothers was seen to be bound up with the degree to which the children attained a sophisticated syntax, a wide vocabulary and a degree of abstraction in their choice of words. One would conclude here that the children of the educated mothers had opportunities for hearing good speech denied to their fellows. Parents and close relatives, apparently, operate by presenting young members of the family with a speech model. Jerome Bruner and Nancy Ratner[27] have pointed out other ways in which they help: without thinking consciously about it, they stage the baby's learning for him. Knowing the baby well, they understand what interests him and what he is capable of assimilating and introduce him to words accordingly. You never hear a mother talking about photosynthesis to her young baby, but you do hear her telling him what a nice day it is and how they will go for a walk. When he is a little older, at three, she might explain that the plants like the sun too. The games the other members of the family play with the baby are significant as well. Games, although apparently spontaneous, have a meticulous task structure and constitute valuable rehearsals of real life situations, with each participant being assigned a clear-cut role and given emphasised opportunities to make a contribution. Other broad social variables are less happy in their implications. Observations of disadvantaged children suggest that their speech may be retarded by the constant meaningless noise to which they are subjected. Their homes are full of noise from the television left on all day, from the radio, from shouting neighbours, from pop music and traffic. In such surroundings, the still, small voice of rational language is drowned and lost.

Television is frequently blamed these days for inhibiting conversation in the home. It probably is true that if it is watched every spare minute of the day it deprives young children of the opportunity for speech and the interplay of words. On the other hand, television programmes present a model of language to children which, so far as clarity goes, is a great improvement on what many of them hear in their own homes. The outside world is introduced into the home and with it a sophistication and richness of experience that form a background for the early development of vocabulary and speech.

The influences affecting the maturation of language in children are numerous and diffuse, ranging from broad sociological factors, such as social class, to intensely personal ones like the games played within the family. In spite of this great complexity, recent research has indicated that there is a broad pattern of development, although controversy rages around one or two important questions.

An interesting and fruitful discussion centres on the relative importance of inherited and environmental factors in the development of a language system. This is of great significance to teachers because, if children attain a facility with words merely as a result of the maturation of innate abilities, the part played by the external environment, including the teaching environment, must be correspondingly less. One school of thought holds that infants are equipped at birth to discriminate all the categories of sound present in all the languages of the world. Chomsky is among the most well-known exponents of this view on the interesting grounds, among others, that children are exposed to such inadequate samples of language in the form of ungrammatical speech, hesitations and uncompleted sentences from their parents and others in contact with them, that they must possess strongly innate linguistic ability in order to develop language at all. Going further, this theory presents an intriguing view both of language development and the environment in which it evolves. It sees linguistic experience, which is of course presented to the infant by means of his environment, as breaking down his very broad capacities for speech discrimination, causing some to atrophy because they are not used, while channelling others into the formation of his native language. Education, in this context, is seen as a kind of corruption.

Such a theory can be supported by other evidence. People who have a lot to do with young babies will be well aware of what is sometimes called 'the babbling phase'. This occurs between the ages of about four or five months, when babies will lie for hours happily humming, singing and mouthing. Listening carefully, it is clear that these babies possess a vast repertoire of sounds, some of which the adult listener will have forgotten and can no longer make. This would suggest that the linguistic environment does indeed embellish and emphasise some abilities at the expense of others.

The discussion can be continued by considering the nature of various languages. Whether the language in question is German, Sanskrit or English, it will have something in common with the others: that is a kind of perception, based on the way in which human beings perceive similarities. For example, it has been most shrewdly remarked that there is no language in the world that groups together, under one name, the red and green sections of the spectrum.[31] As well as this, it would seem that all human beings share other more subtle forms of perception. All languages perceive entities, such as people, animals, house and food. This gives rise to nouns and pronouns. All languages perceive events taking place, like the boy running, the woman working, or, if one happens to have been taught French in the old-fashioned way, the cat sitting on the mat. This kind of perception leads to the articulation of verbs and adverbs. All languages perceive that not only are people active, they can be on the receiving end of action and have things done to them. They allow also for the fact that some events happen in the past, some today and some will happen in the future. So arise the passive and active forms of language, and tense. There is indeed a common core in all languages, even when they have evolved independently of each other in time and space and it is likely that this common core is the result of certain basic perceptual abilities shared by all human beings. One would expect to find this same ability, which exists in all children, resulting in at least some shared features of language development.

Are external environmental influences, then, unimportant? This has been shown not to be the case either. Most infants teachers know of at least one speech-deficient child. He or she has usually little out-of-school contact with adults, is rarely spoken to and hardly ever hears a complete sentence. As a result, this child suffers a grave set-back in speech development. Even more irrevocable, on those rare occasions when a child has been separated completely from adult human company, his speech never fully recovers. Significantly it would seem that there are sensitive periods in the acquisition of language, in which, if the environmental influences are not there, or are of the wrong kind, the speech system is irrevocably damaged.

Research with young children indicates the importance of certain environmental factors, although the complete picture has not yet been drawn and all the influences at work have yet to be identified. Jordan, Bruner and Ratner have described some.[27] Another group of psychologists, while recognising that infants of a few months old are able to perceive speech, set out to assess the importance of listening experience.[28] Working with eight babies of six months old, they concluded that it was of great importance. More than that, they suggest that timing is a relevant environmental factor, pointing out that the intervals between presentations should not be too long when presenting speech stimuli to young children. The view of these authors, Eilers, Wilson and Moore, is that innate abilities, maturation and experience all contribute to children's development of language. Perhaps this is where the truth lies.

This brings us to the next area of controversy. If we accept the importance of the external environment in stimulating young children to acquire speech, what factors are of particular relevance? The debate has centred in particular on whether the mere exposure of the child to the environment is enough, or whether it is specifically the linguistic environment that matters.

One group of thinkers believes in cognitive determinism, that is, that simple contact of the young child with the extra-linguistic environment, with natural phenomena and everyday life, will be sufficient to stimulate language. This line of thinking de-emphasises the role of linguistic interaction with adults and stresses the role of individual experience. The other school of thought, holding the hypothesis of linguistic input, maintains that what is crucial is the child's experience of language. It is only language that can impose order on the sheer multitude of occurrences of events, phenomena and relationships that surround us. The language that a young child hears by virtue of those around him influences him in various ways. It enables him, or her, to learn what is going on; it helps him to interpret these events; it is selective and draws his attention to those aspects of experience that are held to be significant; it enables him to attain concepts. A good example would be a parent correcting a child for referring to a lady as 'she' instead of by name. It is not just a matter of grammar; the adult is stressing to the child that personalities are on a higher scale than, say, chairs and tables, and consequently must be treated respectfully. A very good and clear discussion of the issues involved is given by I. M. Schlesinger in the June, 1977, issue of the *Journal of Child Language*.[31] He concludes, as probably most of us would, that the two theories are not mutually exclusive and that the child in all likelihood uses both kinds of experience in developing language. There may also be individual differences between children, some being inspired by everyday perception and others being stimulated to a much greater degree by hearing actual words.

This leds one to reflect rather more deeply on the nature of both kinds of experience and the relationship between them. It is true that words cannot be used to describe what has already not been perceived. The sky is not blue unless it has been seen to be so. On the other hand, only a small part of experience is ever expressed in words. The human mind is layered; one part of it watches incessantly, remembers and feels, sending up sensations and suggestions to the expressive, controlling part above. Only some of these sensations are given shape and order by means of language. Most of us know what it is to search for a word to describe what we have seen, or felt, or thought, and yet be unable to find one, because it does not exist. Sometimes, but not very often, new words are found to express unique experience, and then language soars into poetry. It may be the case that extra-linguistic experience has an initiating, regenerative role to play in keeping language alive throughout life, while linguistic teaching refines the actual skills.

A third debate concentrates on whether all children develop their language skills in the same way, or whether each child follows an individual pattern and, if so, how? These too are important matters for teachers for on them depends how much provision should be made for individual differences. Not nearly enough research has been done to make possible any definitive answers to these questions, but it seems to be the case that there exists a broad pattern of development, within which are many individual strategies. Research into language development is, of course, one of the most difficult areas, because so much of the evidence is inside the child's head and is not of a quantifiable nature.

In a detailed observation of four children from the age of under one year to the point when they were two, it was found that each baby had its own distinct strategy in acquiring a sound system.[32] In a study of the corrections made by five- and six-year-olds to their own speech, it was noticed that every child had his or her own pattern of approach to learning. Some would ask for a passage to be repeated, some would not.[33] Bearing in mind the importance of the family and of parent-child interaction, one would expect differences in strategy to arise from this source, too.

Nevertheless, it would seem that young children, in broad outline, follow a similar pattern in the acquisition of language.

Speech is rooted in the human environment. All children learn to use speech as a means of satisfying their needs. These needs are many and are not necessarily physical; from early babyhood children use speech, even if this consists of crying and gesturing at first, to communicate, to bond with other people, to express their feelings and to find out about the world. The skein of speech is many-stranded.

All children learn to perceive language before they can speak it themselves. Even when they are only a few months old they can discriminate words and they plainly understand their meaning. There is abundant evidence of this in everyday life. I knew a young boy of under one year old who went on a family trip in the car to the seaside. On the way there was an animated conversation in which he took no part as he could not speak. Yet two years later he repeated that conversation to his parents. He had been listening. Listening, then, is a linguistic skill.

During this first year of life, children are intensely aware of sounds and words. While they are listening and, it must be added, doing a good deal of deep thinking as well, they are making their first attempts to speak. At four or five months they can be heard practising, or babbling and over the years they shape these sounds into words, using only those which form part of their own culture. Probably, these early years are the most sensitive of all, and the most crucial to language.

Learning to perceive speech and learning to produce it are therefore two processes that go hand in hand, and speech is used, right from the beginning of life, for many purposes. In the actual acquisition of words, it does seem that children follow a certain pattern, having much in common with each other. In an interesting study,[34] in which the natural oral language of five groups of children ranging in age from two through to six years, was analysed, it was found that children possess a core of frequently used words and sentences at comparable stages of language development. What made it even more interesting was that the study included children from several nations, including Australia, England, Canada and the USA.

In the early years of life children have typical ways of using language, to ask questions and to label what they perceive. Both are examples of children using language as a cognitive tool to find out more about the world; both, also, are proof that they have found out a good deal already. It is impossible to ask a relevant question unless its context has been understood; if a child asks, 'When are the dustmen coming?', it means that she has already taken in both that the dustmen come and why. Naming is a very important operation, as has been mentioned already; once things have names they can be defined, recalled and thought about; further, they have been placed in their cultural context. Their eagerness to name sometimes leads the under-fives to use other parts of speech as nouns, in fact the years from two to five could be called the age of the noun. I know an irritated mother who is trying to stop her three-year-old son from calling all bees, 'No-no's', simply because she spotted him one day about to touch a bee and shrieked out, 'No! No!'

From three years of age onwards, children steadily develop their linguistic skills, not only the obvious ones such as in articulating words, but in their understanding of the rules of language. Umiker-Sebeck, in his study of three- to five-year-olds, found significant differences between the older and younger children.[25] We have already noted how the older ones were more interested and less egocentric listeners; they were also better able to handle complex elements in a narrative and included a greater variety of information in their conversation. The sentences they used were more complicated in structure and were composed of a greater number of clauses. Further, they were able to go beyond their own immediate experience in recounting a story; the percentage of outside events included in the conversation showed a striking increase with age. At three years it was 11 per cent of the total; at four years it constituted 49 per cent, while at five years it was 53 per cent.

The author notes that the conversation of children of this age group is usually in the form of a narrative, and typically that narrative is based on the personal experience of the speaker. Most of us would agree with this.

Further light is thrown on the way in which young children come to understand the rules of language by the novel approach of analysing the corrections they make to their own speech. These indicate the extent to which they have grasped structure and syntax. Sinclair Rogers analysed the corrections two groups of children made. One group consisted of five-year-olds, the other group was composed of six-year-olds. The two groups produced different patterns of corrections, the older children possessing a better grasp of the rules of sentence construction and being more critical of their own speech. For this reason they corrected themselves more frequently. They were also more aware of the effect of their speech and were better able to match their performance with the rules they had internalised.[33] Sinclair Rogers noted that a large number of corrections concerned the verb and concluded that it is in the usage of this part of speech that five- to six-year-olds have most difficulty. He found, as we have previously noted, that individual children formed their own strategies for understanding what was presented to them.

Language is both the filter and the mirror of experience. The way in which it is used reflects the growing mental abilities of children, and conversely, these bring about an ever-increasing facility in the use of words. Language helps children as they grow older to embark upon a more abstract, complex conceptualisation of the world around them. In the early years this conceptualisation is tied to what is occurring in their own experience. This is indicated by observations of the questions children ask. At about three years of age, when the period of extensive questioning begins, 'what?' and 'where?' questions are the most frequently asked. This is partly because this kind of question is tied more firmly to nouns, which are easier to handle than verbs. As a result, lack of linguistic ability is, at this point, holding back the development of concept. A little later, young children release a flood of 'how's?' and 'when's?' which are rooted in the much more abstract concepts of cause, manner and time.[35]

It takes a long time before children grasp the nature of causality, which is deeply rooted in social culture. We would not, for example, account for rainfall in the same way as an African witch-doctor. One distinction that has to be made is between the kind of causality that results from social convention and the kind that springs from natural law. One can change one's habit of crooking the little finger while drinking a cup of tea in genteel company, but not the succession of night and day. Children of between six and seven years of age have been found not to distinguish between the two sorts of regularity, and hence between the two kinds of causation. They believed it was impossible to change social convention. Those of eight thought it might be possible, but that physical laws could be changed as well. Only ten and eleven-year-olds were able to make an accurate distinction.[36]

Understanding human behaviour takes even longer. It is many years before children can build up a concept of causality that can take account of people's actions, and of the events which result from those actions. At seven it has been observed that a child has little idea as to what constitutes normal human behaviour; he has no normative framework by which to judge people, and his assessments are idiosyncratic. Between the ages of ten to thirteen, however, he has a concept of what is normal, but only on the basis of clearly observable, overt behaviour. The seventeen-year-old, in contrast, possesses a true psychological perspective, making an accurate assessment of both social norms and the uniqueness of the individual.[37]

Such work is ample illustration of the way in which the development of children's mental power goes hand in hand with that of their language. The issues are even broader than this. Language can only be fully comprehended if it is understood in its fullest context, social as well as intellectual. One is reminded of the little girl who, when her mother pointed out that she had her shoes on the wrong feet, replied indignantly, 'But these are the only feet I have.' She had grasped the meaning of the words perfectly, but not the way in which they could be used.

Linguistic skills are a vital and living part of the young child's environmental strategy, but not all the factors contributing to them are within the teacher's control. As we have seen, the years before the age of five are crucial. Apart from this, some of the most significant influences on the development of speech lie in the family, way beyond the confines of the classroom. Further, language is so much a part of every aspect of life that it can be difficult to pin-point exactly how it can be enhanced by teaching. It is, after all, not enough to remark vaguely that children develop their understanding of language through experience, and to leave it at that.

There are, however, ways in which young children can be helped. In general, what they need is opportunity; the opportunity to come into contact with all sorts of experience, both extralinguistic and linguistic; the opportunity to use language for all its many purposes, for communication, for self-expression and for thinking. They cannot be hurried through the stages of development, for each must be peacefully lived through, but they can be helped if their teachers are sensitive to their needs as they mature and if they are aware of what is to come.

A great deal can be gained by organising small excursions from school. This is how one teacher used such a visit for her group of four-year-olds. She took them to a little group of shops, not five minutes away from the classroom. There they helped her with some shopping. They brought back carrots, potatoes, sugar and tea and found they had a lot to talk about when they returned. Not only did they learn the words for the articles, which were written up for them, they searched for new words to describe the glowing colour of the carrots and the rustling noise the sugar made when it was shaken in its packet. They also talked at length about what they had seen happening; a dog was tethered outside the shop and he kept whining. Why?, they were asked, what was he waiting for? Some of the children had noticed an old lady in the shop. She could not see very well and they saw her feeling round a fifty-pence piece when she paid for her groceries. They felt round a fifty-pence piece as well when they returned to the classroom and compared it with the milled edges of other coins. They were asked to find words by which to express the differences. Their teacher edged them carefully into a full discussion, not being content merely with enlarging their vocabulary, but introducing them to the concepts of 'how?', 'when?', and 'why?' by asking them questions. The whole adventure took about half an hour and was worth its weight in gold.

The needs of older children should not be forgotten. It is comparatively easy to think of interesting adventures for young children, but less so for the eight- and nine-year-olds who are much less orientated towards adults and who indeed are often intent on slipping away from them and following their own pursuits. They, too, can benefit from being taken away from humdrum surroundings on a visit that really interests them. To give but two examples, boys and girls of this age are often football fanatics and would love an excursion to the nearest club to see the dressing rooms and meet the trainer. Many football clubs are glad to welcome school parties. Alternatively, girls of this age are usually crazy about horses; they would thoroughly enjoy an hour or so at the local riding stables, where they can see the busy life that goes on there and enjoy the companionship of the horses. There are a surprising number of riding schools, even in inner cities.

Other incidents can be taken from the children's own lives. They may be of the exceptional kind, like a factory fire in their own district, or alternatively, the children can capture the tiny events that make up the fabric of life, like skipping along the streets to school.

The atmosphere within the classroom is important for speech development in children. Some classrooms actually inhibit it. Children need a certain atmosphere to use words freely and to experiment with them. In many ways, speech is the most sensitive human faculty of all, thriving on peace of mind and self-confidence and being totally wrecked by anxiety or fear. Teachers of young children will have noticed how, in times of stress, some children stop speaking completely, and become silent. What is needed, therefore, is the sort of classroom where every child is listened to and respected and, indeed, loved, and where the listeners have the good manners to wait quietly if a young speaker has to search for the right word. It is not necessary to interrupt if children mispronounce a word, as they frequently do. It has not been proved that progress in pronunciation lies along a straight line from speaking a word incorrectly to speaking it correctly, rather has it been suggested that there comes in between a phase of experimentation. In this case, it is doubtful whether asking children to repeat a word they have mispronounced helps them a great deal. The best way to help their pronunciation is to speak clearly oneself and to ensure that they hear plenty of good speech. Older children enjoy recording their own voices and playing the tape back, slang, mispronunciation and all. They learn more from this than from formal correction in the classroom.

Adults, teachers included, should never be too quick to understand and respond to the needs of young children. This may sound hard, but a very good way of encouraging the speechless to speak is to create small situations in which the children need a little assistance and are inspired to ask for it. This works to good effect in some special schools. If a young boy needs help with his wellingtons at playtime, it is not in his interest to leap forward immediately and help him; it might be better to wait for him to ask. It might be better still, if he is not keen on using words, to place his wellingtons out of reach so that he *has* to ask.

Older children, as well as the younger ones, need an atmosphere conducive to speech. Actually, their need is often greater. While adults will usually talk to the under-fives in a warm, encouraging way, they do not often do so to the seven- to nine-year-olds. These children are often starved of conversation with adults, playing in the streets at night by themselves. Their classrooms can be noticeably more repressive, places where chatting to one's neighbour is seen as a matter for punishment. These older children, also, need to have opportunities arranged for them for talking to adults and each other in group work or in conversation.

The importance of modelling in the development of children's language has been amply demonstrated. Children learn words and linguistic styles by listening to other people, therefore both listening experience and opportunities for talking to others are needed. The children can be helped, by good teaching, towards a listening strategy. Teaching them to appreciate silence is, paradoxically, a good way of enabling them to hear language. Most of the time we have to listen to speech against a background of distracting and often ugly noise. Hearing words in peace and quiet allows us to appreciate them fully, both in form and meaning. Also, as Yehudi Menuhin has remarked, 'Silence focuses the personality', and the personality has to be focused for speech.

Another aspect of the listening strategy is to have a method of finding out what the speaker means. It has been shown that in this area, too, it is possible to give children a plan for effective listening. Working with six- and seven-year-olds, two researchers introduced a game in which a speaker had to describe an object, or a picture, and the listener had to decide what it was.[38] When the children were reminded that they could ask questions and were helped to formulate these, their performance in speedily finding the correct answer greatly improved. They benefited from assistance and practice.

Significant in the modelling process is familiarity with the ways in which other people use language. Children need the opportunity of listening to others, both adults and other children, as much as possible. It has been shown that, with an adult, a child's language is often less fluent but more organised than with another child. In other words, his ideas may not be expressed so readily, but he pays greater attention to how he speaks and the structure of language.[39] Obviously he can profit from both kinds of conversation.

Conversations with other people not only present to young children models of speech, they bring them into contact with those realities of viewpoint and living-styles which underpin language. It is usually possible to invite people into the classroom, just to talk. They do not have to be special, just people, like ourselves, occupied with the everyday necessities of living. Parents are an obvious choice, or the kitchen ladies might find time to come in for a chat, or friends of the teacher, or lonely old people living nearby, who have a fund of interesting stories and great patience with young children. They are usually very flattered to be invited in. There are periods during the school week that lend themselves to becoming 'talking times'. They are the times when the children tend to be tranquil and the atmosphere relaxed. Friday afternoon may be one. Introducing comparative strangers, as they will be at first, into the classroom, takes a little tact, particularly as the situation has to be unforced. It is easier if only two or three come in at a time and if they just sit quietly there in odd corners, knitting or reading. Sooner or later the children will wander over to talk to them, it being an unwritten rule among them that everybody must be drawn in. I once heard a fascinating conversation between an eight-year-old boy and a dustman. They were talking, not about collecting dust-bins, but about how the dustman had come to join the Salvation Army. A ten-year-old girl became deep in conversation with a middle-aged housewife about the star of a popular television serial, while both were working at a jigsaw. To the little girl, the actress was a person of enviable glamour; the lady to whom she was talking, however, had read about her in the papers and was explaining how she was bringing up a baby on her own and had a great deal of worry. Young girl and older woman were modifying each other's view, exchanging experience, looking at the world together, and talking.

Children also need the time and opportunity to teach each other. They do just this if they are allowed to. Often they choose to do it by means of word games. Two examples illustrate children's ingenuity and inventiveness. Two four-year-olds had got hold of a big plastic toy truck, but they were not using it for loading bricks. They were sitting about twenty feet apart and one would write a message on a piece of paper, put it in the truck and send it speeding to his companion. The other would reply and back the truck would come. So the game went on, a kind of conversation at long distance.

Another game was invented by two six-year-olds. One drew on a piece of paper what he said was a monster with terrible powers. He described these to his friend. This monster could turn people to dust just by breathing on them, or it could freeze them solid. In response, his friend drew a creature of his own and explained why the first creature's powers would be to no avail. *His* creature had a thermal suit that could withstand both heat and cold; anyway, he'd made a trap for the monster. He explained how it worked. But, said the first little boy, that wouldn't work because . . . So the game continued, springing from fantasy but concerned with the exploration of natural laws and deeply rooted in verbal reasoning. These children had found their own way of exploring language.

Some things the teacher can do. The following are suggestions, some of which are already popular in the schools, and most teachers have a wealth of good ideas of their own. All the suggestions have the purpose of bringing the stimulus and interest of the outside world into the classroom and of encouraging children to use words in the fullest possible way.

Children benefit greatly from being able to talk to their teacher. As we have seen, the speech of young children generally takes a narrative form and the question 'Why?' comes late to them. Causality is not an easy concept to grasp. But the teacher can ask 'Why?' when listening to their stories. Without hurrying the children, because hurrying never works in the classroom, especially with so delicate a faculty as speech, she can at least make them aware that things usually happen for a reason. Suppose Beth was sick after eating an ice-cream, it could have been because she'd eaten too much, or because there was something wrong with the ice-cream, or because ice-cream simply does not agree with Beth. Any discussion of causality usually comes down to the uncovering of a whole network of circumstances. This is what one guides children towards, an appreciation of the situation in its entirety.

Using pictures in the classroom can be of great help here; in fact, pictures have certain advantages over real-life situations when it comes to stimulating language. A picture is a representation of events occurring in the environment. It takes a scene that the children are familiar with, for example, the lollipop lady guiding them safely across the road, and reproduces it in essentials. A picture is designed to make a point and so its message is easy to perceive. The lollipop lady will be given a position central to the picture, while the less important buildings can be seen faintly blurred in the background. In this way, the attention of the children is focussed. More than this, the picture reduces a moving scene to a still one, and it can be looked at for as long as necessary, so that it can be carefully scrutinised. A piece of research which demonstrates the differences in the way children of various age-groups interpret pictures will be of interest to all teachers.[40]

Three groups of children, of four to five years, of six to seven years and of eight to nine years, were given picture recognition tasks. The youngest children based their entire interpretation primarily on the central figure; in our case it would be the lollipop lady. The middle group utilised the entire scene and everything in it; having labelled everything they could see, they felt that the picture had been interpreted adequately. The eight-to nine-year-olds, in contrast, were able to recognise situation and action.

Young children need to be guided towards perceiving everything that is going on, not just the central event. In this way also, incidentally, they will be weaned away from their constant use of the noun and towards an appreciation of the other parts of speech, like the verb, the adverb and the adjective. There is usually a main event in a picture but also minor little dramas going on as well. Children may indeed be guided over the road, but there may also be a cat sitting on a doorstep, a girl may have dropped her hat, or two people may be chatting on a street corner.

It has been shown that young children can be helped towards forming a strategy for the fullest possible appreciation of a picture. In particular, they need to ask appropriate questions. It helps them to retain the information they glean if the picture is described to them before they see it.[41]

Pictures are easy to obtain. A variety can be collected for use in the classroom; those that stimulate speech and language most effectively are those which portray a situation. This may be everyday, like a street scene, or of a unique and exciting occurrence, like landing on the moon. It is much harder for children to talk about a merely descriptive scene like 'Winter in the countryside'. Educational suppliers produce a wealth of material for schools, some of which has already been mentioned. As an example, Philip and Tacey publish *People Who Work for Us* pictures, portraying people the children would see almost every day on their way to and from school, like the milkman, the nurse, the policeman and the shop assistant. Another source lies in the journals published, usually monthly, for teachers. *Child Education* and *Junior Education* both often contain large and colourful pictures just right for nursery, infant and junior children. The special issues of *Child Education* offer pictures of special interest, like those of a fun-fair, which invariably capture the imagination of children (*Child Education*, Special Number 6, 1979). Another entrancing issue was 'Under the Sea' (*Child Education*, Special Number 7, 1979) which contained a dramatic illustration of life around a coral reef. These journals are not expensive and, incidentally, offer teachers many interesting ideas on using the material provided.

However, pictures do not necessarily have to be bought. Local newspapers contain photographs of scenes, people and shops that the children actually know and might like to discuss, and we should not forget that pictures painted by the children themselves can stimulate a great deal of discussion. Everybody tries hard to find the right words when they are trying to get their meaning across to others.

Christmas cards and comics, which the children can bring to school themselves, provide all kinds of pictures. They have certain advantages, one being that they are often very funny and humour is a quality that the materials earnestly produced specifically for use in the classroom frequently lack. Consider the story overleaf about 'The Gingerbread Boy' (*Playhour*, 6 August 1977, IPC Magazines). The story is told in three main pictures. Ginger wants to go swimming at the seaside, finds the tide has gone out, so has a nice swim in a bucket of sea-water instead. This kind of strip is particularly good because even young children have to consider the total situation arising out of Ginger's dilemma. The story cannot be interpreted otherwise. It will not have escaped notice that the little man is only about two inches tall. This element of fantasy is intriguing to children; it is fun to imagine what life would be like were one this height. To put it more sombrely, having to consider a world where circumstances are not the same as in our world teaches a young reader about the rules governing his own environment.

THE GINGERBREAD BOY

"I will soon be swimming in the warm sea," thought Ginger. But the tide was out, and the sea was a long way away. "I'll come back when the tide is in," said Ginger. Then a bucket of sea water caught his eye, and he swam in that!

(Reproduced by permission of IPC Magazines Ltd)

The best pictures tell a story. Stories, whether read to children or told, go further, because they mirror someone's view of reality. For this reason, no two authors write in the same way, even if we are comparing the *Mr Men* stories by Roger Hargreaves (Thurman) with the *Paddington Books* by Michael Bond (Collins). Michael Bond and Roger Hargreaves have different views of the world, even if these differences are intangible and elusive. Stories reflect not merely physical phenomena and their ceaselessly changing nature, but the human environment as well. This is carried further in their content, for stories are invariably about people and even if those people are invented, they throw light on the human predicament. For these reasons, the value of stories in stimulating children's use of language goes far beyond the mere enrichment of vocabulary, because the children are introduced to life itself; life, that is, as it is thought. Stories invest the environment with a peculiar kind of order. This is so in terms of time, because every story has a beginning, a middle and an end; it is so in terms of events, which shape the sequence, and it is so in terms of the writer's perspective.

Let us not forget the stories children make up for themselves. Their lives are full of incident and everything is interesting to them. Encouraged to talk about the events in their lives they must be and a teacher can pick up some of the words they use and help them to enlarge their meaning. If we consider again the visit to the shop by the four-year-olds, some of them noticed the old lady's hands trembling as she fumbled for her change. 'What does "tremble" mean?' Do the children ever tremble, perhaps when they watch a horror film? Then again they saw the orange of the carrots. What other things are orange and are they exactly alike in other respects?

Children are fascinated by television. They often like the kinds of programmes that adults would love to see banned altogether, like cartoons, violent fantasies, cops and robbers series and the commercials. I know a child who, left to herself, will switch on for the commercials and then switch off. Such an interest on the part of children is worthy of careful consideration, for they rarely waste time on what is not useful. Television programmes are attractive, but beneath the superficial attractiveness lies a significance in that they act as a commentary on the world. This vivid portrayal can be used in the classroom.

Not everything can happen in the world in which we live; events are conditioned by both the physical laws controlling the universe and the constraints of human convention. The television programmes most popular with children usually explore what might happen when these regularities are over-turned or reversed. The best examples of this are the ever popular *Dr Who* and the perennial *Star Trek* (BBC 1). In their adventures, the crews are continually meeting creatures and worlds bound by laws quite different from our own.

In the cartoons, it is the sudden reversal or denial of physical laws that causes the greatest amusement in young children. In *Tom and Jerry* (BBC 1), Tom's teeth fall out with a clatter when he bites on something hard; he might fall over a cliff-top, but he paws the air desperately for several seconds before finally plummeting to the ground; having fallen 500 feet he cheerfully picks himself up, regains his normal shape and rushes off to seek revenge. The space fantasies and the cartoons have a lot in common. They are a kind of witty commentary on the way in which our world runs itself, and in making these contrasts they tacitly emphasise to children how their lives are lived. This understanding is the very cornerstone of language.

Such episodes can be used as discussion points in the classroom.

Some television programmes, especially the cartoons, explore the deeper levels of human nature. Their messages are all the more pointed because the characters frequently come in the form of animals or puppets. The popular *Muppet Show* on ITV illustrates this; the Muppets portray human charaacters in a way that children can understand. We have probably all met in real life the terrible Miss Piggy in her pursuit of the sensitive Kermit. Sometimes the humour of the Muppets is built on a desperate truth of human existence. Such was the case when the turkey, the porker, the cattle and finally the vegetables intended for Christmas dinner, rebelled against the chef who was trying to cook them, so that in the end everyone had to eat vitamin pills, with a knife and fork.

Mere exposure to these situations is an education to children. They can be used in the classroom to enlarge their horizons and enrich their vocabulary. As a bonus, publishers often produce the stories behind the television series in book form, so that the gap between the spoken and the written word is bridged: *Muppets go Camping* and *Muppet Manners* are published by Sphere while the *Muppet Show Book* is published by the Souvenir Press.

The commercials on ITV are very popular, especially with really young children. The reasons are instructive, particularly for teachers. Commercials are short and to the point, never lasting longer than about two minutes, so they match the attention-span of the under-fives. They are beautifully produced and sung words and catchy tunes bring out the rhythms of the spoken word and are repeated several times. The phrases are the common ones of everyday life. Of course, such material has to be used with great care in the classroom – nobody would condone the brain-washing of very young children – but perhaps if they are heard humming the tunes, as they often are, the words could be explored.

If they are given the opportunity and the materials children will recreate situations and enhance their own language. Very helpful to them are models, that they can handle, of people, cars and buildings, in fact, anything that they come across in normal living. These little models can be purchased or brought from the children's homes, or made. A street scene can easily be constructed, as so many children collect model cars. A model shop can be made from empty cartons, and vegetables and cakes moulded in playdough. Many classrooms possess dolls' houses and farms, and little models of people, about six inches high that are easy for children to handle, are easily obtainable.

A lot of time is needed for free play in an unforced, relaxed atmosphere. Apart from this, the models can be used by the teacher to focus attention on various aspects of language, particularly that of using words with precision. For example, one child could feed the animals on the farm and bring them in for the night, describing what he is doing. Alternatively, one could carry out the actions while another provides the commentary. Someone else could be persuaded to work with one animal instead of several, thus gaining practice in making the verb agree with the subject; or a child could switch from describing what happens today to recounting what happened yesterday and so be helped to handle tense.

Equipment like telephones, real if possible, and dressing-up clothes and furniture such as toy ironing-boards, cooker and wheelbarrows encourage children to act out situations from real life and so increase their vocabulary. Most of us will have heard them re-enacting the drama of sending for the doctor when someone is ill, or reliving the fun of a Saturday afternoon spent helping in the garden. The older children, too, love both role-play and interesting object lessons. One of the best lessons in vocabulary I ever heard was taken by a young teacher with a class of eight-year-olds with learning difficulties. He took his motor bike along to the English lesson.

The more structured games are likewise a form of role-play. Games have great advantages in the classroom, in that they reduce a situation to its essentials so that these are easy for young children to perceive, they focus their attention and, above all, they are fun. One should cast the net far and wide in searching out games that act as a stimulus to language. As we have seen, children are good at inventing their own games. Apart from this, teachers can take advantage of their fascination for some of the television parlour games. The way in which these intrigue people, adults as well as children incidentally, surely points to their tapping a deeper interest than that of mere entertainment. If we consider two simple games that are very popular, we can see why. *Twenty Questions* and *Animal, Vegetable and Mineral* are really games of verbal reasoning. Played in the classroom, a teacher or a child holds in the hand an object, like a rubber or a sweet, and someone else has to guess what it is. They do this by asking a limited number of questions; ten would be enough for young children. A boy or girl might ask, 'Is it alive?', 'Is it big or little?', 'What colour is it?', 'What is it used for?' After ten questions, he or she must have a guess, before if the answer seems obvious. Such an exercise helps both the listening and the analysing strategies of children. It could be that a small team of children do the questioning, in which case they can reason together.

There is a connection between being able to use the spoken word and being able to read, but the connection is not a simple one. Bernard, at five, was bright and loquacious, with a fund of general knowledge gathered from intelligent parents and lively relationships with other children, but he showed no inclination to read. He was too busy. Never still, he spent most of his day travelling round his open-plan classroom in order to see what everyone else was doing. In contrast it was difficult to get a word out of Tracey who was six. Too shy to speak, she buried herself in books. She joined the local library and, by the time she was eight, was reading a whole book a day. Her parents were worried. As her working-class father put it, 'She spends all day with her head in a book and never goes out.'

Robert's parents were worried too. When he was a baby, he uttered not a sound. When other young children were babbling away and practising the basic sounds of speech, Robert said nothing. But at the age of four, Robert blossomed into speech, speaking perfectly in complex sentences with clauses. At the same time, he taught himself to read by studying the labels on jam jars and bottles he found at home. He proved to be exceptionally intelligent.

Sandra was ten. I taught her years ago and I still think about her. She spoke only in monosyllables and would neither read nor write, achieving very little of any kind, yet she was intelligent. Her mother had died when she was two and she herself had been badly burned in a fire in a caravan while on holiday. She was still shocked. The combined efforts of all the teachers in the school did very little to help Sandra, though we did find that she liked acting. Given a part to act, which she therefore was in almost every lesson, she would speak well. Sandra's was not a success story, for she remained below average in nearly everything; perhaps life has been kinder to her as an adult than it was to her as a child.

These children's cases show how complex and various are the influences which affect the ability of young children to speak, read and write. Some abilities have a genetic basis, like perceptional skills and intelligence; there are social variables like the influence of parents; there are highly personal and unique factors, like that which made Robert store up his knowledge of semantics for a sudden dramatic debut, and Sandra react to grief and shock by turning her back on the written and spoken word.

Being able to read is almost as important a part of a young child's environmental strategy as being able to speak; we can see this if we consider what is implied by reading.

The written word is twice removed from immediate experience. In this it differs from the spoken word, which is only once removed. When reading, we have to call up the experience, the wail of the factory hooter or the song of a bird, through first the print and then the word. This means that reading implies a standing-back from the actualities of life and a recognition of a visual symbol. As a result, the environment that can be explored and ordered is made almost boundless in almost every sense of the word. Through books, a child can explore other regions, other times in history, other ideas and other societies. It is easier to do this through reading because the written word, unlike the spoken, is permanent and can be returned to again and again. Reading, then, is a skill that both expands the environment and makes it more manageable.

The content of this environment differs somewhat from that of the spoken word. Basically, written language embodies concepts and ideas that are essential for thinking, whereas the spoken word is primarily used for self-expression and for inspiring action. The information gained from reading is generally of a more abstract kind. Also, it has a much stronger cultural content, being the medium through which the essence of our civilisation is handed down. Learning and true intellectual effort come to us by means of the written word.

What are we asking of a child when he learns to read? What is this environmental skill called reading?

We ask, first, that he or she develops certain perceptual and mechanical abilities, such as will enable him to trace a sentence, move the eyes from left to right and hold the image of the whole sentence in his mind as well as that of an individual word. These skills were mentioned in the discussion of perception. Children develop them slowly. The evidence is that sensory discrimination cannot be considered apart from cognitive and intellectual skills when it comes to reading. Auditory and visual integration are probably connected with intelligence, as are memory and reasoning. This has led to the suggestion that the time has come for a much broader conceptualisation of reading theory than we have at present.[42]

We also ask of the young child learning to read that he goes beyond the mere pronunciation of the written word and understand the reality behind it. Reading does not consist of correct pronunciation, it means understanding. Coming to this involves maturation and effort on the part of the child. As we all know, the child's idea of reality is not the same as our own. In order to develop this understanding, he has constantly to integrate the information he acquires with what he knows already; he has also to grow through egocentricity, for the essence of the written word is that it should mean the same to all of us. The process is somewhat akin to that of understanding the significance of the spoken word; every teacher knows when a child is coming near this, because he suddenly begins to read aloud with expression. Reading involves a combination of intellectual maturity and a social sophistication on the part of the child. This can be illustrated by considering a simple statement, 'John fell over, because he tripped on a stone.' Having recognised the visual symbols, the reader has to equate the written words with his living experience. He must have come across stones and he will have probably fallen over himself, or the words will mean nothing. This translation of second-hand experience into first-hand is, for the child, a creative task of the first order. Even this is not enough for, to understand the written word fully, all the tacit conventions of the subject matter have to be understood as well. Of peculiar subtlety is the way in which causation operates. The writer has directed the attention of the reader to the stone as the cause of the accident, but causality is many-sided. It could be that John tripped over because he wasn't looking, or because his shoes were too big. In order to understand the true significance of one cause, the reader will have at the back of his mind all the other possibilities.

There is another characteristic of reading, one that is at the heart of it. The reader has to develop an empathy with the characters, the subject matter and the author. Here are two extracts from popular books written specially for children. I picked up both books and opened them at random; it so happens that each describes the everyday activity of cooking. The first extract is from Elizabeth Beresford's *The Invisible Womble and Other Stories* (Puffin, 1973). She writes:

And then there is Madame Cholet the cook. She produces the most divine meals out of all kinds of strange things. Her elm-bark pie with fluffy toadstool topping is famous throughout the Womble world. Like all good cooks she stands no nonsense in the kitchen and has been known to rap even Tobermory's paws when he tried to taste one of her bracken jellies before it was set.

The second extract is from *Paddington Abroad* (Puffin, 1967), a perennial favourite by Michael Bond. Paddington is sniffing the air. The narrative continues:

To start with there was a nice warm smell about everything, which he liked very much indeed. It was an interesting smell – not at all like the one in England, or even in Peru for that matter. It seemed to be made up of coffee and newly baked bread as well as several other things he couldn't quite place, and for some strange reason it was getting stronger every minute.

It wasn't until Paddington reached the top of the hill that he discovered the reason for it, and when he did so he had to rub his eyes several times in order to make sure he wasn't dreaming.

To labour on too much about the differences between these two writers would be to destroy the flavour of their work. Suffice it to say that, in the first extract, cooking is an activity that centres on the strong, practical nature of Madame Cholet; in the second, cooking is hardly a practical matter at all. It is nostalgic and evocative and becomes part of Paddington's dream-world.

Reading is an activity which enables the child to flavour the environment in the fullest and most pervasive sense.

We all want to know, firstly, what makes children start to read, and secondly, what makes them go on reading. We have only partial answers to both questions, largely due to the nature of research on the subject. Various influences have been identified but these are invariably global and generalised in nature. There is very little that enables us to estimate the importance of environmental factors as seen from the personal viewpoint of the young child. What we really need are a series of patient, detailed, long-term studies of such children as Bernard, Tracey, Robert and Sandra, which would allow us to study the interaction of all the influences (parental, social, scholastic and personal) which combined to make them the kind of readers they became.

In trying to answer the question why young children begin to read, it does seem that there is a connection between the kind of verbal interaction a child experiences, especially in the pre-school years, and his reading ability later. Cliff Moon and Gordon Wells made a detailed study of home influences on the reading ability of twenty children between the ages of three and seven.[43] They found that attainment in reading at seven years was strongly predicted by knowledge of literacy on entry to school, and that this, in turn was predicted by parental interest in literacy and the quality of verbal interaction with the child in pre-school years. Significantly, and it is a point for teachers to remember, the children's *own* pre-school interest in literacy was not strongly associated with later success. This research indicates that having plenty of opportunity to talk and listen to other people may encouarge children to learn to read. The exact relationship remains obscure, though. There is an interesting discussion of the subject and a review of relevant research by Patrick Groff in *Reading World*, October 1977, in his article 'Oral Language and Reading'.[44] It should be noted also that the work of Cliff Moon and Gordon Wells indicates that the groundwork for reading is laid long before the child comes to school.

The main reason children begin to read must be, quite simply, that they are exposed to books. Reading is not something that could be described as a primary activity, it is not the kind of skill that develops naturally as a result of maturation, like running and jumping; it is not a skill essential to survival. The alphabet and the written word took hundreds and hundreds of years to evolve as the culmination of immense cultural effort; it is doubtful whether any of us could invent them by ourselves. Reading, then, has to be learnt and it is a much more artificial activity than speech. Children probably learn to read because they have become accustomed to words in the form of speech and are also, therefore, interested in words in the form of writing and print. They see the printed word all around them and are aware of the emphasis the adults in their world place on reading. It is not necessarily books that start them off; they see their parents looking at the telephone directory or studying a map; they themselves will be interested in the labels on jam jars and sauce bottles, like Robert, who taught himself to read by them. It is, after all, important to be able to distinguish strawberry from apricot jam, when you don't like one but are very fond of the other.

Exactly how young children should be introduced to books is therefore a matter vital to us all. The observations of teachers have not only revealed the ways in which children react to books but have also thrown light on certain environmental factors that encourage them to read. Drucilla James is a teacher-librarian, so that what she has to say is worth listening to. From her work in schools she has found that displays of pictures and other similar material are not effective in encouraging children to read, 'the only effective display seems to be selections of the books themselves'.[45]

She has found that the visual apperance of the books themselves matters, though. Children tend to choose books that look colourful and attractive, with a pleasing layout; only exceptionally popular books are borrowed if they look tatty and dull. A significant influence is the proximity of books; if children have plenty of books around them they will tend to read; in the words of Ms James, 'Proximity does influence reading readiness.'

Very interesting are the personal relationships that affect what children read. Friends influence each other's reading, so does the teacher. The teacher has most effect on those children with whom she has the firmest personal relationship.

These observations throw some interesting light on reading. In one sense it is an activity that is integral to itself; it is the books themselves that speak to children, not enticing displays of pictures. Yet, in another sense, reading is affected by many diverse environmental factors, a child who has few friends and a poor family background being that much less likely to pick up a book.

Once they have begun to read, children develop their own individual reading strategies. Although there is a great deal in this area about which we remain ignorant, we do know something about the way in which these skills are acquired. A child learns to make sense of what he or she is reading by utilising the cues implicit in the text. These cues may be graphic, that is, concerning the actual writing of the words; they may be syntactic, in which case they are embedded in the construction of the sentence, or they may be semantic and reveal the meaning of what is written. An interesting piece of research was carried out by Elizabeth Burke, who analysed the oral reading miscues of 216 seven- to nine-year-olds in British primary schools.[46] Her aim was to study the strategies used by children in developing skill in reading by probing the importance of graphic, syntactic and semantic cues in the reading material. With age, the greatest improvement occurred in the semantic skills, which, one would suggest, points to the significance of general maturity in making sense of the written word and to the link between reading and social and intellectual development.

The schools studied adopted different approaches to the teaching of reading, some emphasising the importance of reading much more than others. None of this, however, was found to have a significant effect on the children's patterns of miscues. Where the schools did exert influence was by means of what might be described as their general ethos. Pupils in informal schools obtained the highest scores for both syntactic and semantic miscues. This research points to the role played by maturation in the emergence of reading skills in children and also indicates some of the part played by school and teaching. At the end of her article, Elizabeth Burke suggests some areas where our knowledge of children's reading strategies is lamentably scanty. Not yet assessed is the extent to which children are influenced by the particular methods and materials through which they are taught and there has been no careful analysis of the way in which reading strategies are affected by a child's typical style of response to the text. A child may, for example, exhibit a global or analytical style of response.

Broadening the issue rather, it may well be that varying strategies are called for in response to the demands of the text and the purpose of the reader. We may read because we want information, in which case we need to develop a processing ability. We may be reading mathematics or science, and then we must be strictly logical and be able to think in symbols. We may be reading just for the sheer joy of the rhythm, the colour and the sensory qualities of the words, and then to be too stringently intellectual might kill their meaning. We do persist in referring to reading as if it is just one process, whereas in fact it is probably many.

Once the actual techniques of reading have been mastered, some children use books extensively. These are the good readers, and the difference between them and the poor readers is they will read anything and everything, from comics to hardbacks and encyclopaedias. The reading material of children who dislike books tends to remain confined to comics and strip cartoons.

Reading is an important environmental strategy. Quite simply, it opens up the world, and is therefore a significant part of the environmental study, both in its own right and because it is essential to many of the other environmental skills.

The part played by the teacher has to begin in the classroom but it should reach beyond it. The enthusiasm with which young children take to books is, as we have seen, greatly influenced by their personal relationships with parents, friends and teacher. When a teacher forms a good and trusting relationship with the children in her class, she is, indirectly, encouraging them to read. If she can manage to get a friend for the lonely Sandra or the painfully shy Tracey, she is likewise helping them. Nowadays, teachers can also reach parents. The research of Cliff Moon and Gordon Wells has shown how vital is the early parent-child relationship in predicting the literacy of children in later years, being actually a better predictor than the child's own interest in books.[43] Parents, of nursery school children in particular, should have it explained to them, at parents' meetings if possible, how important it is for them to talk to and read to their children, and to have books around the house. They want to help their children and they speedily get the message. Sometimes tact is called for. I remember a girl in a class of eleven-year-olds I taught who was a very poor reader. All my colleagues were delighted when her father turned up to a parents' meeting and we explained to him, one by one, what the problem was. He was a small, tired man, who worked long hours as a plumber. Yes, he said, he knew that Joan wasn't much good at reading, neither was he or her mother and he intended to buy a set of encyclopaedias in order to put matters right. We were aghast; the thought of him spending a lot of his hard-earned money on what might be impossibly difficult material appalled us. However, nobody liked to say anything and we proved to be quite wrong. Joan's father bought the encyclopaedias (on hire purchase), and he and Joan spent many happy hours looking up things together. Joan's homework became distinctly scholarly in character – in fact much of it was copied from the book – but she certainly learnt to read.

It should not be forgotten that the bonds children form with people quite outside school can be used to help their reading. They become very fond of the presenters of the children's programmes on television. Janet, Simon and Peter of *Blue Peter* on BBC 1 (1984), for example, are very popular, as the floods of children's letters to them show. If one can get home in time to watch these programmes at ten past five, and note what the three presenters are doing and the interests they are following up, many ideas can be gleaned for children's reading.

Both the atmosphere and the materials provided in the classroom greatly affect the willingness with which young children take to books. The observations of Elizabeth Burke contain a message here, one that may not be popular in some quarters. Although one has to be careful to define exactly what 'formal' and 'informal' classrooms are before jumping to conclusions, it may well be the case that a settled routine and carefully staged learning are most conducive to reading. The young Bernard, who was always too busy to learn to read, might have done better in a stricter atmosphere.

Every classroom should be full of attractive books with easy to read print and plenty of pictures. Further, these books should be easy for the children to obtain. There are schools where there are so many rules and regulations about the borrowing of books that nobody bothers to take one out. Drucilla James has also found that habit of borrowing books is a strong factor in encouraging children to read. It will help if, apart from being able to take a book down from the classroom shelves when it suits the children, certain times of the day or week are laid aside for them to choose a book of their own. Reading material should range widely in subject matter because good readers want to read everything. This, of course, will encourage the development of various reading strategies, so that the children will vary their approach according to whether they are searching for information, or just enjoying a good story.

Reading, in the true sense, is a matter of comprehension, and comprehension comes to children as a result of maturation and experience. As we have seen, true understanding requires a sensitive and accurate perception of the subtle realities behind the text. In this sense, all experience helps reading, that is, every conversation with someone else, every trip outside school, every personal relationship. Contact with the world outside school is valuable, because that is where life is led. In a more constrained sense, though, it is often possible for a teacher to help young children to understand what they are reading. Children who do not comprehend well may be in difficulties for a number of reasons; they may not possess the vocabulary; they may be emotionally insecure, or they may not yet have grown through their egocentricity. Although much of this is beyond the reach of the teacher, it has been shown that children can be helped by a careful structuring of their reading. Sentences should be presented one at a time, followed by a pause in which the child is encouraged to visualise what is happening. Questions interspersed in the text help the child build up a fuller understanding of the meaning of the text.

Sometimes the transition from the spoken to the printed word can be eased by the use of pictures. Young children practise fitting words appropriately to drawings of scenes. They might place the captions, 'The dog is crossing the road', or 'Mother is cooking the tea', to the correct pictures. In this way, they learn to connect the written word with something that is actually happening, an aspect of reality. They have to read the words first in order to fit them to the picture.

It might be fun to try fitting sounds to words rather than pictures. We place a good deal of emphasis on visual experience, as indeed we do throughout our society, but there is little exploration of the significance of sounds. Some enterprising teacher, using a tape recorder, might compose a 'sound book'; there could be a door opening and closing, footsteps, the clink of tea cups. Children might enjoy finding a word, a phrase or a sentence to describe the sounds they hear; and this might be more vivid to some of them than matching word to picture.

If the written work of young children is based on experiences that are vivid to them, this again reinforces the message that the printed word does indeed have meaning. This is one of the many ways in which the environmental study contributes to their reading. What young children find fascinating and intriguing does not necessarily matter to an adult, and teachers have to be sensitive to this. I watched a little group of under-fives go out to plant some seeds in a little patch in the school grounds. They all went armed with spades and began to dig enthusiastically. They were very interested in a worm they found which some of the Asian children thought might be a snake. Some tiny pieces of patterned china were dug up and, strangely, a bell. The seeds were forgotten. Back in the classroom, the teacher wisely having put aside the matter of seed-planting for the moment as well, they were helped to write a little book. They learnt to recognise the words 'worm' and 'bell,' 'spade' and 'dig'; more important they were tacitly learning that words encapsulate experience.

With help bigger subjects can be undertaken, based on the children's own lives. An attractive topic would be a group of shops near the school, where perhaps they buy their sweets. The subject matter needs to be broken down and set out clearly. Each page might have a picture with a sentence underneath; the picture could be a photograph or a drawing by an individual child. It might look as below.

A child's own reading book

This is the sweet shop.
I buy sweets here.

The green grocer sells
apples, bananas and cabbages.

At the Post Office
my mum buys
stamps.

This dog often sits outside.
He is not allowed in.

Building up their own readers is illuminating to children in several ways. It takes away the fear of books that some children have, as being rather cold and frightening objects; it teaches them about the mechanics of a book, that it has numbered pages and printed words and that you read from front to back; lastly, it is an exercise in handling subject matter, however simple this may be. Analytical thinking and careful organisation always lie behind the printed word. Simple readers can be made by printing the words in fibre-tip, the pages being either stapled or tied together. The paper on which the words are printed is important; children are sensitive to touch, so that the pages should feel, as well as look, pleasing.

All young children love receiving letters, especially 'real' ones brought by the postman. I know a family who encouraged their young son to read by posting him a letter every week. The letters covered all kinds of subjects, but he was intrigued, being about four, by the confrontations that occurred nearly every day between the family cat and the local squirrel over the food put out in the garden. He wanted to know what they were saying to each other. The letters told him. A school could have a post-box and encourage older children to write to the younger ones.

Often parents compose superb stories for their children, unself-consciously and probably unaware of their value. One family with which I am acquainted, looks after the school guinea-pigs during the holidays. They all have names, adventures and wonderful characters, evolving slowly as stories are told by the parents to the children. Matthew is the grandad; he sits in his hutch all day smoking an old pipe and is a strict disciplinarian. Florence is the mother, sweet natured but clever; she has ambitions to be a pop star. Big Boy is a problem, rebellious, noisy and harum-scarum; he has a motor bike on which he roars around all day, annoying his grandad, and if it's taken away from him he roars around pretending to be a motor bike, which is worse. Tiny Boy is humble and hard-working but spirited. He made himself a pair of leather wings, for he would like to be a bird, but one turned out bigger than the other, so he can only fly in circles. At the moment, the family's efforts are concentrated on obtaining Big Boy gainful employment, but they always fail because something always goes wrong. In his last job, he knitted a jumper out of spaghetti. Nobody wore it.

Stories like these should be written down; the parents would enjoy this exercise. They could form a little group of writers for their children.

While we are on the subject of parents, many schools invite them into the classroom to hear children read, for practice is an essential part of reading skill and teachers have not the time to hear each child read every day.

Children are intrigued by the words they find on jam jars and sauce bottles. Robert taught himself to read them and I've certainly come across children who, by examining the labels on objects they see so often, come to realise that a single word is composed of letters. Each child could keep a little booklet of such labels.

A classroom display could centre on, 'Words we see around us'. Included could be, 'Pay as you enter', 'Exact fare please' (as seen on the buses); 'Pedestrians', 'One way only' and 'litter' as seen in the streets; 'Ladies' and 'Gentlemen' can be read outside the toilets and all sorts of words can be found in the shops.

Nearly all children are familiar with nursery rhymes. These, it is suggested by an infants teacher, Klara Turner, can be used to introduce phonics naturally to young children and to help them with words they find difficult.[47] Having sung 'Humpty Dumpty' and got to know it, they can study the printed words of the song and see that 'Humpty' is different from 'Dumpty'. A line like 'Polly put the kettle on' stresses phonics. In order to help them remember unstressed words sentences like 'Jack and Jill went up the hill' can be cut up and the children can practise putting the words together again in the correct order.

We come now to our old friend the television set. Television is frequently seen as the enemy of language and culture and there are certain grounds for this. Time spent watching it is not spent reading, so that television watchers, quite simply, may be deprived of reading practice. Of equal concern is the suspicion that the presentation to children of a stream of vivid visual images, which is what television does, may actually inhibit their formation of a more abstract, verbal image. On the other hand, those on television speak better English than most of us hear around us all day: sentences are not left unfinished and words on the screen are correctly spelt. The newsreaders, in particular, have good manners, assuming that the watcher is civilised, intelligent and a good listener. These tacit assumptions are essential to the use of language, whether spoken or written. In any case, television programmes are now part of our culture and could be used in schools far more than they are at present. Moreover, it has been shown that both the programmes and the commercials of the television companies can be a great stimulus to children learning to read. The commercials, especially, have considerable appeal for the three- to five-year-olds. They have big, gay letters and clear messages. In many ways they are like the flashcards used in the classroom, with the added dimensions of colour and music. Teachers have found that three-year-olds frequently learn to recognise their first letters from them. One might describe commercials as the nursery rhymes of the 1980s. Young children most appreciate those with a simple, clear message; often this is printed at the bottom of the television screen while the words are sung. In the classroom the captions can be studied closely and analysed, used, in fact, in much the same way that Klara Turner has suggested for nursery rhymes. The commercials which advertise the public services are usually suitable and are often funny as well.

Apart from entertaining the children, the television companies produce excellent educational programmes specially concerned with language development. To mention just three, there are *You and Me* (BBC), *Stop, Look and Listen* (ITV) and *Reading with Lenny* (ITV).

Teachers can learn a good deal from the popularity of comics with children. In my early days as a teacher, the first part of every English lesson was spent going round and confiscating all the comics – which the children wanted to read under the desk or hidden in an earnest-looking exercise book – and directing their attention to what I wanted them to read, the class textbook. Eventually I grew secure enough to admit to myself that the comics made very good reading. They contain some pertinent lessons for teachers on how to teach. The subject matter always has a direct appeal for the reader. A popular story in *Tammy* describes the adventures of Bella, a girl gymnast, who is fighting to reach the Olympics even though she is poor and almost friendless; other themes have covered Stella, who lives her life always under the shadow of her older, brilliant sister; yet another episode is about the evil 'Spider Woman', who plans to conquer the world. These themes are near to the hearts of nine-year-olds; some touch on their own lives, others may represent a pleasing gloss on normal school life, as in the case of the girls' boarding-school in which the headmistress turned out to be a vampire (*Misty*, March 1979).

The layout of comics is instructive because it invites children to read. The narrative is expressed in a sequence of pictures, while the printed word is in the form of speech. This does away with the need for a complicated sentence structure. More than this, each story is carefully broken up into steps, each being depicted in a single picture, so that the reader is never expected to take in too much at once. This kind of layout may be best for those children who are just beginning to read, or who dislike reading. It could be adopted for any books produced by the teacher for the class. In any case, comics should not be banned entirely from the classroom library.

Radio Times and *TV Times* can also be used as reading material. One idea is to use the little captions that describe the programmes. As an example, we can consider the adventures of Porky Pig on ITV at 4.15 p.m. on weekdays (week beginning 26 April 1982).

> On Monday, *TV Times* read, 'Porky is given horseshoes instead of mail when he rides for the pony express.'
> On Tuesday, 'Porky Pig sets out on a trek through the jungle.'
> On Wednesday, 'Foreign Legionnaire Porky Pig learns of an impending attack on a desert fort.'
> On Friday, 'Porky Pig is fascinated by an old fur trapper's recollections of his days in the woods of the north.'

It should be pointed out to children that if they read *TV Times* and *Radio Times*, they can find out what is going to happen in their favourite programmes. They could make their own TV reading books, pasting in the descriptions such as those above and then drawing pictures as illustrations or writing fuller accounts for themselves. The television magazines can be studied in the classroom, being used to encourage the recall of words and to enlarge the children's vocabulary. The adventures of Porky Pig may be simple, but some of the words used to describe them are not. What is 'an impending attack'? What does 'fascinated' mean? And what are 'recollections'?

Often teachers of young children are justifiably far from pleased when they find that they are allowed to stay up late at night watching violent television programmes. However, these too should be used, taking advantage of the vivid impression they make on children, for we cannot turn our backs on reality.

On page 74, we asked what makes children begin to read and why they go on reading. Many of the influences that encourage children to begin reading are also significant in ensuring that they continue to do so; the interest of parents, the interchange of ideas with friends and that availability of books are cases in point. Nevertheless, there are two questions here, because we have all come across children who *can* read, but do not bother to. The answer to the question why children grow into avid readers must be that books have captured their interest. All sorts of reasons may lie behind this; it may be because a book can tell a mechanically minded boy or girl how to mend a bike, or because it can whisk them away to another world. It is the teacher's responsibility to ensure that interest in reading is kept strong and alive by providing the children with books that interest them, and also by showing them how to use them. As has been said, there are various ways of reading a book according to what one wants from it. If information about mending a bicycle tyre is what is required, then a child needs to be helped to find what he or she needs, to analyse the text and perhaps to write the key points down.

The subject matter of books has to appeal to young children. Most teachers have a very good idea as to what their children like to read. Also revealing are some of the studies that have been made of children's interests and hobbies. As Kevin McGrath found, in his exploration of what children like to do in their spare time,[6] these hobbies constitute their real learning material, or, as he put it, their 'underground curriculum'. These children had an immense variety of interests. Nearly all the arts and crafts were mentioned and many musical instruments were played. Sport was a universal favourite and in this field there was considerable overlap between the sexes, girls, as well as boys, enjoying football, cricket and judo. Few children, incidentally, chose sport because of its competitive element; most liked it because it provided the company of friends or because it helped them keep fit.

Animals were favourites, especially horses, and a number of children were wildlife enthusiasts. Encouragingly, lots of children liked reading and, heartening to teachers, continued school subjects as hobbies out of school. Most of them liked carrying out their hobbies by themselves and some specifically stated that they disliked the interference of adults. One can see, in this context, how valuable an activity reading is to children, allowing them as it does a great degree of independence. It is also clear that providing them with books based on their hobbies is an excellent way of keeping their interest in reading alive. These books are real to children, and speak to them.

A consideration of language helps us to perceive more clearly the nature of the environment in which we live. The linguistic environment is perhaps the broadest in spectrum and the richest of all, and the skills that children need to explore it must correspondingly be both powerful and sensitive. Rooted, like other environmental skills, in simple perception, language nevertheless carries children beyond what is immediate, into worlds of colour, emotion and thought. The influences affecting its development are of immense diversity, ranging from the broadly social to the intimate and personal. By means of them a child grows through egocentricity and comes to see the world as adults do. The interaction between children and their environment through language is both literal and imaginative, finite and yet endless and full of change.

Above all, it is exciting.

4
Mathematics through the Environment

In the last two chapters we have discussed how the development of perceptual and linguistic skills in young children influence the ways in which they organise, and learn from, the environment. These processes begin the moment they are born and continue throughout life.

At the age of five, or even before, children begin school. We then put a different emphasis on their learning, for we introduce them to the academic disciplines. It is time that children's perceptual and linguistic skills continue to develop, indeed they underpin all education, but school subjects demand something in addition. They have a cultural component, involving terms and concepts which have been evolved by human society over hundreds of years, which no child can acquire by him or herself. Even an apparently simple act of perception, like looking at a buttercup growing in a field, leads to thinking about its petals, roots and living processes, concepts which have been forged by others and which have to be learnt.

We must remember, though, that the academic disciplines themselves represent ways of thinking about the environment. If this were not so, they would not exist. In the absence of an environmental discipline that can stand by itself, we have to think about the environment in subject terms.

Another issue lurks behind all this, one that is of enormous importance to all teachers. It concerns the extent to which findings in psychology about children can be applied to the classroom. Teachers are often mystified, and frequently irritated, when they accept that the intellectual growth of young children evolves in stages, or that children perceive the colour red before that of grey, and they wonder how they can translate this knowledge into classroom practice. Psychological observations are carried out in carefully structured conditions, whereas teaching is not. Research reveals facts about children of immense complexity, which can only be catered for by the teacher in the broadest possible way. In short, the situation in the classroom is not that of the laboratory. Teachers, as usual, find their own intuitive and often ingenious solutions, teaching broadly so that they are both aware of the characteristics their children have in common, and yet give each child the freedom and opportunity to adapt for him or herself. The examples of teachers' work described in this book illustrate this.

Mathematics orders the environment in quantitative terms. It is not concerned with making judgements of value, or with self-expression, as is language, but with the exploration of properties, relationships and transformations. It is this orderliness, this discipline demanded by mathematics, that invests it with its peculiar beauty and, at the same time, strikes fear into the hearts of those who wrestle with it. One of Her Majesty's Inspectors, not long ago, described the purpose of mathematics in the following words: 'Maths is concerned with the discovery of pattern (and sometimes the absence of pattern), and with the communication, in many different ways, of the pattern found. Patterns of all kinds have a mathematical basis; in shape, number and algebra, in natural and man-made forms.'[48] Mathematics, then, is everywhere.

Mathematics uses concepts in order to reveal these patterns; it also uses certain procedures. There are many of these concepts, and their exact nature is coming under a good deal of scrutiny at the present time, particularly from those concerned with the teaching of young children. Early in their lives, we expect children to become acquainted with the nature of number, of size, of weight and many other mathematical ideas, and also to develop an awareness of the relationship between them. More abstract concepts follow, like those of equal point, line and ratio. It is possible to be quite adept at using mathematical procedures without fully understanding the concepts underlying them. Most of us go through life like this, totting up what we owe the milkman without thinking about the function of money as a medium of exchange, changing the gear on our bicycles as we toil up the hill without bothering about the concept of ratio or the properties of circles. Mathematical concepts are not all of the same order; they vary in their degrees of abstraction and in the extent of the generality with which they can be applied. Some remain on an operational level, being useful only in as far as they solve a particular problem or reveal a single relationship. Others, like those applied in the theorems of Pythagoras, have a very high level of generality and can be applied consistently to many phenomena.

Mathematical procedures involve the use of symbols, and these too, we require children to understand. These symbols are a kind of short-hand and they represent elements, classes, functions and relationships. A degree of heat is indicated by the symbol $°$; 'greater than' and 'less than' are represented by $>$ and $<$ respectively; when two properties are equal we use the sign $=$.

Some of these signs have counterparts in spoken language, as have the last two examples, but many have not. π cannot be expressed verbally, neither can the brackets used in algebra; the character we use to denote one degree of heat derives simply from the method we have evolved of measuring temperature and cannot be expressed verbally. From this we can see one of the essential characteristics of mathematics as a discipline, in that it has its own language. To think mathematically we have to use this language, thinking, as it were, in another tongue. It can create great difficulty for children and for many adults, too.

A great deal of thinking is going on at the moment both as to the ways in which children acquire mathematical concepts and the problems they encounter in the struggle, for a struggle it seems to be. This thinking, by implication, places the part played by the environmental study in the teaching of mathematics in quite a new perspective. We will let some recent research speak for itself. Gerard Vergnaud, of the Department of Education at Cambridge, makes the following valuable observations.[49] Children's difficulties in arithmetic stem more from the concepts involved than in the handling of the actual calculations; solving a problem by choosing the right calculation is a strong criteria for the acquisition of concepts, although a problem-solving procedure is not a true concept in itself. When pupils use a procedure in order to solve a problem, they are using a 'theorem in action', which is not a true theorem. A true concept has to be explained in terms of properties and relationships.

In spite of this apparent abstraction, mathematical concepts are firmly rooted in human experience. Vergnaud points out that the concept of number itself would not exist had man, in the past, not come up against the practical problem of measurement. Further, there are many ways of getting to the right answer in mathematics; there is no one route. Vergnaud is himself investigating the various questions that eleven-year-old children invent and find meaningful when they are presented with a mass of mathematical data and given no guidance as to how to reduce it to order. He suggests that what is needed in mathematics teaching is a task-centred psychology; in other words, we need to seek out for children tasks in which the symbolic representation of mathematics helps them to solve problems.

All this, of course, has important implications for the way in which mathematics is taught in schools. For the moment, let us note that, as a subject, mathematics is firmly rooted in human experience and yet possesses a high degree of abstraction.

Although mathematics, like the other disciplines, has its elements of uniqueness, like them, too, it has elements in common. Conservation is a case in point. The realisation of the unchanging nature of matter is as essential to physics and chemistry as it is to mathematics. Sooner or later, young children come to understand that if they build a pile of bricks into another shape, the number of bricks remains the same although they may look different; likewise, when playing with water, children come to realise that a pint of water remains a pint whether it is poured into a shallow saucepan or a tall bottle. In this way, they make a beginning in both mathematics and physics. In an even broader sense, all the disciplines make emotional demands on the individual. They all, in their various ways, demand a standing-back from oneself, a relinquishing of a particular and idiosyncratic viewpoint, in order to achieve objectivity. Only when this has been achieved can a child accept the existence of universal, unchanging laws and recognise that there are situations in life that have a general application. This is partly what we mean by mental maturity. Some recent evidence suggests that young children are not as egocentric, either in terms of sensory perception or emotionally, as has hitherto been supposed. Paul Light, of the University of Southampton, observed the reactions of sixty four-year-olds, of various social groups.[50] When playing a 'hide-and-seek' game, most were able to hide an object, a doll in this case, bearing in mind the visual perception of the speaker. The children were also sensitive to the emotional reactions of others. Told a story about a boy called Ben, they were good at choosing a face whose expression matched the outcome of his adventures, for example, a sad face when Ben fell off his bicycle. The link between the responses of the four-year-olds and the development of their academic abilities is not as tenuous as it might at first sight seem. To enter into any discipline one has first to leave one's own particular viewpoint behind; being able to adapt to varying visual perspectives is an essential mathematical skill, especially in geometry and mechanics.

In common also with the other subject areas, many of the approaches and ideas in mathematics are culturally determined, so that it is a product of the social environment. Other cultures find our mathematics impossible to understand. A hilarious account was given a year or two ago of research undertaken by a Cambridge lecturer among students in Papua New Guinea.[51]

These 16- to 26-year-old students were unable to generalise or to use hypotheses because, in their culture, every problem arose from a particular set of circumstances and could only be solved within the context of those circumstances. General rules, abstract logic and symbolic representation were, therefore, not only unnecessary, but totally incomprehensible. One student was asked to find the area of a rectangular piece of paper and replied, 'Multiply length by width.' How did his people judge the area of their gardens? 'By adding length and width.' When his questioner pursued the matter, the student explained that one problem referred to a piece of paper and the other to a garden. Further pursued, and asked which of two gardens he would prefer to have, both being represented on paper by a diagram, one bigger than the other, the student explained that this would depend on many things, the soil, the shade, and so on.

This episode, amusing as it is, demonstrates the truth that the ways in which mathematics orders the environment in our society are culturally determined. This can be seen by looking at what is generally considered to be a concept fundamental to mathematics, that of number. Numbers are the means by which we estimate transformations and magnitudes. Counting is one of the operations in which children engage themselves very early on. Many toddlers get their first introduction to arithmetic by counting the stairs as they trudge with their mothers on their way to bed. Yet the concept of number is not an easy one. It demands of the child that he or she recognises an entity. But of what does the entity consist? What is 'a one'? The square, coloured bricks with which many young children explore number in the classroom has six planes and twelve edges, yet we demand that they perceive it as one unit. This may be why one so often observes children carefully turning these bricks over in their hands before they use them, thinking. The truth is that mathematical concepts, like others, are matters of directed perception, that is, in the sense of the action of the physical senses being directed by the mind. What is in the mind is there partly because our culture decrees it.

This brings us to another consideration, one that is quite crucial in any consideration of the part played by mathematics in the environmental study. Mathematics is probably the most practical subject of all, the most firmly embedded in the necessities of everyday living, in spite of the reputation it now has as being the most abstract of disciplines. It can even be claimed that animals use a simple form of arithmetic; how else does a bitch recognise that one of her puppies is missing?

It has been said that mathematics evolved thousands of years ago because mankind itself could not have survived without it. It was used for recording, measuring and assessing relationships, when often the accuracy of these measurements was a matter of life and death. The height of the Nile was recorded by the Ancient Egyptians, so that they knew whether to expect famine or an abundance of food to see them through to the next harvest; Red Indians hacked notches on a pole in order to record the number of scalps they had taken, a way of using arithmetic that has a great appeal to junior school children. The practical side of mathematics existed long before brilliant questioning and enquiring minds gave rise to its concepts. Concepts merely recognised the fact that these practical applications had a degree of generality and could be used in many situations; hence a theory could be worked out. Even the most abstract concepts originated as new and better ways of making calculations. Take place values, for example, which have been found by the Schools Council to cause great difficulty among our ten-year-olds.[52] These were hit upon in a stroke of genius by Arab mathematicians hundreds of years ago, and are simply a more economical means of handling numbers.

Practicalities have always underpinned mathematics and continue to do so. Without these enquiries and this continuous creative inventiveness, there would be no houses built, no tills in the supermarket, no space travel. One of the most exciting challenges is to find a way of measuring what appears, at first sight, to be unmeasurable. How many of us could think up ways of measuring gas, or electricity, both of them essential to most houses? Devising a means of recording temperature proved beyond man's ingenuity for hundreds of years, the resulting thermometer proving to be a most delicate and accurate instrument for measuring that elusive phenomenon, heat. We are apt to lose sight of the fact that mathematics is not merely concerned with abstractions, it comes to grips with the environment in a most concrete and down-to-earth way.

Individuals use mathematics for similar purposes in their personal lives. They aim to explore, to order and to make life easier. When the two-year-old counts the stairs as he (she) goes on his way to bed, the counting gives him terms of reference. He is helped to map his journey; he knows how many stairs he has to climb the next night; later, perhaps, he may be able to compare his house with a friend's. Even later, he may discover the countless patterns numbers make and feel for himself the aesthetic quality of mathematics.

Just because so much mathematical experience is gained from the immediate environment, children find it much easier to apply basic mathematical knowledge to familiar settings. This has been demonstrated by the findings of several government sponsored investigations.[53] It comes as no surprise to anybody who has much to do with children, for we all know the child who is unable to work out interest rates on money sums but who can work out Geoff Boycott's batting average in a flash.

We must remember, too, that the kind of reasoning used in mathematics is basically the same as that used in everyday life. This applies even to the computer, so frequently represented as the embodiment of abstract logic. Although the information fed into it has to be quantative, in terms of number, the processes the computer uses in order to solve a problem, namely the elimination of possibilities, is the same that we use in verbal reasoning. In other words, the computer thinks in a similar fashion to the contestants in the popular television variation of *Twenty Questions*.

There is no clear and generally accepted theory as to the ways in which young children come to understand mathematics. We can, however, be brave and hazard some suggestions, based partly on what research has revealed and partly on the observations of teachers and all those who have a lot to do with children.

Babies, early on in their lives, teach themselves mathematics through their own play. That is, they use their own bodies as measuring instruments and their own actions as hypotheses. A clear and pointed account of this has been given by Bob Green and Veronica Laxton.[54] Through playing with the popular stacking cups and nesting dolls, babies come to grips with the concepts of size, identity, fit, belongingness and serial order. Hammering wooden pegs into their correct holes gives them a similar grasp of mathematical ideas. When they play at sorting, they are teaching themselves about categories and sets, which are quite advanced concepts. Babies do not even need much equipment for their mathematical activities; most of us will have played peek-a-boo with a child of about nine months old; its great popularity seems to lie in the fact that the 'lost' object, whether it is a face hidden behind a hand or a rattle flung out of the pram, always reappears. It is a way of learning constancy. Two- and three-year-olds love posting letters; they are teaching themselves about fit. They love poking things into holes, pushing plasticine into keyholes and mud into cracks in the pavement. These activities may not make young children over-popular with their parents, but they are illuminating the concepts of area and volume.

Such considerations provoke us to make some important observations about the ways in which young children come to mathematics. The mathematical ideas of young children are not separated from their thinking in other areas; they spring from everyday activities and ordinary experience; their own bodies and actions constitute the first measuring instruments, as Green and Laxton neatly put it, they are the children's 'data-gathering machinery'. For children, mathematics is discovered rather than learnt, experienced rather than taught. As these authors express it, 'Maths is not meant to be ladled down like brimstone and treacle'.

Resulting from this, it is possible to make another suggestion that, though the concepts of mathematics are many and complex, the young child does not master them one by one, but all together, as they present themselves to him from the external environment. One day, a little boy of about three-and-a-half years old wandered into the green grocer's. He began examining the sprouts. He picked one up and remarked, 'This is a big one.' He found another and said, 'This is little.' He went on sorting busily. Then he held up the price ticket, 14p per pound, and asked, 'What's this?' The lady nearest to him explained it was the price you had to pay and that the green grocer weighed out the vegetables. He watched this being done for a moment. Then he began comparing all the sprouts with the big one still in his hand. Eventually, he found a huge sprout and announced to us all, 'This is the champion.' At this point his distraught mother rushed in and took him away.

What was interesting was the way in which this little boy worked. He was assimilating several concepts at once, of size, progression and value. He used one line of thinking in order to illuminate others. He was greatly helped by his ability to handle language, using it to clarify his discoveries and also to formulate appropriate questions. He was socially adept, enlisted the help of friendly adults and was ready to assimilate ideas from them. In the broadest possible way, he was full of mathematical ideas.

Here is another anecdote, full of pointers as to the ways in which children acquire mathematical experience and the difficulties they may come across in so doing. Recently, a ten-year-old friend was asked what she would like to find out through sums. She replied in a series of question. 'I'd like to find out about the concept of adding,' she said, 'why do we have it?' Then she asked, 'What are logs? I'd like to find that out too.' The conversation returned to the subject of addition. 'Why do we need adding when we have subtraction?' she demanded. 'Are they the same?'

Now this young girl counts as very good at maths in school, carrying out addition, subtraction, multiplication and division with ease, not to say fractions and decimals. Yet her understanding remains operational and she is struggling to grasp the true nature of the concepts behind the operations. She knows that they exist; she even uses the word 'concept' but while she is working through addition and subtraction sums every day in school, she cannot really understand the difference between them, as her questions show. Social influences are also at work in the mathematical thinking of this ten-year-old. She has already assimilated the cultural outlook that determines the intellectual perspective in our society. This can be seen by the way in which she is already thinking to some degree in abstract terms, quite unlike the students of New Guinea. Interestingly, she wants to know about logarithms. She is nowhere near using them herself in school, but her elder sister is. The young sister has managed to purloin the elder one's scientific calculator and spend happy hours entering numbers and seeing what happens when she presses such buttons as *log*, *sin* and *cos*. She is suceptible, then, in this most academic of subjects, to all kinds of social influences, ranging from those that apply throughout society to those that work in an intimate family framework.

For the ten-year-old, as for the three-year-old, language is of great importance in conceptual thinking. Both she and the little boy working industriously among the sprouts use language to describe and to define, to formulate questions and to clarify what is puzzling them. Questions enable them to reach beyond their own personal horizons into the wealth of knowledge beyond.

Most people would accept that the ways in which children acquire mathematical concepts change as they grow older. There is no absolute proof of this, but it is seen by those who have experience of children. Very young children use their own bodies more and experiment through physical handling and movement. As they grow older, their memories and their powers of abstraction develop so that they rely less on concrete experience. To put it simply, they do less and think more. Older children are capable of assimilating a much broader spectrum of cultural infor-mation; they can pick up mathematical ideas from television, hobbies, brothers and sisters and comics.

We know very little about individual differences between children. There is evidence, however, that suggests that the acquisition of mathe-matical concepts is not a straightforward process and that it is a more com-plex evolution than has hitherto been supposed. Counting, for example, is usually thought of as one of the earliest mathematical operations, yet it has been shown recently that young children have methods of determin-ing number other than by counting. Apparently they can do this by recognising small arrays of objects, such as a group of four, in number patterns.[55]

This early conceptualisation of number must be replaced, at a later stage of development, by a more mature approach. Moreover, it seems that concepts such as conservation are not acquired by a method of simple accumulation. Experiments on the ability of five-year-olds to conserve numbers indicate that they acquire the concept with small numbers first. At the age of five, they might recognise that two blocks remained the same number if they were rearranged, but would become confused if the number of blocks were greater.

Nowadays there is a great wailing and gnashing of teeth about the state of mathematics in schools. Hardly a day goes past when one does not pick up some hair-raising account of how, after eleven years of education, our school-leavers are unable to do simple sums. This is a godsend to all the editors of the national newspapers, because, in the absence of anything more exciting, there is always this national scandal to fall back upon. For the rest of us, it is depressing. We have to ask why this state of affairs exists, and the people who should be listened to are the teachers themselves. They have some clear ideas on the subject. It is plain from many investigations that mathematics is neither the most popular nor the easiest subject in school. One survey by the Schools Council questioned teachers from forty schools in various local education authorities and tested 2,300 children of ten years old.[52] The teachers tried many approaches to mathematics teaching, they made their own workcards and much of their own classroom material, but they reported that the children were in difficulty on several fronts. They did not find any of the four basic exercises, of addition, subtraction, multiplication and division, easy. Forty per cent of the teachers cited subtraction as causing difficulty and 39 per cent put this down to the misunderstanding of the function of place values. The tests completed by the children themselves showed that 50 per cent of them found multiplication difficult too, as well as fractions and decimals. Here again, an inability to understand place values was blamed. The Working Party found that many children were not learning the convention of starting from the right-hand digit and working left across the columns.

Children not only find mathematics difficult, they fear and dislike it. Often these attitudes stay with them for life. The reason is that the mathematics learnt in school is not the same subject as the mathematics used in real life. Mathematics as an academic discipline is a lonely subject; it has an inherently logical structure and its answers can only be right or wrong. This causes us all, adults as well as children, to be very nervous about it. There is nothing to hide behind; our mistakes are there for all to see.

In contrast, the mathematics of everyday life can be quite a jolly affair. Short cuts are taken, procedures are seen in terms of each other and there are a variety of ways of arriving at the right answer. Rosemary Simmons, herself a teacher, gives some lively examples of this.[56] She points out that the petrol pump attendant, in order to calculate the cost of 4 gallons at 79 pence a gallon, (her article was written in 1978!), does not say '$4 \times 9 = 36$'; he is more likely to say, 'four eights are thirty-two . . . that will be £3.20 less 4 pence.'

Moreover, when Ms Simmons set her junior school children a sum, 3½ pence × 49, without suggesting that they should follow any particular method, they thought of a great variety of solutions. Among their ideas were:

$3\frac{1}{2}$p $+ 3\frac{1}{2}$p (49 times)
50×4p $- 50 \times \frac{1}{2}$p $- 3\frac{1}{2}$p
3p $\times 50 + 50 \div 2 - 3\frac{1}{2}$
3×49p $+ 49$p $\div 2$

Nobody used the conventional: $3\frac{1}{2}$p

$$\times\ 49$$

———

By the end of 1984, of course, children were no longer bothered with the $\frac{1}{2}$p.

The point is clear; conventional mathematics taught in schools and the mathematics used outside have different purposes. The conventional method aims at the concise communication of mathematical processes and favours abstraction. In ordinary life, the aim is to find solutions to problems that are immediate and specific. Here, as Rosemary Simmons puts it so clearly: 'What is required is not the formal application of a generalised rule of thumb but an ability to think with mathematical common-sense'.

School mathematics has also been affected, subtly and pervasively, by the Piagetian approach to learning. This, as it has been interpreted, depicts children as proceeding from stage to stage, finally arriving at a mature conceptualisation of the world. Part of the trouble with this view is that it looks at the concepts rather than the child. It does not look at any one child at a particular point in time, right across the child's experience; because it aims at demonstrating how 'the child' arrives at an adult conceptualisation of the world, it tends to ignore what the child is in actual reality. It is rather like considering the aeroplane constructed by the Wright brothers, perfectly adequate in itself, and indeed a thing of beauty, but in terms of the modern Concorde. Children are much more complex, and at the same time more complete in themselves, than that. Moreover, with its emphasis on inner concepts, Piagetian thought is unable to appreciate the subtle interplay between the child and his environment. The inspiration and the efforts of the three-year-old boy and the ten-year-old girl, described a few pages back, vividly depict that interplay.

Can the problem in the schools be met by making all maths 'real-life', or environmental, mathematics? The answer must be no. The most important reason is that the two aspects of mathematics, which can be termed the philosophical and the useful, are not mutually exclusive at all, but complementary. The lively children in the class of Ms Simmons would not have thought in such versatile ways of solutions to the sum she set them had they not possessed a thorough grounding in all four arithmetical operations. Their answers showed that. They did not see a multiplication sum in terms only of multiplication but in terms of addition, subtraction and division as well. Expertise in one approach leads to expertise in the other. Another reason is that mathematics is a cultural subject, in the sense that its body of knowledge is the culmination of the thinking of great minds over centuries. This is true of all the academic disciplines, and that is why they have to be taught. I could draw dozens of circles in the sand, as the Ancient Greeks did, but would never think of π, because that takes creative brilliance. The properties of the circle were thought out by great thinkers, and while the rest of us can apply their findings, and even get a glimmering of understanding ourselves – if it is all explained to us carefully – we would never have discovered those properties by our own efforts.

Returning to the difficulties of the ten-year-olds as described in the Schools Council survey, the greatest of them arose from the children's inability to handle place values. There are two points here: firstly, it is not surprising that the procedure takes children a long time to understand because this system was a stroke of brilliant improvisation and it took men hundreds of years of civilised existence before they thought of it. Secondly, place values, technical and abstract a convention though they seem, fulfil an intensely practical purpose. They avoid the confusion of having to handle vast numbers of digits. Children might realise this if they were allowed to work out something like 539×7, using only beads and wooden blocks and counting to reach an answer.

Other procedures in mathematics would never be arrived at by children themselves, however gaily and determinedly they explored their environment. An example is the convention of working from the right-hand digit across to the left, a convention which children find puzzling because it is opposite to that demanded in reading. As the writers of the Schools Council Working Paper say firmly and sternly, 'Such conventions cannot be discovered by a child directly from experiments in the environment, but need to be taught.' The point to remember is that these conventions are useful in real life. They always have been.

The cumulative structure of mathematics as a discipline also means that it is not easily 'discovered' in the environment. Although children, like the little boy in the green grocer's, can learn about several ideas at once, they learn best if the material is staged for them. It makes sense to tackle addition before subtraction and then to proceed to multiplication, each step being built on the one before. It is the easiest, most practical route for children to follow.

The cultural disciplines, those whose body of knowledge has been built up slowly over thousands of years, share another characteristic which also means that it is impossible for children to come to an understanding of them simply by mere exposure to the environment. Their concepts are telescoped, abstract and not directly accessible to the senses. If we demand that children master them by themelves, we are asking four- and five-year-olds to encapsulate centuries of endeavour and brilliant discovery into the few years of their lives. It is often possible for a child to build up a mathematical concept from his own experience. The concept of equation, for example, $6 + 2 = 8$, can be built up through weighing on a balance scale. However, as we have noted, more often mathematical concepts are not accessible in this way, and sheer shortage of time means that it is not possible to recreate experience for every child, on every occasion, in this manner. Teachers are very well aware of the problem and cope with it with their usual ingenuity. Rather than building up a concept from the child's experience, they tend to hold up the concept to the child, as it were, and then illuminate it by means of the child's own experience in the environment. They will provide the scales (the concept) and encourage the child to weigh up all sorts of things, and so come to grasp the idea of balance.

There is a significant truth here, and one that applies to geography, history and science, as well as to mathematics. In every study, there must be a continual interplay between what the child finds out for himself and how this is shaped by his culture, a balance between teaching on the one hand and discovery on the other. Good teaching consists in encouraging the child to build up his own concepts whenever he or she can, but when that cannot be, the explanation should be clear, adequately repeated and illuminated by the child's own experience. In other words, the environmental study cannot be taught properly unless the limits of the external environment are plainly understood.

The world outside school has an immensely valuable contribution to make to children's understanding of mathematics. Mathematics is everywhere in rich variety, in the shapes of windows and coal-holes, in the clock ticking away outside the jeweller's, in the numbers on the cars moving along the roads and in the speeds at which they travel. It is in the mechanics of the dustmen's cart as it crunches up the rubbish and in the slow-moving steamroller as it trundles down the highway. It is in ourselves, in the way we are built with two arms, two legs, one nose and the ability to use our bodies as measuring instruments. In the outside world, mathematics is exciting.

More than this, it is where mathematics begins, as a means of solving practical, human problems and as a way of making life better. This interplay between the practical problem and the ingenious solution is the growing-point of creative thinking, as it always has been. This thinking is not confined to mathematics but encompasses other disciplines as well. In life as it is actually lived, there are few purely mathematical issues, most have to be seen in human terms as well. We have a freezer, as do 25 per cent of British households these days. We save by buying ahead of the rising cost of living, or trying to, and also because the price of food bought in bulk is less than when it is purchased in small quantities. However, just because we have a freezer, we tend to buy luxury goods that we did without before, like giant cartons of ice-cream and crinkle-cut chips. In actual fact we do not save much money; we just live better. What seems at first sight to be a simple matter of saving money has turned into something more complex; the issue has to be seen in terms of how a family wants to live.

Even when a problem is one of mere calculation, in real life there are many solutions. The petrol attendant, in totting up what was owed him in a rapid and unconventional way, was making a real contribution to mathematics.[56] I am reminded of an incident that happened in a school in which I taught. We took the children on a visit to the gas-works and the friendly foreman who took us round explained that it was the custom to reward any of the work-force who thought of any bright ideas for improving efficiency. The best idea they had had involved measuring. For years and years the amount of coke going into each sack had been painstakingly weighed; then one of the men pointed out that if they marked the point on each sack where the coke should reach at the correct measure, they need not go to all the trouble of weighing. His idea saved thousands of pounds. It was a simple idea, not thought of before because most people think in mathematical strait-jackets and cannot see weight in terms of volume. In most classrooms this is still the case. It needed a human predicament to crack the mould of rigid thinking.

Society itself puts mathematics to some very human uses. Numbers are used to identify houses, cars and telephone boxes. Statistics both identify and help to solve problems which involve people. The census is a case in point. Once we know the size of families we have a good idea as to what kind of housing we need; if we can estimate the number of old people there are likely to be, and the number is growing every year, we can work out what provision is needed for the elderly. Often a delicate issue is revealed that is fraught with controversy, as when certain groups refused to answer questions about their ethnic origins in a recent government census, so that the questions were dropped. Older children are well able to appreciate such sensitive areas.

From the point of view of the individual child, the phenomena and events of the external environment act both as stimuli and as interpreters of mathematical concepts. Interesting events occur continually: Dad wallpapers the sitting-room and the whole family goes shopping; a new zebra crossing is planned for a road on the way to school and a space satellite is launched. Not only are these events interesting, children are familiar with them in a way that is lacking in the classroom and they have subconsciously already half assimilated the concepts evolved, of length, width, area, number and speed. The containment of these concepts within what is easy, indeed obvious, in terms of perception, limits their implications and makes them easier to grasp. The divorce of the theory of mathematics from its application in practice, which so bedevils our attitudes, is mercifully absent. Examples of the kind of symbolic representation mentioned by Vergnaud,[49] that is, those which actually help in the clear presentation of a mathematical situation, can actually be found in the external environment. Sets are a case in point. Everything that is going on in the world outside school lends itself to those ways of working that come naturally to young children, to talking, asking questions and using language accurately, to exploring concepts that range right across all subjects.

In their early days, young children explore the significance of general mathematical ideas. These general concepts are common to other disciplines also. They involve skills such as the ability to recognise likenesses and differences, to discern entities, to put objects into serial order, and to see that certain objects or quantities are bigger, greater or smaller than others. There is an enormous amount of interesting material for children to use and much of it they will enjoy collecting for themselves. Take, for example, two sticks picked up in a local park; they differ in size, thickness, texture and shape, but they weigh the same. Or, consider two stones which look the same size, yet the light coloured one weighs considerably less; it is sandstone. Measuring, weighing and exploring such materials, children come to realise that size, shape and weight are concepts that can be differentiated, yet are also related to each other. Language is important; the children will need words like 'small', 'big', 'heavy', 'larger than', and many more. In early childhood the language of mathematics is the language of everyday life.

It also speaks to the children through quite everyday experience, experience which might strike most people as not mathematical at all. It is interesting for young children to be allowed to explore other people's houses, neighbours' houses in particular. For there they will see that most houses are set out in the same way; most interesting of all are semi-detached houses, where the designs are identical, but reversed in terms of left and right. In this way the children are introduced to the concepts of equivalence and similarity.

Likewise, there is an abundance of material when the children come to experiment with sorting (putting objects into serial order) and with conservation. There are leaves, flowers, animals, insects, themselves, and all the interesting things they can bring from home. Young children love bottles, so every teacher should build up a collection; a few interestingly shaped bottles are illustrated opposite. They can be used to teach both serial order and conservation, as is shown.

In most nursery and infant schools, young children continue to consider volume, shape and area. Although adults think of volume as the most difficult to grasp because it is three-dimensional, children naturally come to it first. This is probably because they are natural diggers and pokers of objects into holes. They can be encouraged to ask questions such as the following. How much plasticine will it take to fill up the big crack in the path leading up to the school door? If they have dug a deep hole in the sand-pit, how many bucketfuls of sand will it take to fill it up again? Sea shells brought back from a summer holiday make interesting and beautiful materials for experiments in volume. Cockle and mussel shells can be filled with plasticine and their various capacities compared. Volume can also be explored by experimenting with the children's drinks. Bottles and tins of Coca-Cola, Lucozade, Tizer, and school milk can be brought along and compared. The bottles vary in shape and size; which holds most? How can the contents be measured? Which gives the best value for money?

The concept of area is more advanced because one dimension, depth, is missing. A true understanding of area involves much more than an ability to apply the dictum, 'length $\times$ breadth $=$ area', it is linked to spatial perception.

The world is full of natural shapes that can be used to help young

Bottles arranged in order of height

Bottles used to teach conservation

Which bottle holds the most water?

children gain this understanding. For example, the leaves of trees are large enough to be drawn round on squared paper; the numbers of squares can then be counted and compared with those comprising the area of another leaf. A child can cut the squares up and fit them together again in order to convince himself or herself that the totals remain constant. The operation is illustrated below.

The concept of area illustrated by leaves

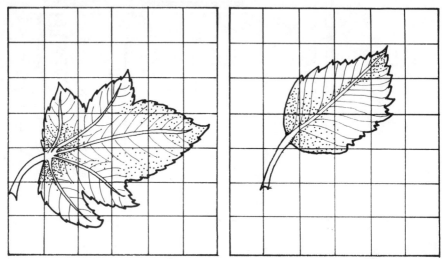

A Sycamore leaf. Its area is **6** squares and some pieces over.

A Birch leaf. Its area is **3** squares and some pieces over.

The word 'area' can be introduced to the children early, and the idea of accurate measurement later. At first, all that matters is that they see that the two leaves differ and that there are ways of assessing their differences.

Small children sometimes find leaves flimsy to hold and hard to keep flat, but they could use cardboard cut-outs to make the task easier. Educational suppliers have produced an abundance of materials aimed at helping children understand area. Apart from those whose addresses are given in the Appendix (pages 233, 235), Oliver and Boyd of Edinburgh, a division of Longman, produce TaK tiles, packs of tiles which can be fitted together in various ways.

Some equipment can be brought from home. Pastry cutters are great favourties. They are made in intriguing shapes these days and the children enjoy experimenting with the equipment they see their parents use to make delicious things to eat.

It is both instructive and fun to try to think of as many ways of estimating area as possible. How many children can sit comfortably on the square of carpet used at story-telling time? How many can squeeze into the Wendy house, or sit in the shade under the big tree in the playground?

A true understanding of area is linked to the ways in which children perceive space in the environment; some of this has already been discussed in the chapter on perception. Sooner or later the children will need to explore geometric shapes, because these are the corner-stones of mathematics and mechanics. A small, but pleasing, piece of research[57] has shown that children find them easier to reproduce for themselves if they are provided with paper cut into the shapes they are drawing, that is, a triangle on a triangular piece of paper and a square on a squared piece, as below. The children practise drawing inside the shapes.

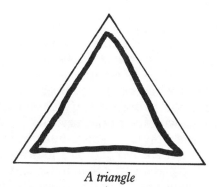

A triangle   *A square*

Young children's understanding of the concepts of space and volume can be carried much further. They need to see how space and volume are related to each other as they truly are in the everyday environment. They should be allowed to make their own shapes and to see how they can be changed. They can roll a lump of plasticine flat with a rolling-pin and press out shapes with pastry cutters; they can turn a flat surface into a three-dimensional one by crushing or folding paper and tin foil; they can reverse the process by unfolding a carton and turning it into a flat shape, then put it together again. They will be learning much more than the properties of shape and volume and the relationships between them; they will be exploring conservation.

Children are natural mechanics and builders and do not themselves divorce theoretical knowledge from its practical applications. Therefore, they learn a great deal from building and the materials need not be expensive; it is actually better if they are drawn from the children's everyday working environment. Cardboard boxes of interesting shapes are easily handled by young children; some of them, especially chocolate boxes or those used for toiletries, are intriguing hexagonals and ovals, and they can always be coated with brightly coloured paint. Odd lengths of wood and wheels can be brought from home, so can cog-wheels. Learning through practical experience and bodily contact as they do, children should be allowed to construct things for themselves.

Some ingenious constructional equipment has been developed recently, specially designed by an enterprising teacher to introduce young children to the theory of engineering. Francis Evans of Sheffield Polytechnic, has designed, among other things, a suspension bridge, a hump-backed bridge and a periscope which children can actually put together themselves and use, and also a spinning-wheel which can be used to make a thread from cotton wool. See Appendix (page 235).

It should not be forgotten that children explore large areas by means of bodily movement. This is seen in the games they play spontaneously. Hop-scotch is a good 'area' game, an estimate of area being gained by the number of hops, the turn of the body and by visual impression. Perhaps teachers can think of other games.

Having been introduced to general mathematical concepts such as like and unlike, size, order and conservation, space and volume, young children continue to explore more specialised concepts. In doing so, they discover various mathematical operations, such as addition and subtraction, multiplication and division. The raw material for number work is everywhere in the environment. There is the natural world with its infinite diversity of pattern; there are the shops with their price tags and goods ready for sorting; there are the streets where the houses are numbered and the cars and buses have number plates; there are the children's homes with stairs, electricity and gas-meters, and also parents with their never-ending task of making the family wage-packets go round. Then there are the children themselves.

There is no one way of looking at the environment. The world outside school illuminates mathematical concepts; more than that, there they can be seen in action, for both human and natural phenomenon are ordered in terms of mathematics. A teacher may choose for his or her class to make a special study of one concept at a time, such as number, but sometimes children will profit from a much wider approach, in which they are able to observe mathematical ideas in action.

We must not forget the importance of the games children play among themselves in illuminating these ideas. Julia Matthews, a teacher herself, has produced many suggestions as to how a visit to the Fair, and all the amusements found there, can provide a lively stimulus to learning for children.[58]

We will discuss in detail two aspects of the environment, widely different from each other, and the ways in which they can illuminate mathematics for young children.

Nowadays we all have to live with traffic, which, nuisance though it may be, suggests many projects and thought-provoking problems.

Numbering is an umbrella term which embraces several related operations. Number plates are used to identify cars, lorries and trucks, all much beloved by young children, many of whom acquire an astonishing knowledge of the specification of cars, their make, capacity and horsepower. They would enjoy collecting the numbers from all the number plates they can spot, for example from the cars parked in their own road. The number plate of a car gives us its exact identity, each one being unique. This enables the car to be traced to its owner if it is lost, involved in an accident or used for law-breaking activity. What children will find much more interesting is that the number plate tells us when the car was made. Until August 1983 this was denoted by the letter at the end of the number, as in PRS 639 S. Below is a list of these end letters, coupled with the corresponding year of registration.

February 1963–31 December 1963	A	1 August 1973–31 July 1974	M
1 January 1964–31 December 1964	B	1 August 1974–31 July 1975	N
1 January 1965–31 December 1965	C	1 August 1975–31 July 1976	P
1 January 1966–31 December 1966	D	1 August 1976–31 July 1977	R
1 January 1967–31 July 1967	E	1 August 1977–31 July 1978	S
1 August 1967–31 July 1968	F	1 August 1978–31 July 1979	T
1 August 1968–31 July 1969	G	1 August 1979–31 July 1980	V
1 August 1969–31 July 1970	H	1 August 1980–31 July 1981	W
1 August 1970–31 July 1971	J	1 August 1981–31 July 1982	X
1 August 1971–31 July 1972	K	1 August 1982–31 July 1983	Y
1 August 1972–31 July 1973	L		

In August 1983 the system was altered slightly because the end of the usable letters of the alphabet had been reached, and letters are now used as prefixes rather than suffixes, for example, A 840 JKP. The figures and letters are also transposed.

By looking at the number plate it is usually possible to tell whether a car is very new or very old. One exception is where the owner has been allowed to keep an old number on his or her new car because he or she is fond of it. This is called a 'cherished number'. Since the suffix system was introduced only in 1963, a number plate with no letter at the end, and no prefix either, might mean a valuable car by virtue of that car's age. Does anyone know of a car with a 'cherished number'?

Once a few numbers have been collected, children can work out the ages of the cars. They can continue to reflect on some of the other characteristics of number plates. Some letters were missed out (I, O, Q, U, and Z). The reason is that *O* and *Q* can easily be mistaken for each other, while the letter *I* could be confused with the number 'one'; *U* could be confused with *V* and the letter *Z* with the number 'two'. The children might reflect on the fact that the suffixes and prefixes are used in exactly the same way as we use numbers for identification. Actually, it does not matter whether letters or numbers are used; both are symbols.

In any district where there is a large railway station, some children will be eager train-spotters. Railway engines are described and identified by means of numbers in like fashion to cars, only in their case the numbers tell the train-spotters how powerful the locomotives are and the depots from which they come. Every locomotive has a five digit number painted on its side, such as 37 214. The first two digits denote the class of engine: the higher the number, the more power it has, so that 45 indicates more power than 37. The last three digits indicate the locomotive's depot. To identify these the spotter needs a Code Book. I know of a London school which could be considered among the dreariest. It is bounded by a derelict factory, a row of humble little dwellings, a railway and, on the fourth side by a trunk road leading to a huge roundabout. There is ceaseless, noisy traffic and the road and railway can be seen from the classrooms. But the road provided some fascinating material from which the children could build up sets. If they watched the roundabout for five minutes, some could count the red cars, some the blue and some the green. They could build up sets as illustrated below.

Cars going round a roundabout

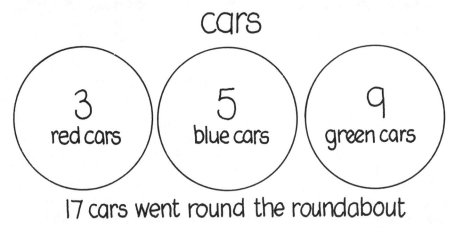

Slightly older children enjoy recording the makes of cars, or their ages as denoted by the suffix letters on their number plates, or the number of private vehicles as opposed to vans and lorries. A whole project could be based on motor vehicles.

Most children are well acquainted with heavy road traffic. The diagram opposite illustrates a typical traffic hold-up occurring every weekday morning between 8 a.m. and 9.30 a.m. Traffic at the crossroads builds up and prevents traffic from the side roads entering the main stream. There are many accidents, caused partly by cars trying to edge in, and also because pedestrians, including school children, find it impossible to cross the road safely and are forced to try to dodge cars. The older children will probably know of similar black-spots in their own locality. They can bring all their mathematical expertise to bear on finding a solution. They will need first to make an accurate assessment of the situation by gathering some information. If they worked from our diagram, they would need to know how many vehicles pass along both minor and major roads during the rush-hour period; they need also to know the amount of road space each vehicle takes up, both in terms of length and width. To obtain this information they could measure stationary cars in their own street or in a

A traffic hold-up. Can mathematics solve this problem?

car-park. Then they must ask how many pedestrians wish to cross the road and how long it will take them; the lady with the pram will take longer than the others.

Conceivably, the children might make the following suggestions in order to render this hazardous situation safer for both pedestrians and motorists. Traffic-lights might be needed at Junctions A and B. The phasing of them will have to be adjusted to the flow of traffic; there are fewer vehicles coming along the minor road at Junction B, so the green phase there can be comparatively short; at Junction A the phasing must allow pedestrians to cross.

The lorry at Junction A has blocked the traffic moving from west to east. Yellow criss-cross lines might be needed there, indicating that traffic cannot proceed unless the way is clear.

A bus is blocking part of the main road from south to north, causing another car to overtake when it is not safe to do so. The solution might be a lay-by for the bus. If this is so, what width and what shape should it be, bearing in mind that space must be used as economically as possible and also the track made by the bus as it turns into the road? Most lay-bys are segments of a circle.

Is it possible to widen the road, so that there can be several lanes of traffic?

Lastly, the children can consider that while in the morning the main flow of traffic is from south to north, in the evening the situation is reversed and the heavy traffic travels from north to south. Are there ways of coping with this situation, either by adjusting the number of lanes in use, or by phasing the traffic lights?

For older children the solution of the innumerable problems that arise from traffic demonstrate the mathematical ingenuity used in everyday life. Thinking has to be adaptable, intelligent and full of common-sense. Children very much enjoy this approach. They do not have to be confined to a consideration of road traffic; air traffic is just as exciting. They can at least be acquainted with all the calculations associated with aeroplane flights. Airspace has to be allotted, with safety margins; landing times have to be worked out, taking into consideration the number of runways available and the number of aeroplanes that wish to use them. Then there are all the problems associated with the passengers, such as handling their luggage, seeing them through customs and arranging the catering. The youngest children could be set to work on some of this, armed with model aeroplanes and an airfield.

To take a contrasting topic, children are great lovers of flowers, leaves and animals, indeed of the whole natural world.

In nature we see the careful ordering, in terms of number, of an amazing abundance and variety of objects. There are many pairs, for example, shells, leaf-buds, sycamore seeds and the wings of birds and butterflies. There are complex patterns and relationships within apparent units, as in the segmentations of leaves and earth-worms. There is change and development and function to be observed. There a wealth of mathematical ideas in nature.

An interesting mathematical exercise for young children is to build up multiplication tables from the objects they have found. In the spring and summer there are flowers and leaves to be collected; in the autumn there are seeds; after the summer holidays there will be shells in the classroom. When they have handled and explored this material the children can build up a multiplication table. A table built from sycamore seeds might look as below:

Sycamore seeds

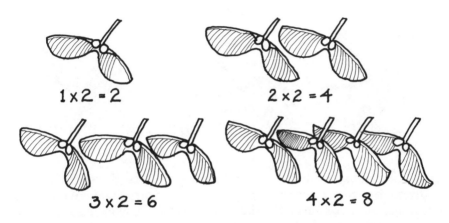

Other multiplication tables can be built up in a similar fashion. The children can begin by recognising number in leaves, petals and in themselves, finding a 'one', a 'two', a 'three' and so on, and recording them in a table. Overleaf is an illustration of what they might discover.

Various plants and leaves are particularly useful because they show variation in the number of petals they have, or the points on their leaves. The hawthorn, oak and dandelion are cases in point. Certain precautions should be taken with young children; berries should never be used because they are so tempting to eat and the most attractive are highly poisonous; sea shells should be thoroughly scrubbed before being handled and, of course, all poisonous plants must be avoided.

As we said before some young children may find fragile leaves and petals difficult to handle, but they can then work with cardboard cut-outs, as has already been suggested. Alternatively, thick plastic templates of leaves are produced commercially (see page 235).

Young children find division much harder to grasp than multiplication. It is intrinsically less attractive to them because it involves making quantities smaller, which is not nearly so enchanting as making them bigger and bigger, as happens in multiplication. There is a procedural complication because division sums are worked in the opposite direction

Number in nature

1. Beech leaf   2. Mussel Shell   3. Clover

4. Speedwell   5. Buttercup   Ever so many. Fir

to addition sums, subtraction and multiplication; also, division is concep-
tually more complex. It really involves holding in the mind two concepts at
once, that of the whole and of the equal parts of the whole. It demands a
firm grasp of the principle of conservation. Division can be understood by
applying the idea of sharing to the environment; it is an idea readily
accepted by young children, who are frequently concerned about either
ensuring that other people get a fair share, but more often that they get
theirs. There may be three guinea-pigs in the classroom and six carrots for
their supper, so how many should each have? The answer can at first be
found by dealing the carrots out. The inquiry should be pushed as far as
possible; one carrot may be much bigger than the other two; is it fair to
give it all to one guinea-pig? If the children have 30 pence to spend on
sweets for a brother and two sisters, how much should be spent on
each? How can the seating for school dinners be arranged if there are 36
children and four tables? The children can experiment until they find the
answers.

At a later stage, problems of sharing can be set out on workcards, as
opposite, above.

Even young children can be introduced to advanced mathematical ideas
through the environmental study. One such idea is that of categories. Not
only are these a basic concern of advanced mathematics but a recognition
of sets encourages a child to think symbolically, in true mathematical
idiom. Sets, also, can be introduced to children through their interest in
their own pets, or in butterflies, birds and wild animals.

Sharing nuts among squirrels

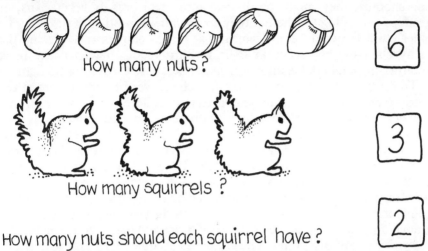

How many nuts?

6

How many squirrels?

3

How many nuts should each squirrel have?

2

The sub-sets (cats, dogs, birds and horses) can be further divided into the various kinds of cats, birds, dogs and horses. Mathematics in the classroom often suffers from being presented to children in a static way, whereas, like all the other disciplines, it is a subject of constant change. Seen in its environmental perspective, mathematics is dynamic.

Animals

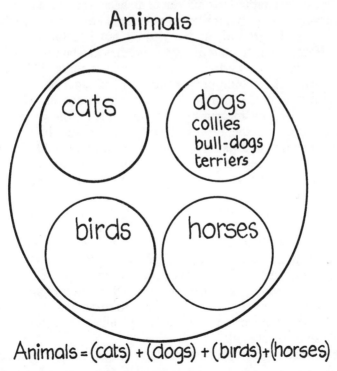

Animals = (cats) + (dogs) + (birds) + (horses)

Animals can be classified in all sorts of ways accounting to the criteria one chooses; they might be divided into carnivores or vegetarians, or grouped according to whether they are mammals, reptiles or insects. The older children would enjoy working at more complex sets, tracing the many changes that occur in their favourite football teams; the most enterprising could delve into sequences, like those used in traffic-lights.

To return to the subject of traffic, such an ever-present feature of the modern environment, it can demonstrate to children an important function of mathematics, that of making a prognostication or forecast.

Suppose John and Mary are both going off on holiday; John is setting out at 9 a.m. and is going by car, whereas Mary has a lift in her Dad's lorry and will not be on the road until 11 a.m. If they both start from the same place, with the car travelling at 30 m.p.h. and the lorry at 50 m.p.h., when will Mary catch John up so that they can both have a drink and a rest before going on? This kind of calculation, vital in the plotting of aeroplane and guided missile routes, as well as those of trains and road traffic, can best be shown by means of a graph. The graph has become a language in itself. In the case of Mary and John, the lorry will catch the car up at 2 p.m., when both have travelled 150 miles, as is shown opposite. If Mary and John looked at a road map they would be able to arrange a meeting place.

There is not the space in this chapter to discuss the many other ways in which mathematics speaks to children through their environment. One more example, however, we will include, because it is exciting and because it can be adapted to children of all ages. It is the nature trail.

For the very young, the trail need not lead them very far, perhaps as far as the school playground, and it should not last longer than twenty minutes. Four things to do is enough, and they can be discussed either on the spot or when the children return to the classroom. Sallying out one morning, every child could press a thin sheet of paper on to a brick in the school wall, tracing the outline. The children will obtain various shapes which can be used for measuring; they might learn the word 'rectangle'. They should notice the bricks on the corners and how they are all cemented together in a pattern. There is a lot in a brick! The next task might be for everyone to press plasticine into a small hole or crevice in the playground. There are usually plenty of them and the children will know where they are. The children can discuss the amount of plasticine needed to fill their crevices and arrive at a notion of volume. Then everyone can hold hands and find out how many children holding hands it will take to go round the edge of the sand-pit, or the length and width of the playground. The measurements can be compared and words like 'length', 'width' and 'perimeter' introduced. Lastly, everyone can pick up a stick and a stone. Back in the classroom, these can be arranged in order of size. Possibly, a problem will arise when the children have to think of a way of comparing two very different objects. The vocabulary 'longer', 'shorter', 'bigger' and 'smaller' can be discussed.

Older children can travel further afield. Groups of teachers sometimes

Mary and John go on a day-trip. When will they meet?

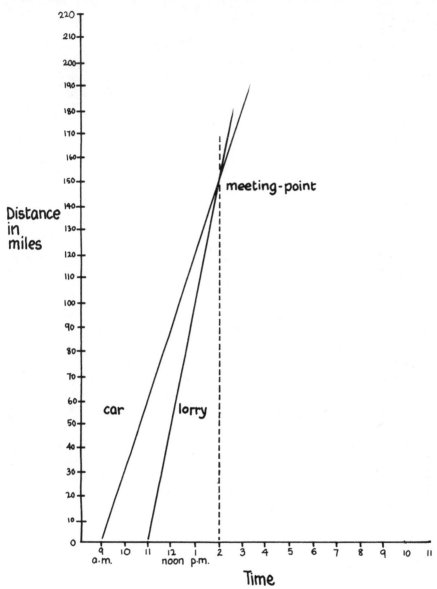

get together and devise mathematics trails for their children. Some Newcastle teachers have worked out two maths trails for their city, one for eight- to ten-year-olds and the other for eleven- to thirteen-year-olds. Over the page are reproduced the tasks set on Castle Garth for the younger age-group. They have to draw the well as if they are looking at it from above, notice whether the stones are all the same size and measure the circumference of the wall in handspans and footlengths. There are lots of

Castle Garth

Draw the well as if looking from above. Mark in the various stones.

Are all the stones the same size?

....

How many children need to hold hands to make a close circle around the well? (Stretch out your arms as far as possible)

....

You have now measured the circumference of the outside of the well.

Measure the circumference,

a) in Handspans: ....

b) in Footlengths: ....

PROBLEM FOR LATER: COMPARE THE MEASUREMENTS YOU MADE OF THE SAME CIRCUMFERENCE WITH THOSE OF YOUR FRIENDS. ARE THEY THE SAME, IF NOT, WHY NOT?

Look at the Keep.
How old do you think this building is?

....

When was the building of the present Keep completed?

....

PROBLEM FOR LATER: WORK OUT HOW OLD THE KEEP IS. HOW NEAR WAS YOUR ESTIMATE?

The Keep is 27 metres high.

Look at the Bridge Hotel.
Estimate its height.

....

Part of a mathematics trail devised by teachers for eight- to ten-year-olds

ideas in these little booklets. They are obtainable for a few pence from 'Town Teacher', at the address given on page 235.

Nine-year-olds are capable of understanding the significance of quite advanced concepts in their maths trail. Tree trunks can start them thinking about the properties of a circle and the terms 'diameter', 'radius' and 'circumference', as illustrated below.

A tree trunk

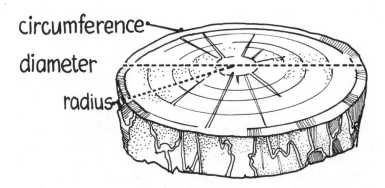

circumference

diameter

radius

If they live in a hilly district, the chldren will probably have spotted a road sign with a legend like, '1 in 7'. This is a ratio and the sign warns road-users of the extent to which the road slopes. It does not matter which unit of measurement is taken; it can be a mile, a foot or a centimetre, the road still slopes one unit in every seven. Can the children apply the concept of ratio to any other features of the environment?

These ways of working are real and they are fun. They involve all sorts of mathematical calculations. Indeed, some of the calculations may not be mathematical at all, but that is how mathematics is used in the environment, in a human context.

5
History through the Environment

History orders the environment in terms of time. Time is all around us, for our lives are lived within it. We cannot escape from it, although most of us have a deep longing to live our lives free from its shackles. We use history in our everyday lives, whether as a means of arranging the commonplace details of earning our livings and shaping the day, or whether we use it on a much grander scale in order to glean information from the past that might help us solve the problems of our present day society. When a mother draws on the experience she has had with her first child to help her bring up the second, she is thinking historically; when her child makes up his (her) mind not to play with his friend today because he quarrelled with him yesterday, he, too, is thinking historically. This way of thinking is not only natural to us, it is enjoyable too. Stories and plays are all written in time, and a glance along the shelves of the public library or down the columns of radio and television programmes shows how extremely popular history is as a recreation. History is, then, an important part of the environment.

It is, however, essentially of the intellectual environment. To gaze at the houses, the shops and the local church in one's surroundings is not necessarily to think of them historically, but to see them in the context of the past is. Historical significance is not accessible directly to the senses; it has to filter through a myriad of ideas before it dawns on the individual; these ideas can be complex even if unarticulated. They imply a certain emotional and intellectual development on the part of individuals and on integration with their own culture. Western ideas of the passing of time, of what constitutes an event and of what is cause and effect in human affairs, do not necessarily apply in other cultures. As a great historian put it many years ago, 'For history, the object to be discussed is not the mere event, but the thought expressed in it.'[59]

What do young children need in order to understand history? They need, first of all, an awareness of the passage of time. The development of time-sense is a key process in the development of children's historical understanding and there was some discussion of this in Chapter 2. There is a great deal of evidence to suggest that children develop a sense of time very early on in their lives, even though there is disagreement as to whether their concept of time is linked to that of space, or whether it develops independently. Even children as young as three, four and five years of age have been shown to be capable of distinguishing between the spatial and temporal meanings of words like 'first', 'last', 'behind' and 'ahead of'.[19]

Another piece of research previously referred to, indicated that the time concepts of nursery school children are indeed temporal in nature, even though the children are apt to be confused by factors like the speed at which an event takes place, or the physical space involved.[24]

Confused they may be, as we all are as we struggle towards mental clarity, but children know when time has gone by. In the early days, this sense of the passing of time is limited to what immediately concerns the individual and to short passages of time, like an hour, a day, or a week. Later, however, the passing of much longer periods of time is noted and assimilated. Events in their own lives and cues in their own environment enable children to accomplish this. Which of us has not a childhood memory of trying on our wellingtons of last winter, or a pretty dress or shirt from the previous summer, and finding that they will not fit because we have grown? The family itself is continually changing. Babies arrive, children grow, grandparents die. Even young children, in these days of rapid development, will have seen the sweet shop on the corner taken over and run by another family, or a new zebra crossing arrive in a busy road. To these young children, the passing of time is indicated by change. By the same token, however, these changes in time are indicative of continuity. It is possible to perceive change only if one is also aware that what lies behind it is unchanging. When a new baby arrives, the family is still there; when someone else takes over the sweet shop you can still buy sweets. A sense of history implies an acknowledgment of both development and the continuity that lies behind it.

Very early on, young children learn to order their own mental processes in terms of time. They speak in narrative and they all love stories. Later on they write in narrative, which is, of course, a form of historical writing. A survey of 595 junior and secondary school teachers in England a few years ago revealed that the most frequent forms in which children write naturally are narratives of their own personal experiences.[60]

At this point we have to make a careful distinction. We have referred so far to the development of a sense of time in so far as it applies to the events of a child's own life. Historical time-sense is a much broader and more complex concept, and when psychologists and historians talk about a sense of time they usually mean quite different things. Historical time-sense is more than the ability which we all develop to order our individual lives along a time-scale. It refers, not to the individual, but to society, and it involves thinking about the past in terms of a sophisticated discipline that has been built up over hundreds of years. The ideas that shape this perspective are always changing and historians themselves frequently disagree. How far, for example, can cause and effect be applied to historical events and what kind of deduction is possible? Apart from philosophical issues, historians themselves are creatures of their age and quite sincerely interpret the past differently from each other. King Henry

VIII can be thought of either as a wicked king or a great statesman according to whether one is Anglican or Catholic, has an instinctive revulsion or a secret admiration for his goings-on with his wives, or has always wanted to play real tennis. Historical truth is like a prism, reflected through many facets and a thing of many colours. That is why history is such a valuable discipline, demanding tolerance, judgement and flexibility of thinking.

Nowhere is this better illustrated than in what we ask of children in developing a sense of historical time, for what we mean by this term is culturally determined and is conditioned by the society in which we live. Gustav Jahoda has described this lucidly.[61] He has written perceptively, 'Our conceptual image of time is that of an even and continuous flow from a remote past to an indefinite future; and we regard history as the ever-changing pattern of events which are, as it were, the ripples on the stream of time.' Other historical concepts, such as the philosophy of change, the significance of events and the rationale of cause and effect are defined in accordance with this perspective. It is essentially linear, events being seen as stretching in a long, straight line from past to future. Other cultures do not conceive of history in this way and do not divide time up in the way that Western society does, into weeks, years and centuries.

One can reflect that individual human beings, whether children or adults, do not, deep down, perceive the events of their lives in a linear manner either. Rather do they feel themselves to be enveloped in time, with the beginning and the end of their lives very close. The events in a life do not happen and finish, rather do they continue to gain in significance and meaning as time goes on. Certain memories, like the face of a dog, an old swing or running water, travel with us throughout our lives, as old friends. Certain happenings come with us too, helping us to learn, go forward or retreat according to what they have taught us. We suppress this circular, embracing view of time in favour of a linear, intellectual perspective. At first, though, to the young child, chronological history has little meaning. To quote Jahoda again, 'The past is thus a kind of shallow-mosaic of disparate impressions, whose interrelations are determined by factors other than chronological sequence.'

We ask young children to relinquish their personal view of time-sense, or at least to push it to the back of their consciousness and to develop a linear, historical view of time. How is this accomplished? And in what stages?

Young children develop a sense of time by interpreting myriads of cues from their own environment. As we have noted, a girl (in this chapter we shall refer to girls) notices changes in herself and in those close to her. Sequences are also made manifest in the environment, in the puppy growing into a dog, in the ice-cream getting smaller and smaller as it is sucked. She becomes aware of simple cause and effect. Before the age of five, children can only encompass events that occurred in the immediate past; they learn the significance of such words as 'yesterday', 'today' and 'tomorrow', but as they grow older they are able to order a much longer span of time and to sort out events of increasing complexity. While they are developing this personal perception of time passing and all that it implies, children are also building up a historical time-sense. They do this very early on; in our culture the beginning is seen in young children's great love of stories of all kinds. Stories are always written in time, they have a beginning, a middle and an end; they are pieces of miniature history. What enables historical time-sense to develop from a simple perception of time? We ask a child, firstly, to recognise that time is not just part of her life, but part of everybody else's as well. In other words, she has to be objective, recognising that time is outside herself. She has also to make the great acceptance that she is just part of total existence, not the whole of it. This new perspective confronts the child with a great challenge, as she now has to order all the phenomena, events and sequences of the external environment in accordance with this view.

Parents and teachers see their children struggling towards this; they usually reach this point by the time they are eight. Round about then, children accept that other people have existed before they themselves were born; before then they often firmly hold two popular beliefs. One is that nothing existed before they did; I once heard a child say, 'Oh, dinosaurs can't have existed because I wasn't here then.' In other words, children claim that time, and indeed life, belongs to them and has no identity outside themselves. Having thought themselves through this phase, children cherish another belief. It is that anyone older than they are can remember everything. We have to put up with being asked what it was like to be chased by a dinosaur, or to live through the Great Plague of 1665, or to go to tea with Queen Victoria. Slowly, however, it dawns on young children that historical time is divided into the parts of a continuum, with people's lives, centuries and historical ages occupying sections. It is primarily a working through of egocentricity that enables young children to begin to develop a sense of historical time. This perspective shapes the events of the past into a certain definite structure, the one postulated by Jahoda. To employ a different metaphor, the child now stands on a mountain-top, with the past stretching out below. Events stand out like the contours of the earth. Those events that occurred recently are not necessarily easier to understand, often those farther away emerge more clearly, being uncluttered by irrelevant detail. It is certainly true that young children find it easier to study the distant past than the twentieth century.

The young child needs other skills in order to develop historical time-sense. She has to be able to construct the kind of associative complexes that will enable her, one day, to know that Tudor houses, spicy food and a deep concern with religious issues go together and are part of the sixteenth century, while disco music, a high standard of living and nuclear armament belong to the 1980s. For this she needs considerable skill in the use and understanding of language. Language gives form and definition to concepts; it enables the thinker to generalise, to identify what belongs to the many and to distinguish this from the unique. It holds the user firmly in her own culture and conveys ideas considered vital to her own society; it is evocative and, by facilitating the association of ideas, allows access to what otherwise remains inaccessible. In history, this is the past. Moreover, it is through the acquisition of the meaning of words that the child builds up an accurate picture of times long ago. There has been a great deal of research into this process, the general conclusion being that children perceive meanings by using contextual cues, so that their concepts grow by becoming increasingly precise and relevant. To take an example, a child may read the sentence, 'A village in mediaeval times had three large fields, on which people grew their crops.' The word 'village' has changed its meaning over the years; a twentieth-century child probably thinks of it as a small group of houses in the country, surrounded by fields, and with just one or two shops. In medieval times, the village was the economic unit of society, agriculturally self-sufficient and with methods of agriculture vastly different from our own. The child reading the sentence would not realise this all at once, but she would have a clue from 'the three large fields'. The meaning of words she does know would in this way lend meaning to the word she does not fully understand.

The process takes time. Coltham, in a well-known piece of research,[62] asked junior school pupils what they thought were the meanings of words commonly used in history. One of the words was 'king'. The youngest children associated the word with pomp and show; the slightly older ones thought of a king as possessing power, while, to the oldest children, the word 'king' denoted both the possession of power and the ability to bring about change. These oldest children showed an awareness of the passage of time, one writing, 'Kings had power but not now.'

The development of historical time-sense is but one element in historical understanding; albeit the most important one. Children need other qualities. Some of these are intellectual, some are emotional. Some, when described, take adults by surprise, because it is so long ago since we ourselves acquired them that we take them for granted.

A true understanding of historical events implies not only a considerable insight into the behaviour of people, but also an ability to distinguish between the physical laws and the social conventions that govern our existence. Physical laws are more or less inevitable, but social conventions are not. To take a case in point, it is just possible that, on the bitter January day in 1649 when Charles I was executed, someone might have stayed the hand of the executioner, but no one could have stopped the falling of a snowflake. Some of the rules by which we live in society are mere artefacts, to be changed at will, though not easily; others dictate the physical world and are irreversible. To understand the difference between the two is to perceive both the possibilities and the limitations of human action and must surely be a prerequisite of any study of human affairs in the form of history. Adults hold this kind of understanding so securely that they are hardly aware of it, but the evidence is that young children do not. Investigations indicate that many six- and seven-year-olds think that human behaviour is immutable, while there are eight- and nine-year-olds who believe that physical laws can be changed by human intervention.[36] An understanding of the limitations and possibilities of human action is won through sheer experience of the environment. It is something we work at and experiment with throughout our lives. Let us say at once that because this knowledge is hard won, is not a reason why young children should not study history, rather it is very much the reverse. History itself is essentially about people and helps children to gain an insight into the ways in which they act.

The ability to perceive the nature of the laws which govern human existence is closely connected to an understanding of human nature. Research suggests that the ability to assess human behaviour and its motives comes very slowly in stages and is not mature until adolescence. One investigation looked at the thinking of children of seven, ten, 13 and 17 years of age.[37] These groups of children were asked to make judgements about two story characters of their own age, whose behaviour was, by adult standards, deviant. One character was uncontrolled and aggressive, the other was paranoid. The children, in making their judgements, also gave their reasons. It was found that only the 17-year-olds possessed a rationally based framework for the assessment of behaviour, and only they had the insight to understand both individual irrationality and the social norms that decree that certain behaviour is abnormal. At the other end of the scale, the seven-year-olds were superficial in their judgements. Aggressive behaviour, to them, was always the result of provocation, and fear was a response to genuine threat. The ten-year-olds did possess a kind of normative framework, but they tended to make judgements on the basis of observable behaviour and rarely tried to look into a person's mind, as it were. Such conclusions are in keeping with many other lines of research and with what we daily experience with young children. If they find difficulty in assessing the people of their own time, how much more difficult is it for them to judge the people of the past, who often lived and thought quite differently from ourselves? We are presenting children with a double-edged task; they have to interpret the actions of mature people when they have not acquired the experience to do so; further, they have to judge them in the context of the conventions and conditions of a period of time with which they are not acquainted. Some people would say, straight away, that these are excellent reasons for not including history in the syllabus at all. Others of us would disagree; we would argue that this is the very reason why history should be studied. We will explain why by means of an example, that of a six-year-old hearing about the story of Sir Francis Drake.

The story of Drake playing bowls as the Spanish Aramada approached Plymouth is an exciting one, but a six-year-old will have little understanding of why England and Spain were fighting each other, and still less what bowls had to do with it, unless her grandad plays bowls down at the local club. However, it is not fair to describe the situation quite so baldly, because the story of Drake has a universal application which we all understand. It is about keeping calm in the face of crisis. This is echoed in everyone's experience, even that of the six-year-old when she loses her crayons or her mother is late collecting her from school. The six-year-old uses her own experience in order to understand Drake's action; at the same time, the story of Drake enhances her insight. She may go on to learn that Drake sailed round the world, that there is a picture of his ship on the old halfpenny, that he forbade his men to swear, and that another Tudor ship, the 'Mary Rose', has been salvaged from where it sank, hundreds of years ago, and can tell us all kinds of things about a seaman's life in the sixteenth century. Regular reports were made about it on the children's television programme *Blue Peter* (BBC 1). In this way history can be a source of tremendous enrichment to a very young child. Children themselves are very aware of this, being avid readers of history books and viewers of historical programmes on television. They know that it teaches them about people, and life, and that it is not beyond them at all.

There is an emotional component in historical understanding. Children often possess it to a greater degree than adults. It is there when a child can see the old copper in the scullery of a run-down house and sense what it was like to do the family washing in it; it is when she can feel the pride and workmanship that went into the building of an early railway locomotive and imagine the excitement of the first journey. We see it in adults when, after a week's hard work earning their living, they stream off to join the local history society. Real historical understanding requires a creative leap forward, the action of the mind to put all things together so that the individual actually feels what it was like to live in the past. We call this empathy. A teacher once described this element in historical understanding when he wrote, 'A people's relation to its own history is mysterious, for history is not something we discover; it is also, in a sense, something which we create.'[63]

The study of history at its ultimate level, that is, in the way that it is taught at university, and even in secondary schools, demands intellectual qualities of a high order. Among these skills are the ability to form a comprehensive judgement taking into account all the possibilities inherent in a situation, the formation of hypotheses which can be confirmed, or otherwise, by the available data, and the ability to make comparisons and reason at an abstract level. A great deal of interesting research has shown that children have not developed these skills until adolescence and that, until then, their judgements are illogical and fragmentary.[64] This is not to say that we should not teach history to young children. Mark Roberts, the teacher who described so clearly the creative element in historical understanding, also has this to say. 'An art', he writes, 'can make its impact on all kinds of conditions of people, at many levels of understanding, in ways which are indefinable but none the less powerful. So it can be with history.'[63] Mark Roberts teaches pupils with learning difficulties.

Let us remember, also, that not understanding is the first step on the road towards understanding. Were it not so, there would be no point at all in sending our children to school.

There are two parts to our consideration of the environmental study. On the one hand, we have to consider the evolution of a child's strategy in ordering the environment through an intellectual discipline; on the other, we are at pains to perceive the many ways in which the environment itself can be used for the purpose of helping the formation of this strategy.

History enables young children to order the environment in terms of the past. They have to do this by being sensitive to thoughts and feelings that are not their own, and possibly different from those of the people in their own society. They have to order the past in accordance with the views and ideas of their own culture. They have to develop a historical time-sense, implying both an awareness of change and of the continuity that underlies it. For all this they need a degree of both intellectual and emotional maturity, it being necessary to relinquish their natural egocentricity, to develop qualities of reasoning, and, finally, to make the creative leap forward that makes the subject their own. Then they carry the past and the present together, inside themselves.

How can the environment, with its phenomena, events and relationships, be presented to young children in such a way as to aid the development of their environmental strategies? It matters a great deal how teachers and educationists themselves perceive the environment. In recent years, a strong line of research has attempted to apply Piagetian theory to the historical thinking of young children. This depicts the thinking of children as evolving through stages and finally arriving at that point where formal logic is possible. Piagetian thinking, or rather the way in which it has been applied to education, seriously underestimates and indeed distorts the significance of environmental factors in the cognitive development of children. It is concerned with how the individual comes to perceive equivalence and orderly relationships in the world; it is concerned with the emergence of universal laws and with logic. Moreover, as we have noted already in another connection, this theory takes the adult concept first and then traces the way in which the young child reaches it; it is not concerned with how the child thinks in everyday situations as they crop up in life. The environment does not have to be conceptualised in an abstract, logical way and it is almost certainly not seen like this by children. Just as important and every bit as instructive are the constantly occurring irregularities, the pluralities and the phenomena occurring at various levels simultaneously, as we see, for example, in a round plate, a round worm and a round person. Piagetian theory, as it has been applied, also ignores the effect of situation in the environment, possibly the most potent stimulus to learning that there is. It has been shown that human beings, adults as well as children, do not think consistently in concrete or operational terms; they adapt their thinking to the situations in which they find themselves. Significantly, they think in concrete and experimental terms when faced with a problem with which they are unfamiliar; children as well as adults can think formally about a situation they know really well. We can note, also, that Piagetian theory conceptualises children in a limited way and structures their responses. They are made to respond, in tests, to highly specialised situations which have been devised and imposed on them by a stranger. The demands made are not those made in the course of everyday living, and the responses called forth are not necessarily those the children would make in an unstructured context.

Further, logic and abstract powers of thought are not the inevitable products of maturation, they are the hard-won fruits of experience. There is no reason to suppose that a quantity of liquid, when poured from one vessel to another of a different shape, remains the same, unless one has proved it for oneself; one could well believe that it might have been possible to stop the snowflake falling at the scene of the execution of Charles I, unless one had oneself tried to stop the snow falling on a wintry afternoon.

Once the environment is conceptualised in more pragmatic and yet more subtle terms, its educational significance becomes clearer. It includes all the people, the events and the situations that make up a child's life. Children learn through seeing and proving for themselves that things *do* happen in a certain way. The interaction taking place between children and the environment is active, complex and ever-changing, children adapting their thinking to the demands made upon them. Each new experience modifies children and they, in turn, modify the environment. Learning can be described as the enlargement of experience, which itself may be seen as a journey from what is known to what is unknown. What is not known provides a basis and a structure for coming to terms with what is new, as when the little girl used her own experience as a basis for understanding the actions of Sir Francis Drake. History, and other subjects too, gain in meaning and significance.

The environmental study can greatly aid the young child's development of a complex sense of time. It is in the immediate environment that the passing of time can be most convincingly and vividly perceived. Creatures and phenomena are to be observed evolving through various time-scales, from the slow drip of a tap to the growth of a plant, through to the slow unfolding of the child's own life as she grows out of her shoes, enters another class at school and acquires a younger brother or sister. The time-scales in the child's immediate environment provide the stepping stones to the historical time-scale, the one that involves the whole of society. An infants school teacher has expressed this very well.[65] Young children's sense of time, she writes, springs from 'the feeling of belonging to a continuing pattern of living.' She helps her children weave this pattern of living through activities that arise spontaneously through their own interests.

Crucial to the development of historical time-sense is the ability of the child to relinquish egocentricity and to accept that time stands outside herself. These lessons, too, are learnt by reference to the environment. The lives of other people are abundant proof that some people were alive before we were, some will be alive after we are gone, and that time is an objective criterion.

The associations children make in their everyday lives help them to build associative complexes that reveal the past. Today's children know that Queen Elizabeth is on the throne; they are aware of how people dress; they know their parents work for a living. Later, they may link Queen Victoria with ladies in long dresses, children working in factories and the existence of a wealthy middle class. The two groups of associations are the same in essentials, different in details. One provides a stepping-stone to the other.

Experience of the human environment likewise enables children to perceive the ways in which social conventions and natural laws operate and that they are not the same thing. The noise of a thunderstorm cannot be prevented but the noise a little sister makes banging on her drum can.

An understanding of these regularities underpins an understanding of society and hence that of society in the past. The same experiences teach children about human nature. The little girl learning about the exploits of Sir Francis Drake has probably fought down her own panic in a personal crisis; she may have avoided confrontation with a bully in the school playground; almost certainly she will have wheedled her parents to let her stay up late watching television on one or two occasions. Such experiences provide her with an insight into the lives of the people of the past. The people she talks to will enhance her vocabulary and provide her with many contextual cues by means of which she can interpret what has gone before. She will learn that 'king' and 'village' meant something different in the Middle Ages.

Imagine the impact the following discovery would make on a class of young children. Sylvia Collicott, who teaches infants in a school in North London, borrowed a box of Roman finds from a local dig while studying local history with her class. There, on a Roman roof-tile, was the imprint of a cat's paw.[66] Cats, it would seem, were the same in Roman times as they are now, and, as today, liked sitting on roof-tops; this cat could not resist putting a paw into the soft clay of the tile. Here is a link with the past, and of a kind to draw children away from a personalised sense of history towards a general one.

Other teachers of older children use back copies of newspapers in order to bring history alive. Michael Winton, teaching in a school in King's Lynn, Norfolk, found the following comment concerning a major outbreak of typhoid in King's Lynn in *The Times* newspaper of 1897. 'The people of Lynn have little taste for pure water,' wrote the commentator, 'they evidently prefer sewage, and they like it neat.'[67] A back copy of the local newspaper contained, in 1921, a fascinating advertisement for false teeth. 'Why Bradleys teeth are best – sets from 21 shillings' was proclaimed from the page. Let us hope that these persuasive words were not accompanied by an illustration.

In the last resort, true historical understanding goes hand in hand with empathy, or a feeling for the past. This is an element that enters into the learning of every subject, although its influence is frequently underestimated by educationists. We all know when we have achieved it. It is when the subject leaps into life, when we feel at once at ease and yet excited about it, when we have made it our own and can go forward and make our own discoveries. Teachers sometimes sense this happening in a classroom, when the children are suddenly silent and work with a will. They are there. Empathy is linked to the conviction that the past is real. Attaining it involves a creative leap of the imagination. How does it happen? We do not know the full answer because creativity in children has only comparatively recently come under investigation. We can, however, hazard a guess at some of the influences present. We have mentioned the conviction that the past is alive; another influence is probably sheer familiarity with the material. It has been shown that both children and adults bring conceptualisation of a higher order to bear on that with which they are familiar; if anything is certain about the exceptional achiever, or the genius, it is that she knows her field extremely well. One would suggest that it is this familiarity that enables a child to integrate all she knows and make the subject part of herself. Familiarity, of course, is part of the environment, and this must represent a great contribution by the environmental study towards historical understanding. The child's emotional involvement with what is immediately perceived provides the stimulus for making an intellectual effort and reaching out. She shapes her perceptions into concepts. These concepts are living, in that they span both past and present; they are evolutionary in that the child can see for herself the process through time. She has not worked from the present backwards; rather has she come to see past and present as one organic whole.

For the purposes of detailed discussion we will consider two topics, one that is particularly suitable for very young children, and one that is enthusiastically received by eight- to ten-year-olds.

Young children spend their early years almost totally within their families, and it is these early experiences which shape their strategies in ordering the environment in terms of historical time. It is in the family that they first notice change and development in human affairs; it is there that they build complexes of associations that are basically historical in nature, like the fact that watching television, putting on nylon socks and shopping in the supermarket all go together and belong to modern times. It is from the family that children absorb the values of their own culture; this provides the stepping-stone for the understanding of others. The family also has more obvious lessons to teach, for its members are the patient story-tellers, the users of language and the clearers-up of mental confusion. It is here, too, that children first learn about human nature and its norms. They may note that Aunt Ada insists on sleeping with her slippers under her pillow and Dad hates spring onions in his salad; they have to make up their minds whether such behaviour is normal, tolerable or unalterable – such experience is the bedrock of historical judgement later.

For the purposes of the teacher, family history offers a great many easily accessible sources and a variety of interesting approaches. Very young children might simply enjoy hearing the memories of their older relatives, who make the past come alive and are proof that it is part of us all. Some relatives, invited into the classroom, will remember events that have had an immediate impact on the children's lives, like the building of a new road or even of their school. Some parents, certainly some grandparents, will be able to talk about past events of world-wide significance, like those of World War II which can be carefully structured into a project for older children. This is how one teacher accomplished it in a project on the last war, using the relatives of the children in her class. A naval airman, an uncle, came to one lesson, attired in the full naval dress of 1942 and bringing along his Mae West. This was a life jacket which inflated automatically when a cord was pulled and saved many men's lives. Another uncle, who had been in the RAF, brought along his old flying helmet, complete with oxygen apparatus, and allowed the children to try it on. The helmet was made of thin leather and seemed pathetically flimsy. Parents and grandparents on another occasion painted a picture of life on the home front; laid out on a plate, unbelievably to these eight-year-olds, were the food rations one person was allowed per week. There was only one egg, for example. Ration books and identity cards were examined. Many stories were recounted, some of them funny; for example, there was the typically British story of the Squander Bug. A horrific looking insect with huge teeth, the Squander Bug appeared on hoardings in a government-sponsored effort to persuade everyone not to waste money. However, as could have been foreseen, the British public grew so fond of him that he made an abrupt disappearance.

Incidentally, these children came from a multinational background; some were American, one was German and there were two Japanese. These children had different stories to tell and, tactfully handled by the teacher, provided a way of presenting history in the round.

People's living memories only go back so far, but family photographs and albums can take the children back much further. On page 126 is the kind of photograph that could be found in many a family album, of two typical working-class Londoners, Charlie and Victoria. The photograph was taken in 1916, in the middle of the First World War. The lives of these two ordinary looking people were full of the most vivid history.

Charlie was born in the East End of London in the late 1880s, a true Cockney, born within the sound of Bow Bells. He could be a great-grandfather of a primary school child of the present day. The London he knew then was a terrible place for children. His family was desperately

A photo from a family album.
Charlie and Victoria

poor, poorer even than most because his mother was a widow who made and sold wooden clothes-pegs in order to provide for her children. Often Charlie would be given ¼d (one old farthing) with which to buy fish and chips for the day. You could get a good portion for that in those days. Many a time Charlie ran away from home for days, sleeping rough. He was a naughty boy and once stayed away for a week because he'd shot through his sister's finger with a home-made bow and arrow. He was afraid of the hiding he'd get.

Few strangers ventured into the East End in those days. The Salvation Army did, singing their hymns as they marched along the narrow streets. They were met with a barrage of missiles from the residents, who would lean out of their windows and hurl anything they could, slops included, down on to the heads below. The soldiers of the Lord would simply shout, 'Praise be the Lord,' and march on.

The most hated figure to Charlie and his family was the school attendance officer, the 'truant man', as he was called. It was his job to round up all the truants and drag them into school, often literally; Charlie hated school, for it wasn't a pleasant place in those days. Teachers were strict and armed with canes, and great emphasis was placed on neat handwriting and learning facts by heart. Inability to write neatly and do mental arithmetic was seen as sheer perversity on the part of the children and punished accordingly. Charlie spent a lot of time playing truant. He and his friends rarely escaped from the dismal London streets. A favourite street game was 'Knock down Ginger', which involved banging on a neighbour's front door and running away before a child was caught and had his ears boxed.

When he was twelve, Charlie left school and got a job. He was a cleaner-out of huge factory furnaces; he had to crawl inside them when they were cool and hack away the hard deposit. He was so thin that he wore a dog collar to keep his trousers up; he had no need of a belt.

As soon as he could, Charlie ran away and joined the army, and fought in the Great War of 1914. While on leave, he met and married Victoria. Victoria, too, had an interesting background. She was named after the great Queen and, like Charlie, was a Londoner, although her parents were Scots. They had come down from the Highlands, where both had been domestic servants on a big estate, in order to better themselves. Victoria's father got himself a respectable job as a butler in the House of Commons. There he took to finishing off all the dregs in the members' glasses, ending up with an over-fondness for drink. This was a closely guarded secret in Victoria's family.

When she finally escaped from school, which she hated as much as Charlie, Victoria took a job as an assistant in a shoe shop. Many years later she told her grandchildren what this was like. The hours were long, six days a week, but Victoria enjoyed her work. She made it a rule never to allow a customer to leave the shop dissatisfied, and her simple psychology was so successful that within a few years Victoria was being sent round from branch to branch of the firm in order to build up sales. The money taken by each shop-girl had to balance exactly with the prices of the shoes she had sold; the great moment came on Saturday night, when the takings were counted. To Victoria's delight, in her first week at work, her accounts did balance. The manager was pleased, too, and gave her a gold sovereign.

Charlie and Victoria met when Charlie came into the shop to buy a pair of boots. Victoria's family were not pleased when she and Charlie became engaged to be married. Charlie lived until he was eighty-eight; Victoria until she was eighty. Londoners to the last, they spent their remaining days in a little terraced house with a sleepy old cat.

Victoria and Charlie were ordinary people, yet their lives tell us far more history than a book, and in a vivid way that appeals to children. One thing is true above all others; hearing their story, we know that they lived; their lives are proof that history is real. Most families keep photograph albums and someone will know the stories behind the pictures. They might talk about their memories to the children in the classroom; older children could listen to a tape recorded version.

Such history does not have to remain on an anecdotal level, indeed it should not, for young children are well capable of appreciating historical trends, especially when they see these in the context of the lives of people they know well and love. Here are some suggestions as to how such material can be shaped and analysed in the classroom.

The children could begin by looking at the characteristics of the people in their families. All children are interested in physical appearances and frequently characteristics run in families. Can they get their parents and grandparents to tell them who were the fair-haired people in the family, who the big and who the tiny? They can map out their findings. Charlie's family were fair-haired and blue-eyed, though his Irish mother had red hair. Victoria's family who came down from Scotland, were big, solid people, the men being usually over six feet tall. They had light-brown hair and blue-grey eyes.

The children can trace less usual physical traits, such as left-handedness or a tendency to have more children of one sex in a family. Victoria's family contained a high proportion of left-handed children and an unusual number of twins.

Recent research shows that quite complex traits of behaviour and inclination can run in families. Members of a family frequently follow the same occupation; miners, dockers, printers and fairground people often hand down jobs from father to son. The children could also consider personality traits, which can also be handed down. Charlie's and Victoria's families mainly consisted of practical, out-of-doors people, with a love of games. One of their children, a girl, became a skilled carpenter; an uncle was a deep-sea diver.

Young children are usually intrigued by names, being usually very possessive about their own because they are part of their self-image. Some families have favourite names, handed down, like jobs, through the generations. Are there any favourite names in their families? Christian, or first names, are also greatly influenced by fashion. Victoria had three sisters and a brother. They were called Ethel, Ivy, Lily and Archibald. Would such names be popular now? The children may be able to find out something about their ancestors by considering their surnames. Surnames can indicate the occupations or physical characteristics of ancestors, or the place where they lived. The Coopers of the past made barrels for beer; the Cruikshanks ('crooked-legs') probably walked lopsidedly or with a limp, disabilities which were common in the days of poor diet and no National Health Service; 'Miller' speaks for itself. The millers were none too popular in mediaeval times, having the monopoly of grinding the villagers' corn for a price. The Smiths, judging from the number of them in the telephone directory, must have been a vigorous and prolific group.

Specialised books in the children's reference library will help the older boys and girls to look into names more deeply. *Your Book of Surnames*, by

Pennethorne Hughes (Faber and Faber, 1967), is specially written for children. A more advanced book, suitable for teachers, is W. O. Hassall's *History through Surnames* (Pergamon Press, 1967). These are established reference texts.

Children enjoy drawing profiles of their own families and this convinces them of the reality of history; they are embarking on a study of a unit basic to social history, one that is of great interest to historians at this very moment.

Going farther afield, important social trends can be illustrated by family histories. The mobility of the population is one. Charlie and Victoria were only first generation Londoners; Charlie's mother had come over from Ireland in order to escape the grinding poverty there, while Victoria's parents had come from Scotland. Their motives were similar to those of thousands of other people in the nineteenth and twentieth centuries; the

Roller-skating before the First World War

Ready for a roller-disco today
(Reproduced by permission of
Associated Newspapers Ltd)

great cities, London in particular, always act as magnets for the poor, the desperate and the ambitious. The children can probably trace this in their own family histories.

Let us look at some more photographs, one of them from the same album as the portrait of Charlie and Victoria. On page 129 are two photographs of Victoria and her sister Ivy, dressed for the roller-skating rink at Brixton in 1913, and a picture published in the *Daily Mail* (1 September 1980) of a present day roller-skater. Roller-skating was a popular pastime in London before the First World War, as it is now, but what a difference! In Victoria and Ivy's day, it was the thing to go as someone sweetly romantic. Victoria is dressed as Cinderella. Nowadays, people go roller-skating for rhythm, trendiness and fun. Such photographs could start the children off on a topic of 'Amusements, then and now'. The leisure-time pursuits of the people portrayed in the children's photograph albums could be investigated. There were few amusements in Victoria's day and what did exist was usually of the people's own making. There was no television. The girls spent a lot of time sewing for their bottom drawer, the drawer, that is, where they stored all their bed-linen, table-mats, napkins, table-runners and goodness knows what else, ready for the day when they married. The true sign of success in life for a respectable working-class family was a piano, carefully placed in the parlour so that the neighbours could see (and admire) it through the net curtains. The whole family would gather round it and sing – only respectable songs, of course; the others were kept for the music-hall.

Other themes can be shaped from the contents of family albums. The children could investigate the lives of children in the nineteenth century, which are in sharp contrast to their own. They could carry out a project on the homes of nineteenth century people, or on World War I.

If a teacher is lucky, the children can provide other sources of history which give depth to the lives of the people illustrated. Some of these are vivid and unexpected. My husband's grandfather kept an allotment in the early years of this century; a working man, he grew vegetables on it with which to feed his family. Meticulously, he kept a record of expenditure, profit and loss for every single year. The page for 1906 is reproduced overleaf. It can be seen that in those days people grew strains of vegetables that we never hear of now: for example Duke of York peas, Alexandra lettuce and Titan runner-beans. Note also the prices, two old pence for a packet of cabbage seeds. Lastly, this working-class family man kept his accounts in meticulously neat handwriting, using not one of the ballpoints of today, but an old-fashioned pen with a scratchy nib. He was a product of the kind of school that Victoria and Charlie hated so much.

Most families keep records of the past in the form of albums, letters, notebooks and even furniture and clothes. The mothers of today's infant school children may well have been the mini-skirted young girls of the sixties; going even further back, their grandmas will remember Elvis Presley and the first wave of rock-and-roll. An infants class would enjoy dressing up in the clothes of the past. Should anyone wish to make a more formal study with older children using conventional historical sources, D. J. Steel and L. Taylor have written a very helpful book, *Family History in Schools* (Phillimore, 1973). Unfortunately, this book is now out of print, although it is available from libraries. As well as describing how family and school records can be put to use by children, the authors explain how to unearth available sources in the County Record Office, possibly documents concerned with the enclosure movement, tithes, estate maps and town plans of the nineteenth century. They also include many examples of children's project work. More and more people are interested in tracing their ancestry these days, and the BBC has responded with its popular television series, *Family History*. A book has also been produced to go with series entitled *Discovering your Family History* by Don Steel (BBC, 1980). In it there are many clues and ideas to start children off on investigating the story of their families' past. Family history can lead on to other fruitful and related themes: one is the theme of work.

Work unites both past and present in the lives of people, and so has appeal for children; further, it has a particular relevance for them because they are aware of the bearing that the work their parents and teachers do

Expenditure 1906		£	s	d
Date	Particulars			
26.9.05	Rent	5	0	
6.2.06	Shallots		3	0
5.3.06	Onions (1 oz up-to-date)	1	0	
ditto	Parsnip (Lisbonais)		2	0
14.3.06	Peas (Gracus & Albany)		9	0
"	Lettuce (Hexanian)		2	0
2.4.06	Pea. (Duke of York)		4	0
6.4.06	Carrot (Intermediate)		2	0
"	Beetroot. (Dells & Covent)		4	0
"	Potatoes (6 Rose & Llewell)	1	3	
11.4.06	Runner Beans (Titan)		8	0
"	Potatoes (Sect: Trium)	2	0	
4.5.06	Pea Sticks (6 bundles)	3	0	
10.5.06	Turnips & Radishes		2+1	
18.6.06	Celery (Red)		6	0
"	Cabbage Seed		2	0
"	Winter greens	1	4	4
		17	4	

Receipts 1906		£	s	d
Date	Particulars			
15.6.06	Cabbage			5
"	Lettuce		4	6½
23.6.06	Spring Onions			4
14.7.06	Lettuce		2	6½
"	Cabbage			6
"	Peas		1	8
24.7.06	Broad Beans			4
28.7.06	Onions			2
1.5.06	Potatoes		1	8
"	Rhubarb			1
4.8.06	Runner Beans		3	3½
"	Potatoes		4	0½
"	Lettuce			1
11.8.06	Beetroot			11½
18.8.06	Marrows			2
30.8.06	Potatoes		2	11
1.9.06	Marrows			5½
		1	4	2

A record of an allotment in 1906

has on their own lives. The children, too, will enter the world of work one day.

The youngest children will learn a great deal simply by considering the work carried out by some of the people in their lives, such as their mothers and fathers, the school dinner ladies, the dustmen and even the popular commentators on television. They will see how important their work is, and also how many of these jobs have changed, even in the last few years. The children will be studying living history. We will consider, for a moment, the housewife, still the corner-stone of society, but the ways in which she carries out her work have changed radically, even in the last twenty years. Washing, cooking and cleaning are the main tasks. Many little terraced houses in working-class districts still have old sculleries with coppers and also old-fashioned cooking ranges dating from the early years of this century; as a result the children may well have evidence to hand. Forty or fifty years ago, housewives did the family wash on Monday. They filled the copper in the scullery with water, added soap, then lit a fire underneath and boiled up the clothes. These were hauled out after a few hours, scrubbed clean with soap and brush on the wash-board, rinsed and put through the mangle. The mangle was fearsome; old ones can still be found today. It consisted basically of two big, wooden rollers through which the clothes were squeezed so that the water ran out. To turn the rollers a big wheel had to be heaved round by hand; it was very hard work. Mangling was also an art; one skill was to get all the shirts through without crushing the buttons; another skill, equally important, was to get the clothes through without crushing one's fingers either. Having survived the mangle, the clothes were hung up on the clothes-line in the garden to dry. The line was kept high by a clothes-prop. After washing and drying came the ironing, done, not with a modern electric iron, but with an old flat-iron. This had to be heated up on the stove or the gas-ring; housewives devised their own ways of telling whether the iron was of the right heat, usually by spitting on a finger and judging the sizzle when it was held briefly against the hot metal.

Washing-day was the hardest day of the week for the housewife, as some of the children's relatives may well remember. This is not so today. The washing machine, modern detergents which do away with the need for rubbing and scrubbing, and the electric iron, have changed the work of the housewife.

Cooking and cleaning have likewise been transformed. Fifty years ago most houses had gas-stoves, which came before electric ones, but even in the cities many women used the old-fashioned range as well. This meant getting up early, often before dawn, in order to clean out the ashes and get the fire going. Usually the main meal of the day, which was eaten when the men came home from work in the evening, was cooked slowly in the range all day. There was one disadvantage in that the housewife had to keep an eye on the fire all the time, but there were advantages. This method of cooking was cheap, for almost any cut of meat was tender after simmering away for eight hours. It also had the bonus of filling the house with a delicious dinnery smell all day. Modern cooking methods, including the microwave oven, have transformed the housewives' work in this area as well.

The children themselves will be able to list all the modern aids there are for cleaning. Then they can cut out pictures of the items and pin them on the classroom walls. The vacuum cleaner is an important and vital aid, but others, less obvious, have exerted equal influence. Plastic surfaces and new kinds of paint have, for example, made household surfaces much easier to clean.

Through discussion, the children can be brought to perceive how, as the work of the housewife has changed, so has her role in the family and the kind of life she leads. Fifty years ago it was almost impossible for women to go out to work, looking after the home and family was so arduous that it took all their time. Now they can, and do. This, in turn has meant that the task of looking after the home is shared by other members of the family, which is not only right, but fun as well.

Other kinds of work besides that of the housewife will be known to the children. Some may have parents whose jobs have also changed in character recently, like those of carpenter, miner and policeman/woman. Some may have jobs that did not exist a short while ago, like that of a television cameraman; some may carry out work that has continued down the centuries like that of the shepherd.

There is a wealth of supplementary material available for the classroom. We will consider the less conventional.

A pleasing development has taken place recently, in that local communities are showing a growing interest in the working lives of their own people. Hackney, in London, is one such locality, and their Community Publishing Project produced in the late 1970s a book on the people of Hackney, written by themselves. Two of the authors appeared on television and read extracts from their own writings. One was a woman working in a factory; she told how she always had to be out of bed first in the morning in order to get breakfast for her children before going off to work herself; usually she was up by six o'clock. She described how, hours after she had left it, she saw the factory bench in front of her eyes.

A postman spoke about his work. Some letter-boxes he did not mind emptying in the least, but others he hated – one always had glass and rubbish poked into it. He always carried a piece of chocolate with him, with which to bribe an unfriendly dog; however, his worst attack had come from a cat which had pounced on him. He remarked, wryly, that he had not been carrying a saucer of milk at the time.

These recollections carry the ring of truth. Unlike the polite generalised accounts issued by certain organisations, they tell us what the jobs are really like. Any local authority may have some worthwhile material and it is worth enquiring; sometimes information comes through the local newspaper. In my own district, the industrial Chaplain organised an exhibition entitled 'World of Work', illustrating, by means of models and written explanation, the huge variety of enterprise going on in the district. This was advertised in the Church news. The children would have enjoyed a visit.

Television programmes, not necessarily those produced just for children, can paint a vivid picture of past industries and of the lives of the people who worked in them. For example, ITV once broadcast a fascinating account of two now defunct industries in Devon, those of ice-making and peat, which flourished in the late nineteenth century. The ice was manufactured on the moors for use by the wealthier households. These were, of course, the days before the refrigerator. It was taken by cart to the large Devon towns and half of it melted on the way.

A former peat-worker described what it was like hacking out peat from the moors in the early years of this century. He began his work at 7.30 in the morning, after a five-mile walk to the site. He hacked out the peat with a long curved knife and, after a day's work, walked the five miles back. He was paid seventeen shillings a week.

Pictures and books for both children and teachers are easy to find. The teacher's journals frequently develop work as a theme, for example, *Junior Education* (see the Appendix, page 234, for the address).

The theme of work, and indeed all those topics explored in environmental history, will frequently lead children on to examine a more complex historical problem, one that presents itself at a higher level of generality. It is well-nigh impossible to study work and its history, or the histories of transport, agriculture or local industry, without coming across the Industrial Revolution. Similarly, a study of local churches would inevitably lead back to the Reformation. These great movements are just as much a part of the environment as the houses, streets and buses in front of our noses; they are simply perceived on a different level.

Another theme related to the family is that of the home. In our homes is a wealth of historical evidence, testifying to both change and continuity. 'The home' is an excellent theme for young children to explore, because the evidence is easily accessible and the subject is dear to them.

Those in the nursery and infant school, for whom the past is not very far away, need a strong, clear theme. Some themes suggest themselves through looking at photographs, or through hearing their parents talk. 'Cooking dinner' might be one; 'Doing the housework' another; and 'Amusements in the home' yet another, bearing in mind that it was not so very long ago that there were no television sets.

Environmental history should not confine children to what is immediately discernible in their own surroundings; rather should it lead them into a broader historical perspective. A study of their own homes can lead children to a consideration of houses in general and the homes of all classes of people. Homes and houses are historical documents in their own right, telling us a great deal about the lives of people in the past. In most of our cities can be found the stately homes of the aristocracy, the houses built by the prosperous middle classes for their families, and rows of little terraces. Teachers will usually find ample reference material in the local reference library, from their local history society or from that useful periodical, *The Local Historian*. Some fascinating articles can be found in *The Local Historian* and, with luck, one can even find something on the locality of one's own school. Two interesting articles on houses were written by Adrian Henstock, the county architect for Nottinghamshire.[68] Writing on 'Town Houses and Society in Georgian Country Towns', he described some of the beautiful houses built by the prosperous gentlemen of the late eighteenth century in towns like Ashbourne in Derbyshire, Lichfield in Staffordshire and Newark in Nottinghamshire, and he included some excellent photographs. In a second article, the author discussed the architectural qualities of houses. As he put it so well, 'Houses express the life-styles, attitudes, prosperity and personalities of the people who built them.'

As we have seen, the family is an excellent environmental theme for young children; one that can lead them into a perception of history and one that can, further, be enjoyed by older children as well.

The study of the children's own particular area is yet another approach to environmental history. It has a potent appeal, one that can almost be described as instinctive, particularly to children of seven and upwards.

Deep in human make-up are a sense of belonging to one's own piece of territory and a determination to defend it. In a civilised society, this instinctive drive manifests itself in various ways. It is seen in the pride people take in their homes and gardens, and also in complaints about the; neighbours when they impinge, by means of trespass, behaviour or the making of too much noise, on someone else's space. It is seen on a cultural level, in the interest people show in the history of the area in which they live; it is seen on a national level, as in the dispute over the Falkland Islands, in which we were quite prepared to fight a war, thousands of miles away, in defence of territory. Research, as well as observation, shows that children early possess this same sense of territory and that this is quickly transformed into a respect for their own surroundings. By the age of about ten they tend to be strongly preservationist and very much in favour of keeping monuments and other evidence of the past intact. They dislike so-called 'development'. The local study is therefore very much part of the strategy young children spontaneously evolve for themselves. It is looking at the environment through their eyes.

The local study can be approached in several ways. One way is through the lives of people who have lived in the locality in the past. They do not have to be the grand and famous; the lives of ordinary, humble people usually reveal much more. Guess who this is. He lived in the eighteenth century from 1727 to 1771. He kept pigs and sheep and grew peas and oats. He was a clean, neat little man, spending 15 shillings annually on stockings and socks (in those days shoes were five shillings a pair). This gentleman enjoyed taking snuff and spent three shillings and sixpence a year on it. He had a maid called Hester, whom he engaged in 1733 and paid £12 for three years' wages. He also employed a cook-maid and an odd-job man, all out of his income of approximately £233 17 shillings a year. Some of his income he received in goods, not in money. He was a kind man, ever conscious of the needs and sufferings of the poor. In 1739, he paid a local school mistress £3 to teach six poor children.

When I add that this gentleman received tithes, you will probably guess what, if not who, he was. He was the Reverend Edmund Lewin, a country parson of the parish of Westmill in Hertfordshire. He is the subject of an article by W. A. Pemberton in *The Local Historian*.[69] How lucky would be the children of Westmill to be told all about him. Seeing life through the eyes of a character like the Reverend Lewin has great value for children, because it makes history convincingly real. History as a formal subject is usually taught at a high level of generality. It is possible, indeed almost inevitable, that we learn about great movements like the Industrial Revolution or the Napoleonic Wars, or about the ever-present problem of poverty, without actually sensing the underlying human experience. The enormity of the events seems to emasculate the people taking part. Edmund Lewin must have seen some of the effects of the Agricultural Revolution in England, but he would not have been aware of it as a movement; it would have come to him in the guise of better ways of growing his peas and oats, and perhaps of dealing with the troublesome moles. He knew, too, about poverty, because of the six poor children on whom he took pity and had taught to read and write. Great events filtered through to ordinary people dimly, like voices through the mist. It is the same today, and it is an experience that children share with adults.

The other side of the coin is that local history can remain on the level of gossip and anecdote and fail to make possible any kind of analytical thinking. This, however, does not have to be the case, because local people and local events frequently illustrate very well much broader historical issues. Valerie Brierley, for her class, used the diary of another parson of the eighteenth century, the well-known James Woodforde, who was a rector in Norfolk from 1776 to 1803.[70] Although Ms Brierley worked with rather older children than those we are considering, the way in which she worked would be interesting to eight- and nine-year-olds and they would certainly find the material amusing. For example, Woodforde describes what it was like to make a journey in the eighteenth century, giving a graphic account, not just of the dangers and inconveniences, but of his fellow passengers also. He writes thus of the people he shared a coach with on one journey. 'We had four inside Passengers besides: one very stout man of Norwich by name Hix, a Grocer, one single lady and a comical Woman and a little Boy her son – the child sick most of the night as was the single Woman.'

Of another journey Woodforde writes, 'I was bit terribly by Buggs last night, but did not wake me. I was terribly swelled in the face and hands by the Buggs.' In such material lie the beginnings of a whole project on travel in the eighteenth century. Using extracts from Woodforde's diary, Valerie Brierley set the children in her class to work on group topics; Life in the Parsonage, Wages and Bills, and Sport and Culture were some. This venture is described in another valuable journal for teachers, *Teaching History*, the address of which can be found in the Appendix (page 235).

The lives of characters such as Lewin and Woodforde can be set in the broader context of the local community by drawing on sources provided by the public reference library and the local history society. Some teachers have come together and produced resource kits for their children. The teachers of Aberdare, in mid-Glamorgan, have compiled *How they lived then: Aberdare in the Eighteen Fifties* (published by the Mid-Glamorgan Education Authority, 1980). The work-kit includes key documents, which have been reproduced for the children to work on. Local authorities are themselves publishing histories of their own communities. Deptford, in London, has produced *Up the Creek* (1980) about an area in the East End rich in history. The book is well-illustrated, with prints of old photographs, and has proved very popular with the local people.

The teachers of Aberdare describe most lucidly the aim of the local history they have produced. It is, they say, to encourage in children 'the development of concepts of continuity and change in relation to the local communities of which they are members.'

It is almost a truism to say that history is about people and about communities. Without humanity there would be no history, because it is the needs and actions of people that create events and crises, and which engender both the change and the enduring regularity that underlie societies as they evolve. As they are introduced to the people of the past, as they see how the Reverend Lewin worried over his garden and the Reverend Woodforde stolidly endured the bed bugs and his sweating companions on his coach journeys, children are introduced to the human predicament. We are all acquainted with it. There is, in fact, a school of thought which holds that the contact with people that history gives is of inestimable benefit to young children, enabling them to work through their own inner conflicts.[71]

A fruitful approach to local history is to allow children to explore the history of their physical surroundings. They enjoy this, territory-conscious as they are. They can set out to answer questions like the following: why did our village, town or city grow up where it did? What sorts of industries are there and how did they develop? How have the streets and shops changed over the years? How did the streets get their names? A good way of beginning is to take the children on a walk, noting outstanding physical features like rivers, crossroads, hills and valleys, or the sea. Alternatively, they can study a map. Very often, the history of a locality, particularly the way in which it earns its livelihood, has been dictated by its geography. Towns may have grown up near crossroads, busy ports near harbours. Teachers can obtain the background to their school's particular locality by referring, in the first place, to the Victoria

County Histories, which can be found in local reference libraries. One large volume has been written about each county. The local history societies, whose members are invariably great enthusiasts, will always prove helpful; so, often, will the local librarian, who may also be an archivist.

The children will almost certainly find if they live in a town or city, that this has greatly expanded in size over the years. It is possible for them to demonstrate this for themselves. Starting with a map of the original settlement drawn on plain paper, they can draw other maps of the town or village at key points in its history; the Middle Ages, the end of the seventeenth century and the end of the nineteenth century would be good points to choose if they want a long-term view. These maps can be drawn on transparent paper with fibre-tipped pens, a different colour being used for each period. When all the maps are stapled together in chronological order, by turning the pages the children can read, in visual terms, the story of the expansion.

Alternatively, models can be built of the area at different stages in its history. These have the advantage of showing how the streets, houses and shops have changed down the centuries.

The streets of today have a long history, going right back to Roman times when they received their name, 'strata', from the Latin word denoting that they were built in layers. Incidentally, this means that streets are likely to go farther back in time than roads. Children are intrigued by the ways in which shops, coal-holes and pillar-boxes have changed, by street furniture as it is called. They are interested in the pleasing relics from the past that we still keep in our streets, like many-sided pillar-boxes and drinking-troughs from the days of horse-drawn traffic. Teachers' magazines often include short articles and up-to-date information on streets. In the February 1980 issue of *Junior Education* there is a short article on the history of streets and some advice to children on how to make rubbings of coal-holes.

Shops reflect our industrial and commercial history, our trade and our way of life as a nation, and make a very good environmental topic. *Shops and Markets* by Paul White (A and C Black, 1971) traces the history of shops and markets, right up to the mail-order firms and huge department stores of today. Books like this one can be used by children to provide the background for an investigation into the history of the shops in their own locality.

All the children will want to know how their particular street or road acquired its name. Finding this out is not always an easy matter and they will almost certainly need help. Streets have acquired their names for all sorts of reasons. They may denote a physical characteristic, for example, Broad Street, Sandy Lane or Copse Hill. When the urban spread began with the coming of the Industrial Revolution and continued with another spurt in the early years of this century, a number of streets and roads were named after the farmers and families whose land was taken over. Other

.s have origins that will greatly appeal to young children. In my own .rict we have Beverley Way, named after the field where the beavers ,;layed in Anglo-Saxon times ('bever' = 'beaver' and 'lea' = 'field'). Often, too, the name of a street, road or lane will indicate to the children a craft or business that has been carried on there in the past, sometimes down the centuries. Pudding Lane, where the Great Fire of London was sparked off in 1666, was so named because bakers had their shops there. This had been the custom since medieval times. Not so long ago in terms of history, in the latter half of the nineteenth century, the people of Battersea in South London grew lavender. Lavender Hill is now a great inner city road, choked with fumes and traffic, while Lavender Sweep nearby is a huddle of tiny terraced houses, but the history of the district survives in the names of its streets.

The Victoria County Histories and the pamphlets produced by the local history society will help in tracking all this down. Long ago, the English Place-Name Society set out to produce a volume on the place-names of each county in England, which, of course, would be concerned as well with names other than those of streets. The task was never completed, but the volumes that have been published are very useful and can usually be found on library shelves. The *Concise Oxford Dictionary of English Place-Names* by E. Ekwall (fourth edition, 1960) will also be of great help to teachers. The author explains how 'chester' on the name of a town denotes a one-time fort, as in Manchester and Colchester.

Local history provides real opportunities for even young children to carry out some original research of their own. Finding out about how the people of their locality lived in the past, or how industry and agriculture have evolved in the working community are fairly obvious examples. Less frequently undertaken are projects on the local churchyard. The local churchyard or cemetery reveals a good deal of history; gravestones can be unique sources of local history, since the first government census was not taken until 1801, and deaths did not have to be recorded in the parish burial registers until 1813. The children may be very lucky and live near a really ancient graveyard; if not, they can learn a good deal about people's lives in the last century. They will not discover much about the personalities of the people who lie there, because inscriptions are invariably written in pious and complimentary terms, but they will find out a lot about people's life-spans and even the mobility of the local population.

Occasionally, an inscription does record an interesting fact about a person; the children will enjoy making a note of these. There was the army officer, commemorated in a churchyard in Harrow, who died playing polo in Poona in the early years of the nineteenth century. Then there was the unfortunate lady killed by a 'tyger' when it visited her locality in a travelling circus, and escaped. Most people, however, meet their end in less dramatic fashion.

The children can investigate the life-span of the people of the past by noting the names and dates recorded on each headstone. To record them all they can work in groups, pooling their information before working out how long people lived. They will almost certainly find that people in previous centuries did not live as long as they do now; if they are considering the early years of the nineteenth century, the average life-span was only fifty years. More interesting detail can be added to this picture. Although many people died young, in any period there are a few hardy old souls who lived to a ripe age of seventy or eighty. We sometimes meet hardy creatures of today on our television screens, swearing to us that their long lives are due to their drinking pints of water, or smoking only home-cured tobacco, or going to church on Sunday. The children will not know this, but recent research suggests that longevity is due to being unexceptional. Those who are not too big, not too heavy, not very athletic, not particularly adventurous, are the ones who survive into their eighties and nineties. The secret of long life is being ordinary.

The children of past centuries were much more vulnerable to death than adults, and much more vulnerable than are the children of today. This can be seen by counting the number of deaths among those under five years of age and comparing them to those in other age-groups.

Seasonal mortality is interesting. Studies undertaken over the last few years indicate that more people died in the winter and spring months, from November to April, than in the summer. The proportion is roughly 60–40 per cent and this still remains the case today. The children can see whether this applies to the people of their own locality by looking at the headstones; and they might also be interested to know, although of course this will not appear for them to see for themselves, that more people die and more babies are born in the early hours of the morning than at other times.

Other aspects of social history can be explored in the local graveyard. The children might notice that certain surnames occur repeatedly over the years. These might provide the clue to the existence of families who have lived in the district for a very long time. Such families exist even now, especially in rural areas. More about them can be discovered by referring to general sources of local history. Alternatively, children may find that surnames do not repeat themselves over the generations. This indicates a degree of mobility in the population and means that people were continually coming and going; one would expect this pattern in urban areas. How long have their own families lived in the district?

An exercise that the children will enjoy is to analyse the Christian names recorded on the headstones. Fashions in names, as in everything else, are continually changing, but some names remain consistently popular. Nowadays, too, we have a much wider variety of first names. It has been estimated that, between 1650 and 1849, approximately half the male population were called John, William or Thomas. Only in the latter half of the nineteenth century did other names become popular. For girls during a similar period, Mary, Elizabeth and Ann were the most loved names, and have remained so ever since. Even today, the old names remain popular. The new Prince, first child of Prince Charles and Diana, Princess of

Wales, has been christened William. The children could follow up the information they glean from the headstones by making a comparison with their own first names.

Sometimes it can be difficult to read the inscriptions on headstones because of moss and stains. They can be deciphered more easily if a thin piece of paper is pressed over the writing and a rubbing taken, so that the indentations appear.

Incidentally, before we leave the subject of gravestones, if the children do make a study of their local churchyard, this represents a small but valuable piece of research. The local librarian might be glad of their findings for the library shelves.

Every pavingstone, every building, every blade of grass has a history. An environmental trail demonstrates this to children. A group of us took a short walk round part of Isleworth, in Middlesex, to see what we could find. The district, like most others, is a mixture of the very old and the new. We crossed a bridge over the River Crane (which has given its name to one of the surrounding districts, Cranford) and came to some old derelict docks. Great iron rings, which had once been used to moor the barges, were still embedded in the moss-covered walls; then we walked down a narrow lane of charming old houses. Two had intriguing names, 'Buttercup Cottage' and 'Richard Reynolds House'. An old lady standing in the garden of the cottage explained to us that, fifty years ago, there was a field where the cows grazed behind her home and that was how it got its name. Richard Reynolds, we found out later, had been vicar of Isleworth in the reign of Henry VIII and had gone to his death for refusing to accept Henry as Head of the Church. The present house had been built on the site of his home; it had fallen into disrepair and was occupied by squatters.

We came to the church and the graveyard. Part of the church dated back to medieval times, while some of it had been beautifully rebuilt just after the last war when a gang of boys had set fire to it. The graveyard was ancient and overgrown. We examined some of the gravestones of the nineteenth century and noted the kind of age distribution of the population that has just been discussed in this chapter. Many of the people of Isleworth had died pathetically young, while a few had fought through to their seventies and eighties. There was an ancient yew tree, probably hundreds of years old and possibly used as a supply of wood for the piercingly hard arrows used in the Middle Ages. One of the medieval kings had decreed that every churchyard in England should grow a yew tree for this very purpose.

Then we found a plaque that marked a gravepit dating from the year 1665, the year the dreaded Great Plague swept through London. There the victims of Isleworth had been buried, after dying a terrible death from the bubonic plague which was the scourge of the West from the Middle Ages onwards, and which did not retreat from London completely until the nineteenth century.

When we entered the church we found a rare medieval brass. Also, for five pence there was a fascinating history of Isleworth and its parish church, explaining where the parish records were kept and suggesting many avenues of research. Julius Caesar crossed the Thames at Isleworth in 54 BC, on his way to St Albans; William the Conqueror gave the parish to one of his knights, Walter de St Valeri; from the banks of the river near the church, Catherine Howard, one of the wives of Henry VIII, was taken by royal barge to the Tower of London. She met the dreaded end of a wife of Henry VIII; she was beheaded.

Finally, on our way home we passed 'The London Apprentice', a famous local public house overlooking the Thames and so named because the apprentices of the eighteenth century used to stop for a drink there before continuing their tramp up to London. We had not walked more than a quarter of a mile.

How can children make the best possible use of such a wealth of material? It is patently obvious that no time-sequence emerges of its own accord. One house was eighteenth century, while the story of Reynolds went back to the reign of Henry VIII; the church was partly fourteenth century and partly twentieth century, while the plague-pit took us back to the Stuart days; we came across all of them in that order. In these circumstances, the teacher has to set the guidelines for the children's work very firmly. It is possible to choose some things only for them to concentrate on, perhaps those of one period in history, like Richard Reynolds and Catherine Howard of Henry VIII's time. It may well be that the class is studying this period in school. Alternatively, the whole expedition can be treated as an exercise in finding out and research. Here again, the children should set out with clear objectives in mind and a list of what they are going to look for. They can be encouraged to ask questions about what they find and helped to find the answers. For this they will need a good children's reference library and a variety of background books.

It is a happy exercise for the teachers of a particular locality to come together and devise a history trail for all the children in their area. The teachers of Middlesbrough have done this and their trail is described in the Autumn 1979 (Number 6) edition of *Enjoying History*.

Very young children will not have acquired the sense of historical time that gives a history trail meaning. However, they too can enjoy an outing provided it is carefully designed to fit in with their own stage of development. A street I know well is not more than seventy yards long, so that for a group of five-year-olds this would not mean an exhausting journey. Some of the houses are old and some are new. The old houses have much smaller bricks than the modern flats and the children would enjoy measuring a brick from a sample of each, or else taking a rubbing. They would also be intrigued to make a rubbing of a Victorian coal-hole. There is a date inscribed on the frontage of the old houses, 1880. The flats have been named after a television personality of today, while the houses, as a group, are named after a member of one of the ancient families of the district, who

143

owned much of its land for many years. A group of five-year-olds would take at least an hour to complete such a trail. Back in the classroom, it would all have to be discussed; builders used much smaller bricks in the old days than they do now, so providing quite a reliable guide to the age of the house; what exactly does '1880' mean? Why do the old houses have coal-holes, but not the flats? The children would recognise the name of the television personality; they might be interested to hear about the old local family. In the case of this street, a very old lady, who lives in one of the houses, can remember the time when her's was the only house. Very little of the area had been built on and she can remember running over the fields to school. How do the children come to school today?

Some very helpful books have been written on local history, both for teachers and children.

More lively books have been produced recently to arouse the interest of children in their own localities. Macdonald Educational publish the 'Town and Around' series (1981) which explains to young children how to go about tracing the history of their own area. *History Around You* by D. Thornton (Oliver and Boyd, 1983) contains many stimulating ideas as to projects which can be carried out by junior school children. Then there is *History on Your Doorstep* by J. R. Ravendale published by the BBC to accompany their television programmes of the same title. One chapter deals with the history of a house; another is intriguingly titled 'Things Invisible to See'. Lastly, Paul Titley has written *Discovering Local History* (Ebenezer Baylis, 1971) specially for children, telling them the kind of questions to ask and how to find the answers.

Many of our great towns expanded in the nineteenth century, transforming what had once been open countryside. The Ordnance Survey is now reproducing copies of the original Victorian Ordnance Survey maps, on the scale of one inch to the mile. By studying them, and comparing them with maps of their locality today, children can trace the little streams, the woods and the farms that once were part of their neighbourhood not so long ago. The address from which these maps are available is given in the Appendix (page 236).

One source of local history is rarely taken advantage of by schools, but it is a good one. Students studying history in local colleges often carry out small pieces of research on a certain topic as part of their degree, producing a written and illustrated account of up to 20,000 words. One student of my own college made a study of crime in Middlesex in the first half of the nineteenth century, with special reference to the two Houses of Correction to which minor offenders were sent in order to mend their ways.[72]

Young children, even seven-year-olds, were terrible offenders in those days, with pickpocketing their speciality. Most hated of all by the Warders of the Houses of Correction, though, were the women inmates. The women of Middlesex in the nineteenth century were much given to what was described as 'riotous and disorderly conduct'; once in the Houses of Correction, they were fearless and difficult to control, always answering back, whatever the consequences. By collecting and analysing the relevant statistics, this student revealed the pattern of petty crime in Middlesex in the nineteenth century. All age-groups committed crimes, but the dangerous age was the same as today, between fifteen and twenty. Society has always grappled with the problem of the rumbustious teenager. The present-day children of Middlesex might like to hear what their ancestors got up to.

Another student researched Chiswick from 1875 to 1911.[73] She was lucky because, due to the careful records left by a conscientious medical officer, she was able to draw up a picture of the kinds of illnesses people suffered in those days. Young children were the most vulnerable and were carried off, often before they were five, by the same groups of diseases against which we struggle more effectively today, namely gastroenteritis and respiratory infections. Interestingly, illnesses came in much the same time sequences as they do today, every other year being 'a measles year' and influenza striking at regular intervals. This student uncovered a mystery. Chiswick in those days was a district of market gardens, where prosperous farmers grew vegetable produce for nearby London. She found pictures of luscious apples whose names sound strange to our ears and which are no longer grown. The site of one of these farms she was unable to trace, important though it was. Older children might well be intrigued enough to take part in the detective hunt, searching for the whereabouts of this farm and hunting for clues.

Both these studies would be of interest to the children of the area. They throw an unexpected light on the lives of a local community in the past, with a relevance and liveliness that is not usually found in any general textbook. It is worthwhile for teachers to contact the history departments of nearby colleges of further or higher education in order to find out whether there is any interesting work being done. It is a contact that should be made anyway.

In this chapter we have considered just two of the many ways in which environmental history can be approached by the teacher of young children. However, there is no limit to its subject matter and no one way of conceptualising the environment. Many children for example, would enjoy perceiving the environment in terms of the major events in their lives, like visiting the Fair, or taking a trip to the seaside.

Environmental history is concerned with the ways in which the children order the environment in terms of the past. This ordering is based on all that comprises their whole personality, their skills, their perceptions, their emotions and their cultural heritage. All are a part of children, all are a part of their strategies for living.

6

Science through the Environment

The young child playing in the sand-pit is a natural scientist. He sets out to fill his bucket with sand, he puts it down, empties it out and eventually builds a castle. In his own mind, he already has a good idea of the events that will result from his actions; in other words, he has formed a hypothesis, though not a spoken one. Perhaps, when he empties out his bucket, something goes wrong and the whole thing collapses. The sand may have been either too dry or too wet. In that case, the little boy will try all over again, working away until he has eliminated all the possibilities and the castle is built.

In this normal, everyday activity, he displays most of the characteristics of scientific thinking. He has a working hypothesis which he modifies as he works. He is capable of thinking logically and of analysing the variables in the situation, especially if there is a mishap. When all has gone well and the castle is finished, he has acquired a fund of information and an expertise which he may be able to apply later. The next day he might try to build a castle out of earth. This will not be quite the same as using sand because earth has different properties. Both experiences may enable this little boy to generalise, to form a theory about what happens when he uses the building materials of earth, sand and water. In this way he is able to imagine using his skills in circumstances other than those he has just dealt with and to push forward the frontiers of his own knowledge. Incidentally, he will be developing, all this time, another of the skills of the scientist, one in which science is historically rooted: that of controlling the environment.

Scientific thinking is part of everyday living. This is equally true for adults and children; those of us who humbly believe we are no good at science are often adept at working out why the car keeps stalling or the cake has sunk in the middle. Science is often considered a difficult subject for young children in school, one reason being that certain levels of it are highly specialised, abstract, and dependent on higher mathematics, which frightens most of us to death. Another, more significant, reason though is that the mainstream of research into children's thinking has started from the wrong end and has often used inappropriate methods. It has usually been concerned with assessing how children perform in abstract tasks of deduction; that is, it starts with an idea of what the children *will* have attained by the time they reach intellectual maturity and then works backwards in order to describe the various stages through which they go.

Inevitably, having conceptualised the problem in this way, the emphasis is all on how far the intellectual concepts of young children fall short of those of adults. According to this line of reasoning, the little boy's efforts in the sand-pit are dependent on abstract propositional reasoning. One wonders how he ever dared to fill his bucket with sand in the first place.

However, there is another stream of research, gathering strength particularly over the last ten years, which is by nature empirical, sharp-eyed and sensitive to the ways in which young children like to work. This concentrates on examining how children develop their abilities as scientists in their everyday lives. Its findings are important for teachers, because what emerges is the significance of the child's interaction with his environment. We will discuss some of that research here and consider the light it throws on the scientific thinking of young children.

The ability to form a hypothesis and work it through is essential. A hypothesis is a supposition made as a basis for reasoning, or any other form of action; the hypothesis of the little boy in the sand-pit was that if he filled his bucket with sand, patted it down and turned it out, it would emerge in the shape he wanted.

A recent study goes right to the heart of the matter, investigating how well children of various ages are able to form a hypothesis and then modify it, using their common sense.[74] Other skills contribute to the ability to use hypotheses; a child must, for example, be able to discern, manipulate and eliminate the variables inherent in a given situation and also to think in terms of cause and effect.

The children were studied in three age-groups, the mean ages being 7.2 years, 9.3 and 11.3 years respectively. They were presented with a variety of stories about (significantly) situations familiar to them, like baking a cake, making a clay pot or finding the cat. They were told the outcome of the stories and then asked to determine the element which caused the outcome. All the children were able to do this, thinking in terms of cause and effect and holding in their minds the general goal of proving a point. A group of adults was presented by the author of this research, Judith Tschirgi, with the same tasks; interestingly, the general pattern of responses was the same for the children of all three age-groups and the adults. They all employed broadly the same strategy of manipulating the factors in a situation by eliminating them or repeating them strategically, although a developmental trend was discernible in the way in which the situation was handled. We can note also that these children did not have to handle the material themselves in order to reason about it; unlike the little boy in the sand-pit, they dealt with the facts as presented to them in the medium of a story. Their thinking was not dependent upon the availability of concrete evidence.

An understanding of object transformations is critical to scientific thinking. It is at the heart of scientific experiment, for science is basically about changes in state that occur in the physical world. If we heat a metal bar and it expands, we must be able to understand why; further, we have to be able to put this event in a rational context. We will not get very far if we believe that we can transform the iron bar by our thoughts, or that it only exists when we are in the room with it. In order to understand object transformation we have to be able to perceive the appropriate sequences; say, for example, a boy has thrown a stone and shattered a window. This kind of perception underlies the ability to think in terms of causation.

A group of research psychologists set out to discover how far young children are able to understand object transformation. The incidents used were the kind that could occur in everyday life, such as a stone shattering a window. A less usual event would be a hammer breaking the handle off a cup.[75] The children studied were very young, between three and four years of age. They were presented with three item stories, for example the one illustrated below, and asked to reason about the sequence of events.

An object transformation

The children were well able to analyse the situations. They could see the relationship between a transformation and the two states of an object; they could predict a transformation, infer what instrument had been used and retrieve the initial state of the transformed object. Further, amusingly, these three-year-olds were able to reason about unusual sequences with which they could not have been familiar, like sewing a cut banana back together again. The authors state their important conclusions clearly. Young children possess 'a great ability to code event sequences', and this reasoning ability is 'not tied to immediate experience'. If such abilities are not innate, and there is no obvious way of telling whether this is so, they must be acquired very rapidly.

Underlying all kinds of investigation and thinking is the ability to categorise objects and phenomena; underpinning this ability is the kind of conceptualisation we make of the world around us. We know, for instance, that copper and iron are both metals because they possess characteristics in common, characteristics that are more significant to us than their contrasting colouring. There are all kinds of ways of conceptualising phenomena; concepts may differ in their complexity, their degree of concreteness and in the extent to which they are definable. These variations greatly affect the ease with which they are grasped and the strategies adopted in order to understand them. It has recently been hypothesised that taxonomies of concrete objects include two levels, a basic concrete level and a superordinate level. An object on the concrete level would be a chair; on the superordinate we would think of furniture. It takes very little reflection to see that this is exactly the kind of categorisation used in science, and indeed in many other disciplines. Categorisation is a way forward to more detailed and extensive knowledge. Take animals, which are great favourites with children. A child may love the family cat, but she (he) will know more about him when she realises that he is a member of the great cat family, which includes lions, leopards and tigers, and that the cat family belongs to a wider group of mammals, and that she herself is a mammal, having quite a lot in common with her cat.

At what age do children develop this ability to categorise? In what order do they acquire concepts, and is it possible to ease the way for them by good teaching? Psychologists have turned their attention to these questions in recent years. One interesting study involved groups of children ranging from four to 7.4 years, in which their ability to place objects and animals in groups was investigated.[76]

The children in all the age-groups were able to perceive basic level categories, whether or not the criteria for classification were explained to them. When it came to the superordinate categories however, the older children, of 6.8 to 7.4 years, were greatly helped by a discussion of these criteria, whereas the younger children of four to 5.2 years, were not. The authors of this research, M. Horton and E. Markham, conclude that this was not because the younger children could not understand the meaning of words; we know that they can. We also know that they are able to sort objects correctly. In order to use linguistic information fully, a child has to hold a memorised list of criteria in his head and match each piece of newly presented information against it. This is what the four- and five-year-olds were unable to do. In other words, they lacked a kind of computing ability. This is not to say that they cannot acquire superordinate concepts, merely that they can be helped to do so in other ways. As the authors point out, there are other non-linguistic ways of drawing the attention of young children to the existence of these categories and the criteria that delineate them. In the case of tools, for example, they can be allowed to experiment in the use to which they are put. They should always be allowed to handle objects as much as possible. We should never fall into the trap of not explaining criteria to young children, on the grounds that they cannot fully understand what we are saying. In talking to them about what they are doing, frequently and cheerfully, we are presenting them with the possibility of another strategy, one towards which they are struggling.

Of the great amount of work being carried out at the moment into the scientific thinking of children, only a little has been quoted here. It suggests that young children are well able to evaluate their environment in scientific terms, for they can form hypotheses, carry out experiments, understand the nature of transformations and think in terms of categories. Research mentioned in earlier chapters draws attention to other abilities children need. They must come to understand the different influences exerted by social and physical laws in the transformation of the environment;[36] they have to perceive the way in which events occur in space and time,[19] and they must see the world as real in the same sense as we do.[1]

We have, at this point, to be honest. If young children can think so well, what is the difference between them and adults? There seem to be two lines of thought at the moment; one takes us back into the world of childhood, where trees can bite, rabbits talk to each other and vengeance can be wreaked on a thinker of evil thoughts; the other, more recent line of research, reveals that even young children possess surprisingly mature intellectual abilities and are, in fact, like adults. Which is true and can the two be knitted together and seen as a whole?

Let us consider first an imaginative inquiry which pin-points some of the issues involved. The research was aimed at ascertaining how well young children are able to arrive at a true comprehension of the causes of illness and accidents, common enough occurrences in everyday life.[77] The authors of the research, M. Kister and C. Patterson, were concerned with four groups of children with mean ages of 4.8, 5.6, 7.4 and 9.6 years, interviewing and questioning them all. The younger the children, the more likely they were to over-extend the concept of contagion to inappropriate ailments; that is, they were inclined to think that everything was catching. One child thought that distance was a factor in the transmission of toothache, the nearer you were to a sufferer, the more likely you were to get it. The four- and five-year-olds were also more prone to invoke justice explanations of events, believing that accident or illness might strike if they were disobedient to their mothers. The use of such immanent justice explanations was inversely related to the understanding of the rational causes of illness, so that the older children were far less likely to link illness and accident to their own feelings of fear and guilt.

Most of us will recognise the voice of childhood in these findings. We know it well. We can see also the slow struggle towards rationality, which is also a reminder of the inestimable benefit that the good teaching of science can bring to the very young, leading them from the nightmare of superstition and out into the sunlight.

Young children are inclined to think egocentrically, that is, they do not find it easy to see a point of view other than their own. This has been seen when considering the evolution of their ability to grasp the concept of historical time, a six-year-old finding it difficult to accept that dinosaurs were in existence before he was. Young children also think animistically, believing that the wind, trees and stones are alive in the same sense that they and their relatives are. They frequently invoke magic in seeking to find explanations for events and phenomena; in other words, they believe in the existence of forces that have no basis in reason. All these tendencies hang together, being well-known, copiously documented and frequently seen as constituting the great dividing-line between the thinking of children and that of adults.

The explanation of these differences could be simpler than supposed, however, and need not necessarily denote such sharp contrast. These attributes could be due, in large measure, to sheer lack of experience. When a child is born, he knows very little about the world and the laws which govern it. Why should he be expected to know that toothache is not catching when he has no experience to prove it? In his ignorance of the nature of the phenomena he sees around him, it is natural, even intelligent, to assume that everything must be like himself, for this is all he has to go by. If there is a storm and it thunders, the sky may well be angry; a tree ought to have teeth, because how else will it eat? It could be argued that animistic and magical things are healthy signs in a young child, signs of a vigorous exploring and enterprising intellect. Let us remember also, that adults in times of stress, danger and ignorance, readily revert to magic and superstition.

The research of Horton and Markham points to the existence of a difference between children and adults of quite another kind. The four-year-olds, in attempting to grasp the nature of superordinate categories, could not be helped much by verbal discussion because their memories and mental sorting processes were not mature enough for them to evaluate the information offered. The development of such abilities must be due, in part at least, to the maturation of the central nervous system. This is clearly a difference between children and adults and one which must patently affect the kind of thinking of which they are capable.

The part played by language in thinking is so vital that it can hardly be overestimated. Here too, the young child is lacking in resources. Language defines and extends experience; it tests reality accurately and economically, without, that is, the individual going through the costly and time-wasting exercise of becoming involved in physical activity. Language facilitates memorisation and is thus an essential factor in sorting and ordering information. Young children have yet to develop a mature language system, so that they have to a large extent to think by means of concrete, physical experience. Abstract thinking and generalities are not possible for them.

Young children differ from adults along another continuum, in that their thinking has been much less exposed to the social and cultural milieu. They are, in a sense, truly idiosyncratic. The cultural influences of the society in which a young child is reared pervade every aspect of his activity. They shape his perception in a quite literal, physical way; they indicate permissible explanations of phenomena and occurrences in his environment. We have seen how the students of New Guinea possessed widely differing mathematical concepts from those of our culture;[51] the young children's interpretations of the causes of illness which were described a little way back[77] would be quite permissible in more primitive societies.

Simple lack of experience, poverty of language, inadequate memory and a lesser degree of exposure to culture of their society go a long way in illuminating the way in which children think, but they are not enough to explain it fully. One elusive quality is missing, and this may best be described as relating to a differentiation in consciousness. It is now many years since Freud began his pioneer work on the development of the human psyche and his findings have in many ways been modified, but the truths he uncovered remain valid. He conceived of the human mind as a whole, with powerful emotions conditioning what might appear to be purely intellectual processes; the struggle towards maturity is slow, a crucial process being the development of an adult consciousness, free from the distorting pressures of unconscious fears and uncontrollable desires. In this differentiation of consciousness, the formative influence of speech, both inner and outer, is paramount, simultaneously bringing the individual into contact with the outside world, and enabling him to control his inner thoughts. Experience of the outside world is also important, acting as a stimulus to thought and providing a parameter by which reality could be tested.

Young children do not possess this adult consciousness. Theirs has a significance, and sometimes a great charm, of its own. A child might well believe that he has fallen off the kitchen chair because he has been cheeky to his mother, since this is what his inner fears are telling him, and he cannot yet control them. He might believe in magic, because his deep desires would have him believe that anything is possible.

The ways in which children's thinking differs from our own may be considered separately for the purposes of discussion, but in their effects they intermingle and can hardly be distinguished from each other. The maturation of the nervous system underlies the development of speech, perception and the capacity of memory. Interaction with the social and cultural milieu ensures that what is perceived, remembered and thought about, has the flavour of that particular society. The conscious mind is slowly transformed by all these relationships and, in its turn, exerts a powerful influence on them. All this combines to typify the thinking of children and its development towards maturity.

It also suggests a new and coherent model of environmental learning, in which what is crucial is the interaction between the young child and the environment. Both he and the world he perceives are ever-changing, exerting a continual modifying influence on the other. Learning takes place when what is known about phenomena in the environment is used to create a new concept. The three- and four-year-olds, observed by Gelman and his colleagues,[75] were able to reason about sequences they could not possibly have observed in everyday life, like the pieces of a cut banana being sewn back together.

However, although the children had not observed such a process, they would know what a needle and thread were for, they would also have learnt to perceive a banana as a whole. Putting these pieces of experience together, it would not be beyond them to reason about the banana's fate and to see how it could be made whole again. Knowledge is truly built up from experience, and experience is won from the environment.

The two streams of research about early childhood are not incompatible; they have to be seen in terms of each other. Young children are well capable of sophisticated thinking when circumstances call for it; at the same time, as we would expect, their responses bear the hallmark of inexperience and immature personality. What might prove illuminating would be more detailed enquiry into the kinds of situation that stimulate the various kinds of thinking. One suspects that young children think most sophisticatedly when the situation presented to them is familiar, unthreatening, but interesting.

Scientific thinking aims at ordering the environment in various ways. It is concerned only with physical phenomena and aims to describe them and to assess their reactions in objective and, if possible, quantitative terms. When light passes through a prism and is split into the colours of the rainbow, the physicist is not concerned with whether the red band is prettier than the blue. Physical phenomena can be described in all their aspects; they can be categorised; their changes in state, or transformations, can be noted, or their causation examined. The infinite variety in our environment is tested and described by means of hypotheses, the truth of these hypotheses being tried out by means of experiment. The scientific method is at the heart of science, being applied by both the humble searcher in everyday life, like the little boy in the sand-pit, and the deviser of advanced experiments in the laboratory. Most of us would describe it as clear, logical reasoning. The scientific method is not confined to the subject we think of as science; it is used in all the disciplines whenever an objective, indisputable result is needed. We might hypothesise that the metal iron expands on being heated. To test this out, we might first pass an unheated iron ball through a ring. When we heat up the ball, we might find that it will not now pass through the ring because it is bigger, so that our hypothesis that iron expands when it is heated is confirmed. Alternatively we might just find that the heat made no difference, in which case we will amend the hypothesis in order to take account of a new fact. Then we devise a new experiment to test that.

Scientists, by means of deduction and hypothesis, can surmise about certain phenomena long before they have the concrete evidence. The composition of some stars in the universe was understood in this way. Today, the existence of the neutrino, which is too minute to be discerned by any microscope, has been postulated, because its impact has been traced.

The scientific method is demanding. It requires honesty of thought, keen observation and unceasing adaptability. Frequently it takes great courage to accept conclusions that may be unpalatable or even distressing to the people of the time, upsetting cosily-held beliefs. The lives of some of our great scientific thinkers testify to this. Galileo was imprisoned by the Inquisition for saying that the earth moved. Scientific thinking is thus a precious and hard-won part of our culture.

Science has many ways of investigating phenomena in the environment; often it presents its conclusions about them by describing them in terms of models. Thinking in terms of models is common to all areas of knowledge; in history they concern human behaviour and the causation of events; in language they mirror modes of action. Models are a clear, graphic means of explanation. Those employed in science are usually strongly visual, for example, sound is postulated as travelling in waves, and light in straight lines. A molecule is conceptualised as a number of atoms connected to each other, the atoms being regarded as tiny spheres. These models do not themselves represent ultimate truths, but they do enable us to ask the right questions, that is, questions that will give us workable answers. As we push forward to further knowledge, models become obsolete and new ones are found. A hundred years ago, we would not have been accustomed to the illuminating lectures we see now on television, in which popular academics brilliantly expound on the structure of matter using wires and brightly coloured plastic. We did not have the television, the plastic, the modes of description, or the popular academics, for that matter.

Some of the models used by scientists are much looser in nature than those mentioned above, reflecting the values and culture of society. These do not affect the actual structure of concepts, but they do put them into a new context, one that is usually an expression of what a particular society values. Today, botanists and biologists have become increasingly interested in the study of eco-systems, or the interdependence of all forms of life. The life cycles of living creatures are not studies in isolation, but are seen as interacting in their needs and behaviour with all other creatures. A pond is an excellent example, with plants and animals, high and low, sustaining each other. This view of life emphasises a reverence for nature that is typical of Western society in the late twentieth century, a reverence felt more keenly because we feel we may be on the point of destroying an irreplaceable unity, because we are afraid of pollution and, perhaps, because our high and secure standard of living enables us to adopt a more compassionate attitude to other forms of life. The ideas here are not scientific in themselves, but they have shaped the thinking of scientists. Such a view has also greatly influenced teaching in the schools. The humble lichen is no longer seen as a kind of green scum, but as the brave fore-runner of higher life, which could not exist without it. The earthworm has become a hero, as indeed Charles Darwin portrayed him many years ago, transforming the environment for his so-called superiors by dint of long and arduous effort.

Some branches of science, in particular physics, demonstrate human thinking at its most abstract. Here we are taken far beyond what our own senses tell us about the environment. We learn that our eyes, ears, and sense of touch can deceive us about the world in which we spend our lives – at the very least, we exist in one layer of reality only. This travelling beyond the limitations of human perception is an important aspect of science, scientists being continually preoccupied with the invention of new instruments, new methods of calculation. The snowflake is a good example; contrast a snowflake seen with the naked eye with the intricate structure of a snow crystal when it is magnified hundreds of times.

On the other hand, science is arguably the most practical of all disciplines, the one most concerned with what is visible and tangible, the one whose discoveries play most part in the business of everyday living. This side of science is aimed at the control and manipulation of the environment; to put it simply, it aims at helping us to survive. Medicine and mechanical inventions are a part of scientific activity, so are experiments in crop rotation, salmon-breeding and pesticides. This practical aspect of science has great appeal for young children.

Young children are natural scientists; as we have seen, they can work out hypotheses. They are born explorers and think of marvellously creative ideas. They will mix shampoo with the bath water and sugar with salt in order to see what happens. They can classify, order and reason; they have a great love of other living creatures, being eager to know more about them. They are quick to find ways of controlling the environment, being natural builders of Wendy houses and trainers of the family dog. The environmental study is an excellent way of introducing young children to science, because there the evidence is directly in front of them and does not have to be memorised or abstracted; the situations to be investigated are not artefacts but can be thought about naturally. There, too, the sequences and changes which are at the heart of science are in evidence. Science has a great deal to give young children in other ways as well, leading them through the egocentricity and fear of early childhood towards rational thinking. In a word, it is educational.

Yet science is not a popular subject in schools. In nursery, infant and junior schools it is often not taught at all, or is confined to nature study. Even when it is taught there is grave concern over standards. There are several reasons for this state of affairs. One is that society places such a high value on scientific training that, ironically, all those truly interested in science are drawn from the schools to lusher pastures elsewhere. Another reason is that the teaching of science tends to be male-orientated. As the majority of our teachers of young children, that is, those in nursery, infant and junior schools, tend to be women, and, further, with non-specialist training, they feel ill at ease in teaching science. The subject is associated with the setting-up in under-equipped classrooms of dreary and sometimes dangerous experiments which frequently go wrong. The pity of it is that there are whole areas of traditionally women's interests which offer many exciting possibilities in terms of scientific investigation. Cookery is one. All kinds of experiments can be carried out using simple, everyday materials, where the point made is clear and easily understood.

A third reason why science tends to be unpopular is that it is taught to children at the wrong time in their lives. Usually it is introduced seriously to them in the secondary school which, in my experience, is just when they are entering adolescence and losing interest. Certainly adolescents become self-conscious about their own bodies and for that reason will shy away from biology. At a school where I once taught, a class of fourteen-year-olds were each asked to bring a sample of urine to the biology lesson so that it could be analysed. Only one did so, the rest brought lemonade. There were gales of laughter in the staffroom and the science teacher was furious. Contrast the attitude of a four-year-old I encountered recently who had swallowed a loose tooth by mistake and was publicly enquiring, to the chagrin of her crimson-faced parents, just how it was going to work through her body. There is a moral here. It is young children who take enthusiastically to science, for they are inquisitive, adventurous and free from embarrassment.

This chapter will concentrate on ways in which these qualities can be put to good use; meanwhile, there are some excellent books for teachers of young children. Romola Showell has written *Teaching Science to Infants* (Ward Lock Educational, 1979) which gives many ideas and a list of reference books.

An Introduction and Guide to Teaching Primary Science by Diamond (Nuffield/Macdonald Educational, 1978) assumes that the teacher has no scientific background and describes many small, practical experiments that the children can perform by themselves. Also useful is *Using the Environment Part 2, Investigations 1 and 2* by Margaret Collis ('Science 5–13' series, Macdonald Educational). Alan Ward has written a lively book for teachers of primary science, *A Source Book for Primary Science Education* (Hodder and Stoughton, 1983).

Full of suggestions for teachers is the Schools Council Project of the 1970s, *Learning through Science*, in particular the 5–13 project. The *Learning through Science* team have a Resources Centre in London, where examples of science materials for young children are on display. Many of the materials can be produced by the teacher and children themselves. Visitors, including school children, are welcome (the address is given in the Appendix). The 1982 edition of 'Learning through Science' is published by Macdonald Educational in two parts, *Moving Around* and *On the Move*. An excellent science teaching series has been produced for young children. There is one programme for four- to eight-year-olds entitled *First Look!* by C. Gilbert (Addison-Wesley, 1982), and another programme for the seven- to nine-year-olds, entitled *Look! Primary Science*, by C. Gilbert and P. Matthews (Addison-Wesley, 1981). Teachers need no specialised scientific knowledge to use the materials, comprising background guides and unit cards, effectively.

The subject matter for environmental science is all around us in great abundance. Teaching it implies looking at what young children know well and care about, like their family pets, the flowers in the garden and the trees in the park. It means looking at the world with their eyes and entering into activities that are interesting to them, like wading through puddles, peering under stones and building a go-kart. The best materials are those with which they are well acquainted already, the plastic bottles and marbles that they readily pick up and play with. Science can also be seen in the exciting occasions of children's lives, in the day spent at the seaside or a visit to the Fair. The skill of the teacher lies in choosing activities that best reveal those concepts central to science.

Science is less a body of subject matter than a way of investigation, scientific method being central to it. Even young children can understand it because they think along these lines for much of the time anyway. Suppose a class of six-year-olds have in their classroom three guinea-pigs, we will call them Pop-corn, Big-Boy and Florence, and they are investigating what the guinea-pigs like to eat. Their teacher might ask the class for suggestions.

'I think they eat anything,' someone might say.
'Not anything,' another six-year-old might correct, 'carrots and dandelions, things like that.'
'Let's try them with sausages and chips,' a third might add. 'They're my favourites.'

The above contributions constitute hypotheses. An experiment now has to be devised in order to test them. Various methods of observation can be employed, and the merits of each should be carefully discussed. The children might decide to offer each guinea-pig several foods at once, like carrots, dandelions and sausage, and observe which it goes to first, or which it eats most of. Alternatively, they might decide to offer chips for one meal and see what happens, and dandelions the next. They will also be faced with the accurate recording of their discoveries. If Pop-corn eats a great deal of carrots, what does 'a lot' mean? Would it be best to weigh the carrots before and after he's eaten some?

With very young children the enquiry needs to be kept simple. Older children can explore further. They can enquire into the factors that affect the eating habits of the guinea-pig. Florence may be smaller than the other two and eat less of everything; Big-Boy may have been off-colour recently. Individual preferences are always in evidence and are often surprising. I once had a guinea-pig who was very fond of curry. The children could continue by investigating related aspects of eating. *How* do the guinea-pigs eat? What kind of teeth have they and how do they compare with the children's? Do they use their paws at all?

After a series of observations and experiments, the children may arrive at a written conclusion, which can be illustrated to their liking. The conclusion might read, 'Guinea-pigs like to eat lettuce, carrots, dandelions, sow-thistle and cabbage leaves. They do not like chips and sausages. They are vegetarians.' The children will have exercised several scientific skills. They will, for example, have refined their ability to classify, recognising that guinea-pigs, as vegetarians, belong to one group of animals, while cats, as carnivores, belong to another. They will have formed an idea as to cause and effect, they will have begun to form a theory.

To illustrate how science can reveal itself to children through natural and well-loved activities in everyday surroundings, we will examine two possible projects. The first is *Project Puddle*. Puddles are in plentiful supply in Britain and are near to the hearts of children. On a spring day after the rain, nursery and infant school children can put on their wellingtons and select puddles in the play-ground for careful study. What the children see illustrates concepts basic to physics. They can notice the following:

(1) *Reflections.* What can they see? They will see themselves reflected in the water, as well as the sky and the clouds. Their attention should be drawn to the fact that they see their left hand as their right. What happens to the reflections when the children ruffle up the water with a stick? They will enjoy doing this. The reflections shatter and dissolve, only to appear again.

(2) *How light behaves.* If the children hold a stick in the still waters of the puddle, they will see that it appears bent, as in the illustration below. This

How light behaves

A stick appears to bend when placed in a puddle

A leg appears to bend when seen in the bath

is called refraction and they will notice a similar thing happening to their legs when they are sitting in the bath. The explanation is that when light-rays travel from one kind of matter to another, their direction may change. Light from the top of the stick passes through air, while light from the bottom of the stick passes through water and so travels at a different angle. The children can examine for themselves that their sticks are not really bent by pulling them out of the puddle and examining them.

Why can the children see themselves in the water? Light is travelling from the sun, through the water to the dark mud at the bottom, then bouncing back to form an image. A mirror works in the same way.

An explanation of how light travels is not easy for young children to grasp, because light cannot be seen. However, the explanation should be given. The analogy of a bouncing ball can help. If the children bounce a ball up and down in the playground, they will see that it bounces at various angles; so does light.

Light, or white light, as it is called, splits up to form the colours of the rainbow. If a little oil is spread on their puddle, the children will see the colours dancing on the surface and can note them (red, orange, yellow, green, blue, indigo and violet).

(3) *How water behaves*. When a stone is dropped into a puddle, circular ripples move outwards. What happens when the children blow on the water? Can they make waves? Some objects float, while others sink. The children can conduct their own experiments by trying out objects. There will probably be a dead leaf or two and a twig floating on top of the water. A ball will float too. If they are lucky, the children might find little insects, such as water-boatmen, skimming along the surface of the water. How do they manage it? The children can't walk over water. Water has a skin or, in scientific terms, it possesses surface tension. If the children fill a spoon with water and look at it closely from a side angle, they will see that the surface is actually slightly curved. The water in the spoon is held there partly by the tension on the surface. This surface tension is strong enough for a water-boatman to skim happily across it, but not strong enough to support a foot in a wellington boot.

Project Puddle and its findings can be recorded, either in the form of a colourful chart made by the whole class or with each boy or girl making one of their own. The youngest children will not yet be able to remember words like 'reflection' and 'refraction' easily, but they will be interested to hear them. In this way, they slowly become familiar with the terminology and concepts that are essential for structured thinking later.

Project Puddle can be expanded in all sorts of ways. It can be linked to bath-time, and this has the advantage that parents can be drawn in too. Some things float in the bath, while others sink: why? If the children get into the bath carefully, and slowly sit down, they will feel a pleasant lifting sensation as the water buoys them up. When they get out they will feel a sensation of suddenly increased weight. They will have noticed how their sticks appear to bend when poked into a puddle; the same is true of their own bodies in the bath.

Raindrops make an interesting and related study. Children of any age are intrigued by them. If they watch raindrops sliding down the window-pane, they can notice exactly how they move. Each has a shape, rather like a pear, and it isn't flat, but curved, held in shape by its surrounding 'skin'. This skin is the result of the same surface tension that enabled the water-boatman to skim about on the puddle. When a raindrop lands on the window, it starts to slide, slowly at first, then faster and faster, zig-zagging across the glass. It eventually collides with another and they will join together and slide even faster, until finally many of them end up in a small pool of water on the window-sill. The brief life of the raindrop is over.

The observations of the children will illustrate surface tension, friction or 'slideability', and the force of gravity which pulls the heavier raindrops down faster.

Raindrops are the end result of a whole chain of natural events, culminating in rain falling. A simple demonstration can illustrate this chain. If a teacher boils a kettle of water and holds a flat cool surface over the steam, as illustrated below, the steam will condense into droplets and fall down. Rain is formed in a similar fashion; when water evaporates from the rivers and seas, it is condensed as rain when it meets the cooler, upper air levels. This is one experiment that the children should not be allowed to try out themselves, because steam can scald very badly.

How rain is formed

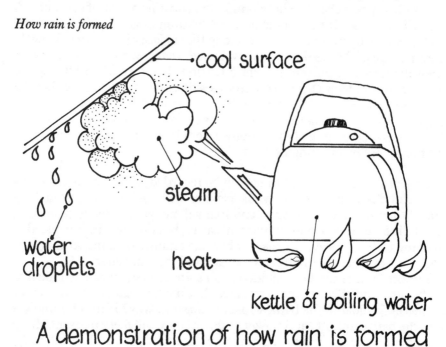

cool surface

steam

water droplets

heat

kettle of boiling water

A demonstration of how rain is formed

Water also demonstrates very well an important scientific concept, that of physical change. It may be winter, and when the snow is on the ground, the children can put a foot on an icy puddle and listen to the sharp crack as the ice breaks. Snow, hail and ice are forms of water. Even very young children can carry out a simple experiment to prove that water, when it turns into ice, expands. They each fill a plastic bottle with water and measure its circumference. A wide bottle is best because the change is easier to discern. All the bottles can be placed in a freezer and measured again when the water has frozen. Their circumferences will be greater. The youngest children may not be able to manage to read a tape-measure, in which case they can use a piece of string and compare the two lengths. When the ice is allowed to melt and turn into water again, the bottles will return to their original measurements.

Water expands when frozen

This characteristic of water, that it expands when frozen, has application in the home. In winter, the water in pipes may freeze and the expansion may crack them. The damage is not noticed then; we have to wait until the ice melts and water seeps through the ceiling. Project puddle has expanded into an investigation of the properties of water. It can also include another favourite pastime of children, blowing bubbles.

This is another interesting scientific project, for bubbles illustrate the working of many of the principles of physics that mould our environment. It is a project, also, that can be studied at greater or lesser depth according to the age and aptitude of the children. No doubt most of us remember from our own childhood how to blow bubbles, but, in case memory has faded, a good bubble-blowing solution can be made from diluted washing-up liquid. Bubble-blowers can be pipes, bottle caps with holes drilled through, straws, or frames of wire and plastic. Children enjoy making their own frames, dipping them into the mixture and seeing what bubble-shapes they can get.

The children should watch closely what happens when they blow a bubble. Each one has a shape, but this changes all the time. As the bubble dangles from the pipe it is egg-shaped; when it is released into the air it becomes spherical. If they look carefully, they can see that it is vibrating, shimmering in the light. The bubble floats away (why?), but it sinks lower and lower. If it lands on a soft surface it may bounce; if it lands on a hard surface, it will break, and that is the end of the bubble. Bubbles are full of colour, and as the light strikes them, the children will see all the colours of the rainbow.

A wonderfully clear and interesting explanation of all this is given by Alan Ward in his article 'Physics concepts from a bubble', in the journal *Natural Science in Schools*, Autumn, 1980.[78] He accounts for the shape of the bubble in the following way (older children will be able to think it out): 'A bubble made with water and liquid detergent is held in shape by the surface tension forces of the detergent molecules lining the inner and outer surfaces of the bubble's envelope.'

This envelope is constructed like a sandwich, with water in the middle. When the bubble dangles from the pipe, the force of its weight, a result of the pull of gravity on its liquid mass, stretches the envelope into an egg-shape. When released, the bubble contracts a little, causing it to vibrate. Air resistance causes it slowly to drop; it may burst when it hits a hard surface, or it may burst in the air. This latter is caused by drainage and evaporation making the bubble-envelope thinner and thinner, until it can no longer hold together.

The rainbow colours seen in bubbles are not caused by the prism mechanism, but by light-wave interference, caused by mixed lengths of light being reflected by both inner and outer surfaces. If the children look closely at the bubbles' surfaces, they will see many images reflected there, some upside down, some up the right way.

The youngest children will learn a great deal simply by being encouraged to observe their bubbles closely and accurately. Older children can work outwards from their observations, to consider aspects of physics such as light, colour and air resistance.

Bubbles appear to be as fascinating to adults as they are to children, so that there is a wealth of scientific material in them. Dr Isenberg opens up new vistas for science teaching in his article, 'Problem Solving with Soap Films', in the *School Science Review*.[79] Audio-Visual Productions have produced a set of 24 slides, or alternatively a film-strip, which demonstrate the geometrical and optical properties of structures made from soap solution. The set is called *Soap Films and Bubbles*, and could start older children on several lines of fruitful inquiry. The address of Audio-Visual Productions is given in the Appendix, page 236.

The natural and well-loved activities of young children, such as playing in puddles, watching raindrops and blowing bubbles, reveal to them a great deal of science, in particular in the examples we have chosen, about the nature of water, light, colour and gravity. A visit to the seaside, an exciting event in most children's lives, provides another perspective.

The sea has immense energy, as we all know from watching the waves crashing on to the sea-shore. This makes life far from easy for the limpet living on a sea-wall, which may have to withstand blows to the equivalent of over 50 tonnes per square metre in a storm. The rest of us, especially children for whom the sea holds a great fascination, can learn a lot about the energy of the waves and the effect its exertion has on the environment.

If they watch the waves as they come rolling in over the sea, rising up as they near the beach and finally crashing down on the shore, questions will arise in the children's minds. What makes the waves? Why do they break on the shore? Are some waves bigger than others, and is it really true, as is frequently asserted, that every fifth, tenth or twentieth wave is a monster? Some of the answers the children can find out for themselves. They can count the waves as the tide comes in and note their size for themselves. They can compare the height of the waves as the tide comes in with their height when the tide goes out.

The answers to other questions the children might ask have to be explained to them. Leslie Morris has written a fascinating account in his articles 'Waves on the shore', in the journal *Natural Science in Schools* Summer, 1980.[80]

Water, in all its manifestations, is a source of never-ending wonder to children. Other childhood interests are equally rewarding. There is, for example, cookery, an activity which not only comes naturally to most teachers in nursery and infant schools, who happen to be women, but which illustrates important scientific principles like physical and chemical change and the action of heat.

Most teachers will have plenty of ideas for simple, attractive recipes, and the children may well want to try out their own. Cookery books specially for children have been produced; two in the 'Ladybird' series are particularly useful, *Cooking with Mother* (1977) and *Easy Meals* (1979) by Lynn Peebles, and an excellent article by Dorothy Diamond, 'Edible Science', appeared in *Junior Education* December, 1979.[81] There are all kinds of ideas for introducing children to science through cookery, using some tempting recipes.

Science is continually used in the home. Mothers and fathers usually find quick ways of getting through household tasks and they are nearly always based on science. The children can find the answers to a questionnaire, or draw up one of their own. Their parents can add to it. Below are some questions to begin with, based on the principles of chemistry, physics and mechanics.

A Science Questionnaire on the Home

(1) Why do we stir hot liquids with a wooden, rather than a metal spoon?
(Wood is a poor conductor of heat whereas metal is a good one, so there is less likelihood of burning our fingers.)
(2) Why does a cold knife cut new bread better?
(Metal contracts when it loses heat, so the blade of the knife is sharper. Also, the new bread does not stick to it.)
(3) Why, when we can't unscrew a metal lid on a jar of jam, can we usually manage it if we immerse the lid in hot water for a few minutes?
(Metal expands when heated, so the lid becomes an easier fit.)
(4) Why is it better to use brass screws for outdoor woodwork?
(Brass does not rust. Rusting is the process by which some metals, like iron, are oxidised through contact with the air.)
(5) Why is it a good tip to rub a screw with soap before putting it in?
(The soap insulates the screw from the air and so helps to prevent rusting. Soap is also greasy, so that it will be easier to remove the screw when necessary. This has to do with friction and the fact that certain substances offer less resistance than others.)
(6) Why do chairs have four legs?
(7) Why is the water tank kept in the loft?
(8) Why do we have glass windows?
(9) Is silicone polish better than the old wax type?

Even the properties of electricity, a source of power basic to most homes, are not difficult to explain to young children. Some of the books recommended in this chapter give clear, safe illustrations by means of simple experiments. Tony Evans, in his article 'Switch on to Science',[82] explains how to demonstrate electrical flow, insulation and electromagnetism in the classroom, using everyday materials like wire and an iron bolt.

We should consider, before we go further, exactly what an experiment should mean to a young child. We still know little about how children come to recognise and apply the models and analogies used in scientific explanation, nor has there been any sustained inquiry into how they develop an understanding of commonly used scientific concepts like those of temperature, energy and force.[83] Nevertheless, an experiment should elucidate, whether this elucidation involves a reaction, a process, a general law, or all these things at once. It will aim at revealing more about what is being investigated, and in terms which children can understand, whether this is puddles, cooking salt or the classroom guinea-pig.

We come now to our second main project, taken from quite a different field of science, that of nature study. Projects in natural history are the most popular in our schools, and for excellent reasons. They introduce children to a new and vibrant conceptualisation of the environment. Other branches of science, such as physics and chemistry, are concerned with material and physical interactions, but the study of plants and animals leads young children towards a consideration of the highest forms of interaction within the environment, those of the learning and survival techniques of living creatures. The glider that the five-year-old makes in the classroom demonstrates the principles of flight, but the seagull uses them for his own purposes.

Biology and botany are ordered by the concepts used in many of the other disciplines and encompass them. The lives of plants and animals illustrate the principles of chemistry and physics. The fish uses oxygen from the water in which it swims, whereas human beings utilise it from the air, it being carried round to the body cells by means of a chemical combination with the red blood cells. All utilise oxygen in order to breathe, but in accordance with their own make-up. Because of this unity, young children are able to perceive the more abstract forms of science in terms of the lives of creatures they know well. In fact, they themselves are part of this rich variety of pattern.

They are even more fortunate in that the study of the phenomena of the natural world is at present given coherence in our society by certain powerful ideas. There is the idea of the interdependence of life, the way in which all forms of life depend upon each other. This is why, in recent years, the study of eco-systems has become such a popular form of science. Then there is the idea of the life cycle, whereby one animal or plant can be studied from its birth to its death, in its growth to maturity, its adaptation to the environment, in the way in which it reproduces, and finally in its death, which can be seen as no true death at all, because its remains become part of the resources of the earth, and the means by which others live. Many animals and plants live out their lives in time-spans sufficiently short for even young children to observe these processes. Such ideas are strong and coherent and help to shape the environmental study in the classroom.

The evidence for such an environmental study is easily accessible to children, existing all around them. Happily, this is the case in the cities as well as in the country; foxes, herons, field-mice, and even owls, can be spotted in parks, on railway embankments and in private gardens. Living creatures have proved adept at making the most of life in the inner city; a colony of rare bees was found living busily off the window-boxes carefully tended by the office workers of central London. Recent studies of foxes have shown that they are particularly fond of Kentucky Fried Chicken, scattering the empty cartons outside their dens. This teeming wildlife in the cities is partly due to the efficiency with which pesticides are used on farmland, killing off the food supply of the animals and birds that survive. More so-called wild birds are to be found now in the suburban rings surrounding our big cities than can be found in agricultural areas. Studies of so-called derelict areas in the inner cities, such as abandoned docks or bomb-sites dating from the last World War, have shown that these are teeming with life. There is a sad side to this revolution, of course, but it does mean that city children, too, can be nature-watchers.

There is another reason why the living world should form part of the environmental study for young children. It is connected with their feeling for nature, and the way in which they see themselves. Most young children have a deep reverence for living creatures; some of them, at a stage in their lives, actually want to *be* a bird, a dog or a fish. I know two, a brother and sister, who are at present taking it in turns to be a dog, practising barking and lapping up water from a bowl. They have tolerant parents. These emotional ties have an educational significance, though it is one that has been almost completely ignored by educationists and psychologists. The great Lorenz, renowned for his work with animals and, in particular, for his discovery of imprinting, has explained that his interest in birds was first aroused when, as a very young child, he felt a deep desire to be a bird himself. His young friend, the girl he was later to marry, felt it too. Lorenz went on, in this television interview (*Nature Watch*, ITV, May 1981), to state his belief that this kind of emotional arousal in individuals leads them on to scientific discovery later. You cannot, he explained simply, watch fish for hours and hours unless you love them. It is certainly true that young children can attain a much higher intellectual standard when studying what they care about. The bond that young children feel for other living creatures should be respected and nurtured, not just because it leads to higher intellectual attainment but because it makes them richer in themselves. Teachers might like to read, *Sharing Nature with Children* by Joseph Bharat Cornell (Exley, 1981).

Many approaches are possible in the environmental study. A theme can be taken, such as Eating, Animal Homes, the Life of a Cress Seed (or a spider, a worm or a cat). The interdependence of life can be studied by looking at a pond, or life on the sea-shore or even in the children's own gardens. The possibilities are endless but we will explore one.

On the whole, younger children enjoy looking at plants and animals in themselves, as personalities in their own right. They are fortunate in that there is a wealth of material ready at hand in their own homes. The family pet is a case in point. Domesticated animals, such as the cat luxuriating in the best position by the fire in the winter, and the puppy chewing up the family's slippers, are of course vastly different from those living in the wild, but, at the same time, they have a lot in common, remaining part of a much wider animal world. The very fact that they can live happily with human beings actually indicates some important biological truths, one being their adaptability shown in survival techniques, another that most living creatures have characteristics in common and can understand each other. That is why the family cat can outwit us when it comes to securing the cosiest place by the fire.

The advantage for young children is that they can be introduced to the animal world through studying pets that they know well and love. They can observe them closely and they do not have to go far afield. What is true of domesticated animals is also true of domesticated plants in the back garden. The grasses, tulips and daisies there have all been bred from ancestors that survived in the wild: they still retain their essential character.

One in five homes in Britain has a cat and one in four has a dog. Contrary to what one might expect, more dogs live in the town than in the country. This means that most children will be well acquainted with both animals. A class might begin a study of their pets by counting up how many of each kind they possess between them; there may be dogs, cats, gerbils, fish, guinea-pigs and birds. The results will probably vary according to the part of the country in which the children live; in the north there will be whippets and pigeons. Older children can express the results of the count in the form of a block graph. One or two of the animals can then be selected for a special study of four related aspects; these are the animal's physical make-up, his life-style, how he learns and adapts, and his links with the wider animal world. We will suppose that the cat and the dog have been chosen. They make an instructive contrast.

The first step is for everybody to draw their own cat, with the teacher's help if necessary. His important features (ears, eyes, nose, mouth, tail, claws, whiskers and fibrils) should be labelled, as below.

A cat

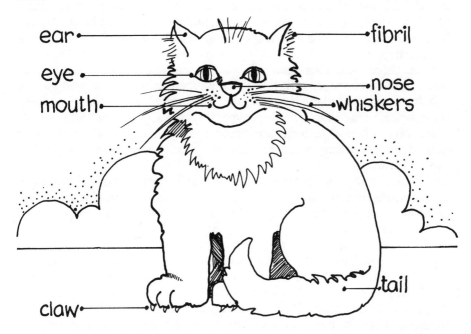

ear   fibril

eye   nose

mouth   whiskers

claw   tail

The children can consider the structure of the cat, how he is formed, and there will be a great deal of discussion, with everyone joining in. Little tasks of observation can be set in order to ensure accuracy. Do cats all have the same number of whiskers? Have they the same number of toes on their back as opposed to their front feet? Everybody can count them up that evening. Slowly a picture of how the cat functions will emerge. Some children will have noticed, and if they have not they can be asked to observe for themselves, how the pupils of a cat's eyes rapidly change when the light fades, as illustrated below. The cat's sensitive pupils ensure that he makes the best use of any light available. He is a night animal, hunting during the hours of darkness, and this is as true of the cat who lives in suburban Leicester as it is of the Bengal tiger.

A cat's eyes

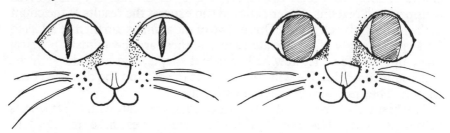

A little experiment will demonstrate how a cat uses his whiskers and fibrils. If the children wait until their cat is asleep and then gently touch the tips of his whiskers and fibrils, he will twitch them and probably wake up. They are extremely sensitive measuring devices, enabling him to feel what is ahead of him in the dark and to estimate the width of any space he is sidling through.

Even three- and four-year-olds can be asked to observe and report exactly how their cat uses his tail. What happens when the cat walks along a shaky or narrow ledge? He varies the position of his tail in order to keep his balance, sometimes, if he is desperate, twirling it round and round. Somebody is bound to point out that cats wag their tails when angry or excited, an interesting reminder that they, like ourselves, have a need to express emotion.

The cat has acute senses of hearing and smell, as well as of sight. He can catch sounds by turning his tall ears; what sounds is he most sensitive to? Does he sometimes appear to be listening to sounds that the children cannot hear?

The cat is a carnivore; that is, he is a meat-eater. The children can prove this by offering him carrots or cabbage for supper and noting his disgust. Of course, there will be intriguing exceptions and these, too, can be noted. I had a cat whose favourite food was chocolate. If the children look carefully, and gently, inside the cat's mouth, they will see that he has pointed teeth and a rough, hairy tongue. These features are linked to the way in which he eats and drinks; he tears off his food and gulps it down without chewing much; a whole plateful can disappear sometimes in less than a minute. This is in sharp contrast to our own eating habits, and in even sharper contrast to those of a cow. If the children get down on the floor, which they like doing, they can see how their cat uses his tongue for drinking. He curls it up into a shape like a spoon and then flicks the liquid to the back of this throat. His claws are also worthy of examination because they are sharp and pointed, and can be retracted at will. They are used for hunting.

The cat's body is ideal for the life he leads. His owners can note his behaviour, how he conducts his life, how he learns and how he adapts himself to new situations. They can keep a time-chart and record when their cat sleeps and when he is at his busiest. What games does he like to play? Most of them are pouncing, jumping games, practice for hunting. What about his coat? They might notice that he moults in the spring and grows a thicker coat in the autumn, which is his way of adapting to a changing climate.

Animal-learning is a vast and complex subject and it would be difficult for young children to conduct their own experiments in this area. They can, however, at least be aware that animals do learn, just as we do. They can collect stories of how their cat has learnt to negotiate the cat-flap, how he avoids a hostile dog (usually by jumping up somewhere high where the dog is unable to reach him), how he has learnt the time when he will be offered food or when a favourite friend comes home. Everybody will, of course, have the best and most intelligent cat.

Finally, the children can enlarge their study to include other members of the great cat family, the lions and the tigers, the panthers and jaguars. Pictures are easy to obtain from magazines and greeting cards.

Because of the British love of pets, all kinds of organisations have produced a wealth of visual and reading material, not just on cats, but on dogs, birds, guinea-pigs, gerbils and rabbits as well. Many useful addresses are given in the Appendix (pages 236–8).

The dog provides an interesting comparison with the cat, because he is basically the same kind of animal, a mammal, and yet his life-style and personality are different. Like the cat, he belongs to an ancient and thriving family; like the cat also, he is very well-known to young children. A picture of the dog will help to draw the children's attention to his characteristics.

Young children can begin by comparing the dog's eyes, whiskers, tail, claws and nose with those of a cat. His eyes do not react so dramatically to a change in light as those of the cat and he cannot see so well in the dark, for he is a day animal. His whiskers are much shorter (the children can measure them); he doesn't need long ones. Young children are usually very amused and intrigued by the contrast in the way dogs and cats use their tails. The dog does use his tail to help him balance to a certain extent, though not as much as a cat; not being a creature who likes height, he has less need to. Where the contrast comes is that the cat wags his tail in order to express anger and arousal, while the dog wags his tail as an expression of pleasure. The children will provide many anecdotes to illustrate this. They can also look carefully at their dog's claws. He has the same number as the cat, but he cannot retract them at will. You can often hear a dog clattering along a hard floor, but the cat walks silently.

A dog

eye
nose
whiskers
mouth

ear
tail
claws

Most dogs have a superb sense of smell and hearing, far better than ours. The children might devise simple little experiments in order to test this for themselves, like finding out from what distance they can open something like a bar of chocolate, of which their dog is fond, before he hears what they are doing.

The dog's teeth and the way in which he eats, or rather gulps his food, show that, like the cat, he is a carnivore. His physical features are at one with the life he leads. The same is true of his behaviour. If the children notice what games their dog likes to play, they will find he enjoys rough, fighting and hunting games. These, though carried out with great good humour, are really rehearsals for life in the wild.

Although the dog, like the cat, is domesticated and has adapted to life with humans, he still retains behaviour that is characteristic of all dogs, even those in the wild. The children might have observed that their dog is happiest of all when the whole family is together; what he likes best is going out in a crowd. This is because, unlike the cat, he is a pack animal. In the wild state, he would be hunting with other dogs, with a co-operative role to play and a well-defined place in the hierarchy. A domestic dog usually singles out one person in the family for a particular show of obedience and devotion. He sees this person as leader of the pack. Who has been chosen in the children's families? The communal instincts of the dog are worth thinking about, for they have enabled him to survive. The children might reflect on the kind of task that can be achieved most satisfactorily when they work co-operatively with each other, instead of by themselves.

The cat and the dog, then, can introduce young children to animal life, in a much wider environment than their own. Both are hunters, both are carnivores, but one is a pack animal while the other is a loner or tends to live in small groups. One is a day animal, while the other hunts at night. Both the cat and the dog have retained their age-old instincts, even though they live with us.

Many books have been written about dogs, enabling children to see their pets in the much wider context of dog-life throughout the world. *The Life of the Dog* by Jan Feder (Hutchinson, 1980) is a title in Hutchinson's 'Animal Lives' series. It is ideal for children to use by themselves, with a short history of the dog included at the back. Two good reference books for slightly older children are *The New Observer's Book of Dogs* by Catherine Sutton (Warne, 1983), and the volume on dogs by W. Boorer in the 'Explorer Guides' series (Latimer House, 1979).

A superb *Child Education Special* (1, 1982) is devoted to dogs. It has some beautiful pictures and plenty of information presented in such an attractive way that young children could use it by themselves.

Older children enjoy studying their family pets as much as younger ones do and their observations can be taken much further. Seven- to nine-year-olds can explore the actual structure of the eyes, mouths and ears of their animals, using a more exact terminology and being introduced to words like retina, cornea and cell. They can use a microscope in order to examine a hair or a whisker. These children will also be able to consider more complex aspects of animal life, such as learning. Learning is the ultimate in adaptation to the environment, a mental and behavioural adaptation which enables a creature to modify its actions in order to use the world to its own advantage. Apart from this, when animals modify their behaviour, they tell us what features of the environment are important to them. All the higher forms of life share this ability. Animal-learning is a vast and complicated area, in which there are hot disputes between animal biologists. One dispute centres on what behaviours are learnt and what are genetically determined, recent research indicating that quite complex behaviours may be inherited. Children can devise some simple experiments of their own in order to begin to answer some broad questions. For example, are there some things that animals can do at birth, like sucking? If they rig up some little runs in the gerbil cage, only one of which leads to a particularly nice piece of food, how long does the gerbil take to find the right way? How does he work it out? Do animals learn in stages, or in a sudden flash of insight? For example, if the family dog is learning to catch a ball on the bounce, does he slowly get better and better at it, or does he suddenly see what to do and get it completely right all at once? During a school holiday, some of the children could set out to teach their pets a simple trick and carefully chart their progress. The task should be a very easy one so as to cause no possible distress to the animal. On page 172 is a picture of a dog being trained to hurdle by a family during a dreary Christmas holiday. Once he had grasped that he was not allowed to slide under the hurdles, or to step over them, he thoroughly enjoyed learning this skill.

Baloo learns a new skill in return for a chocolate drop

All children, however young, can explore wildlife.

They do not have to go far afield, for plenty of wildlife exists in their own homes and in the school grounds. Adults, whether teachers or parents, can help to provide this variety for them; it simply means being tolerant towards the spider who sets up home behind the drain-pipe outside the back door or the wood-lice scurrying in the rockery. All are harmless, and all can teach children a good deal.

Drain-pipes, buckets and pieces of rotting wood are all nature reserves. If young children look behind a drain-pipe, they might find a spider and its web and perhaps a fly caught there. They can observe that the web is the spider's home and that she has built it herself. It is also her larder. If the spider is at home and they touch the edge of the web very gently with a stick, they will see her scurry towards the point of contact. The vibration of the strands of web have told her that something has been caught. If they look closely at the dead fly, they might find that the spider has wrapped it up securely and left it for future use. Then the children can examine the spider. How many legs has she? Are they jointed? They can compare the spider to the fly.

If a plastic bucket is left in one place for a week or two, worms will often come to live beneath it. The worm makes an interesting contrast to the spider and the fly. It has no legs, so how exactly does it move? It has a segmented body. A little thought should convince the children that worms like to live in dark, damp places. If there is any old wood or a rockery nearby, there is almost certain to be a wood-louse, an insect with an interesting segmented body. These four humble creatures are fascinating examples of complexity of structure and variety of life-style. To very young children even their most obvious characteristics are a source of wonder. It really is a source of comment to them that some creatures have eight legs, some have six, some two (themselves) and some have none at all.

A nature reserve for the under-fives; behind a drain-pipe and under a bucket

A nature reserve can easily be made in a quiet place in the school grounds. If the children leave a piece of wood or corrugated iron in one place for several weeks, all kinds of small creatures will come to live there. *Animals at your Feet* by 'Althea' (Dinosaur Publications, 1980) is specially written for children under five. It explains all about the little animals and insects they might find, such as the ant, earwig, earth-worm and lady-bird. It has bold pictures and the author takes the trouble to explain that these are larger than life-size so that the children can see them better.

A Guide to Wild Life in House and Home by Mourier and Winding (Collins, 1977) is also helpful for those unable to go far from home or school. It gives a detailed and well-illustrated description of all the creatures they can find in their own homes and gardens, like spiders, water-boatmen and silver-fish.

It's easy to have a worm to stay by Caroline O'Hagan (Chatto, 1980) is a charming book which explains how to find, keep happily and observe your very own earth-worm. Caroline O'Hagan has also written *It's easy to have a caterpillar to stay* and *It's easy to have a snail to stay,* both published by Chatto and Windus in 1980.

If they can be allowed a tiny patch in the school grounds, nursery and infant children can enjoy attracting and studying butterflies. A clump of nettles in a sunny spot is ideal for attracting the Tortoiseshell and the Red Admiral and might provide an opportunity for studying the life-cycle of a butterfly, from egg, to caterpillar, to chrysalis and finally insect. However, and with good reason, nettles are not popular with young children though perhaps a clump could be fenced off so that nobody falls into it. The children could set out to grow the kinds of plant that attract butterflies; there are those with shallow flowers, so that the nectar is easily reached, such as Buddleia, lavender, catmint, asters and ice plants. Butterflies are particularly attracted to the colours of yellow and purple.

In an edition of *Wildtrack*, the nature programme for schoolchildren broadcast on BBC 1, Su Ingle and Mike Jordan explained how a bird-table constructed for the winter could be converted into a butterfly-table for the summer. Nectar to attract the butterflies can be made from half a teaspoonful of sugar, half a teaspoonful of honey, and a pinch of salt, all dissolved in half a pint of warm water. This solution should be placed in a shallow saucer on the bird table and a small island should be created in the middle so that the butterflies have something to stand on. Su Ingle and Mike Jordan suggested a simple experiment by which the children can find out for themselves which colours butterflies prefer. They can dip pieces of variously coloured cotton wool in the nectar solution and suspend these from the table, noting which colour proves the most popular.

Many species of butterfly are threatened today. Young children, champions as they always are of the under-privileged, can do a great deal to save those we still have. The British Butterfly Conservation Society willingly gives advice (the address can be found in the Appendix, page 237).

Older children will be able to carry their observations of wildlife much further afield. Most wild animals in Britain, like the hedgehog, fox and field-mouse, are nocturnal, so that it is rare to spot them during the day. On the other hand, looking for evidence of their existence can turn into an exciting adventure. In fact, a very good way of beginning an environmental study with junior school children is by taking a wood, a field, or a piece of waste ground, or even the school itself, and asking 'What, or who, lives here?'

There are many clues for which the children can look. There is the evidence of hair or fur caught on fences, brambles and twigs. This can be collected, careful note being made of the height from the ground at which it is found, because that will indicate the size of the animal. The holes of animals can often be seen, those of rabbits at the base of trees, those of water-rats and voles in the river-banks. Sometimes scrape-marks can be seen in the earth, and also droppings. Other clues to look for are the browse-line of the trees and whether the grass has been cropped. If it has, the ends of the grass will be squared, not pointed. Cropped grass and trees indicate the presence of herbivorous animals.

The most exciting clues for children to look for are footprints. The search brings out the hunter in them. Footprints show up best in soft earth or in snow and they tell an enormous amount about the animal who has left them. A good time to search is after rain and in the morning or the evening, when the rays of the sun are slanting. If the print has gone deeply into the ground, deeper than other similar ones around it, its owner is a big animal of its kind. If the animal has a stride and there is a considerable distance between the prints, this again indicates a large specimen. Many excellent charts are available to help children identify the footprints of animals. Overleaf are reproduced the footprints of the mole, cat, rat and hedgehog.

The children might like to make plaster-casts of some of the prints they find, either for the purpose of identifying them later or in order to make a collection. Plaster of paris should be mixed with water until it is the consistency of thick custard, and then poured into a mould, made by surrounding the footprint with cardboard. There should not be too much delay in this part of the operation because this type of plaster is quick-setting. After fifteen minutes the cardboard mount and the cast can be removed, and after twenty-four hours the cast will have set really hard, so that it can be smoothed down, labelled and the cardboard painted to form an attractive surround.

Suppose the children have been searching a piece of land and have found all sorts of clues as to the animals who live there. They will have plaster casts of footprints, scraps of fur, droppings and even bones. Then they will need to interpret these signs and, from them, to build up a picture of the lives these wild creatures live. They can centre their investigations round certain clear questions, such as, Where does this animal live? When can it be seen? What does it eat? Who are its enemies?

Some excellent material is available to help children. Collins publish *A Guide to Animal Tracks and Signs* by Bang and Dahlstrom, which the children can use themselves. There is also a Spotter's Guide, with the same title, by Alfred Leutscher, published by Usborne, 1979.

The School Natural Science Society produce an enormous range of invaluable material for schools, very cheaply. One leaflet would be ideal for the purpose we have just been discussing, *Animal Tracks and Clues*; another contains information and a hundred questions about sparrows, with whom surely all children are well acquainted. The leaflets, together with further information, can be obtained from the address given in the Appendix (page 237).

Often teachers' journals produce special issues devoted to nature study. The August, 1980 edition of *Junior Education* had a special pull-out section on British wild animals, with beautiful, coloured classroom pictures of the fox, grass-snake, wood-mouse, hedgehog and rabbit. Also published was some of the information given above, and much else besides.

In order to build up a picture of the life-styles of the animals they are studying, and in order to trace the pattern of their interactions with the environment, the children will need to refer to a range of specialist books.

Footprints of a mole, cat, rat and hedgehog

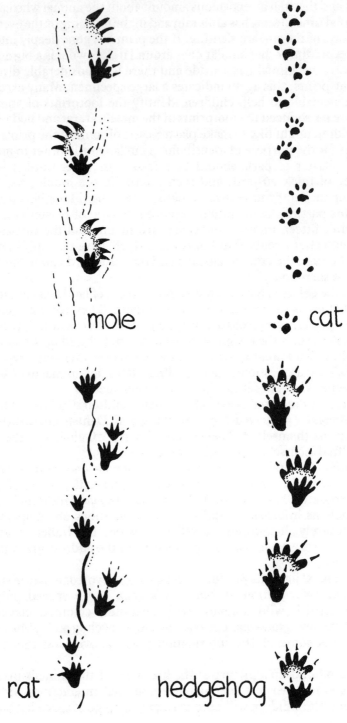

mole

cat

rat

hedgehog

Again they are lucky, because there are many colourful, well-written books for this age-group. I have chosen to mention the following texts because they describe the animals and insects that most children will have come across in everyday life.

The 'Observing Nature' series (Wayland) consists of a number of little books with easy texts about everyday animals and insects, such as ants, snails and grass-hoppers.

Ladybird publish many books on natural history, suitable for young children to read by themselves.

Heinemann produced in 1982 a charming series for very young children called 'Natural Pop-ups'. The beauty of them is that, as the children open a book, up pops a cut-out frog, tadpole or butterfly, as the case may be.

Bodley Head and Beaver publications also produce naturalist series suitable for children. Their books describe the lives of hedgehogs, bats and many other wild animals native to Britain.

Oxford Scientific Films have some outstandingly beautiful films on animals like the harvest mouse, ducks and the honeybee.

There is a continuous stream of excellent television programmes for children on animals, plants and other wildlife. Johnny Morris, David Bellamy and David Attenborough are names of presenters that all children will know. Many of their programmes can supplement work in the classroom – children being asked to watch them at home – this constituting some interesting and demanding homework. Children, as we know, are great dog lovers; the popular and repeated programme on the hunting dogs of the African plains (ITV) would make an intriguing supplement to a study of their own pets.

Programmes specially produced for children are particularly valuable because they often drawn children in to the mainstream of research. Su Ingle and Mike Jordan, for example, in *Wildtrack* (BBC 1, 1984) asked for help in discovering the 'Bird Brain of Britain'. Children were asked to devise intelligence tests for the wild birds that came into their gardens. The entries were ingenious and so were the birds. 'Bird Brain' proved to be a Great Tit from Somerset who was very adept at solving puzzles and getting at peanuts in double-quick time.

It is true that most of us live in an urban society. Thousands of our children go to school in cities, the endless pavements brightened only by a few trees and patches of waste ground. Yet here, too, there is wild life in abundance and nature holds us all in the palm of her hand as surely as if we lived in the country. Anyone who despairs of including wildlife in an environmental study for city children should read the story of the Lower Swansea Valley, described by Stephen Lavender in his article 'The Educational Value of a Derelict Landscape' which appeared in the teachers' journal *Natural Science in Schools*.[84]

The Lower Swansea Valley, prosperous and beautiful in the eighteenth century was, by the 1960s, a derelict waste-tip. It was reclaimed by the combined efforts of the University College of Swansea, the City Council and the local school children. Once the children had been invited to take part, fire-raising and vandalism miraculously decreased. The children planted trees, putting in thousands by 1979. The teachers devised a nature trail, incorporating several school subjects and drawing the children's attention to features like the strange shapes of the old copper tips and the keystone of a bridge. Rare and unusual plants were discovered and a survey of bird-life by the children revealed that many wild birds had survived and actually benefited from the industrial dereliction. There are many valuable lessons to be learnt here. We can see the resilience and adaptability of wildlife, and there is proof of the creativeness and concern that young children show towards living creatures and their surroundings, once they are given a part to play.

It is just possible that other local authorities or prospective builders would allow a school to set to work on a piece of waste land. There is a great deal that can be done, even on a small piece. The youngest children could clear a patch of ground and observe what happens to it. It will not remain unoccupied for long; they can record what animals, plants and insects appear. They can then ask some questions. How have the plants got there? Some, like the ever-present couch grass, have roots that travel underground from the surrounding area, as the children can see by digging it up; other plants grow from seeds dropped by birds or carried on the wind. Other questions will help the children to explore the delicate but very stable balance that prevails among living creatures in the environment. Which plants provide a food supply for birds, rabbits and squirrels? Which compete with each other? *Animals and Plants in the Fields* by Valerie Duncan (A and C Black, 1975) will enable rather older children to identify for themselves the common plants and animals that are found on grassland. *A Piece of Waste Ground* by Wigley (Ginn, 1970) has been written for children of seven onwards. It tells the story of Tom and Ann, who explore a piece of waste land, where once stood houses which have since been pulled down. Many such plots exist in our cities. Tom and Ann use theirs for making collections of interesting objects like stones, for measuring and thinking about mathematics, and for observing wildlife. There are strong, clear pictures.

The children may be able to build their own pond and observe the life there, or there may be water on the waste ground already. Many good books have been written on ponds and pond-life. An excellent one is the *Spotter's Guide to Ponds and Lakes* by Anthony Wootton (Usborne, 1980). The author explains to children not only how to identify what they find and how to make accurate observations, but also how to set about making a pond of their own. Then they can attract to it some of the frogs and water plants whose existence is threatened today.

Another project for a piece of waste land is to build a nature reserve. Project 67 in *School Projects in Natural History* (Heinemann, 1972) describes how to do this on a piece of derelict land. This book will be described in greater detail a little further on.

The work involved in some of these projects can be physically heavy, so that the help of parents and families should be enlisted where possible. City mothers and fathers might well be eager to help. Their assistance should be sought in other respects, and here a note of warning must be sounded, or rather two. Before the children set foot on a piece of waste land, it should be combed for all possible dangers. There can be rusty metal, broken glass and unexpected dips in the ground, sometimes harbouring water. All these should be dealt with. The other warning concerns poisonous plants. Some of the prettiest, the most naturally attractive to young children, can be deadly. The Ministry of Agriculture publishes a guide, *British Poisonous Plants*, and there should be a copy in every staffroom.

Older children might also be able to explore refuse tips. Here again, care must be taken and the local council should be asked what has been dumped there, so that it is quite safe for the children. That having been stated, a great deal of life thrives in refuse tips and there are numerous lessons to be learnt from it. *The Urban Dweller's Wildlife Companion* by Ron Wilson (Blandford, 1983) is an ideal reference book for juniors. Ron Wilson describes what they can find on waste ground, rubbish tips and in parks and ponds. A really beautiful book to accompany it is Jane Burton's *A Natural History of Britain through the Seasons* (Warne, 1983). Illustrated in colour, Jane Burton paints a picture of the changing face of nature, whether seen in the countryside, in parks or on rubbish dumps.

Children can work in an almost infinite variety of ways in a study of nature. The material is all around them, in their own homes, in the family pets, on television and radio and outside school. There is as much life on a rubbish-tip as there is in a field in the heart of the country. Children of between three and nine years of age can act as detectives, conservationists and the builders of nature reserves. They are well capable of working scientifically in the true sense of the word, devising and carrying out experiments of their own choosing. Should anyone be short of ideas, an excellent book has been produced for teachers, *School Projects in Natural History* (Heinemann, 1972). It describes one hundred and fourteen natural history projects that have been carried out in British schools, and was initiated by the Devon Trust for Nature Conservation. The projects are suitable for both rural and city schools and can be adapted for all ages of children. If we consider the younger children, they would enjoy a study of spiders' webs, or an investigation into the climbing habits of plants. Polymorphism, referring to the way in which leaf-shapes vary in certain plants, would also interest them. The ivy is an example. Older children could carry out a soil survey, or an investigation into the influence of weather conditions on toadstools, or a study of weeds and weed seedlings. Project 15, on 'Aggressive and Submissive Behaviour of Horses', is fascinating, revealing as it does to the ignorant observer the complex social behaviour of a group of horses, apparently idly grazing in a field.

A nature trail can awaken the interest of children of all ages to natural

IN THE PARK

Today when you are in the Park, try to think carefully about what you see... hear.... smell... feel. There are lots of things to do and here are some suggestions:

PARK

- See how many different trees you can spot. Draw a leaf from three of them and describe the colour very carefully.
- Look at insects on plants through a nature viewer. Try and sketch or describe them.

view A
quiet in the park
view B
not smoky in the park

Find two views looking outside the Park and sketch them Would you rather be inside or outside the Park? Explain why.

history. Sometimes a local council will produce one for the schools of the neighbourhood. The Parks department of my own borough in London has brought out a pamphlet on the wildlife on the local common, describing also the old Mill House and the remains of the Surrey Iron Railways. Often teachers devise their own nature trails to suit the needs of their children. Across the page is an extract from a trail devised by teachers at the Spencer Park Teachers' Centre in inner London for the children in their locality. This is a heavily built-up area, but there is an abundance of natural life.

In all their projects on natural history, the children will need good reference books that they can explore for themselves.

Just as exciting for the children is studying their own finds under the microscope. Then they can see revealed the intricate structure of the hairy blue-bottle's leg or the stem of a plant. Graebner has written a book, *Using the Microscope* (Lutterworth, 1976), especially for children on the various kinds of microscope and how to use them.

This chapter has ended on a practical note. Yet the excitement of all there is for children to do in science, should not be allowed to obscure one central feature. In studying science in the environment, children are studying life itself and the influences that condition it. It is possible to list the characteristics of life, the ability to adapt, to survive and to recreate, without being able to define life itself. In the last resort, perhaps the most valuable lesson to be learnt from the environmental study is that we do not know everything.

Opposite: A nature trail for an inner city school. Devised by teachers at the Spencer Park Teachers' Centre.

7

Geography through the Environment

Of all the disciplines, geography is most closely linked to the human senses and to survival. Even before he (she) can walk a child must prepare a map of his environment, a complicated map, using his mental abilities as well as his eyes and his sense of touch. It is a map not drawn on one level, but on several all at once, certain of the dimensions being social and emotional. Some of the abilities necessary to perceive the environment are inherited; there is evidence that young children carry within them from the beginning an awareness of depth and height and their attendant dangers, evidence also that people who have been blind from birth are able to draw quite accurate pictures of objects they can never have seen. At a more sophisticated level, human beings have always had to be good geographers in order to survive. It has always been necessary to possess a keen awareness of the physical features of one's surroundings, of where water can be found, of the quickest route to a given point, of the best places in which to grow crops and feed animals, of where there are treacherous bogs, hob-goblins or simply enemies waiting to pounce. All this is deep within everybody. Geography, at its grass roots, bears witness to the complexity of the human environment and the ingenuity necessary to survive there.

As an intellectual discipline, geography can be seen as a refinement of these needs. The need to map surroundings has led to the use of co-ordinates, while later, as huge areas came to be explored, the lines of latitude and longitude were brilliantly invented as a means of mapping the globe. In the days of highly complex, technological societies it is no longer sufficient to be concerned with our own immediate surroundings. In human terms, the globe is shrinking. As we know full well today, the effects of political and religious movements in one country reverberate across the world; poverty and disease in communities thousands of miles away threaten the stability of our own society; parts of the world to which it once took weeks and months to travel, if the lucky traveller arrived at all, can now be reached in a few hours for a week's summer holiday. As the world has grown smaller, the boundaries of geography have extended.

Because of this range and complexity, geography is sometimes hard put to prove its own identity and to carve out a respectable academic area of its own. Geographers themselves are well aware of this. A society under scrutiny at a given point in time cannot easily be understood unless its past development is examined, in which case the geographer is into the realms of history. A study of the methods of food production used by the people of a region implies a considerable knowledge of ecological systems, in which case the geographer is treading on the toes of the scientist. If he seeks to unravel the problems of the under-developed countries of the world, with their seemingly never-ending burden of poverty, he must also consider the clash of cultures within them and their relationships with their richer neighbours. Here the geographer must turn into a politician and an economist.

We have therefore to ask whether there is a heart to the subject of geography. Is there something, a view-point or a perspective, which, if we took it away, would mean that we were no longer studying geography? What seems to be essential is the sense of region; take that away and we are studying something else. These regions may be small or large, consisting of the classroom, the city of Birmingham, or the continent of India. They may hang together for many reasons, not necessarily to do with the physical features of the land. It may be that unique ecological features give a particular region its identity, or the inhabitants of a region may possess a common culture, as in the case of Europe or the world of Islam.

Geographers frequently argue about what makes a region worthy of study, and some point out to others that certain areas have been neglected. It has been alleged recently that the oceans, with their enormous influence on climate and culture, have not received nearly enough attention; bio-geography, that is, zones of vegetation, deserve more study also.[85] New regions are continually being perceived as our preoccupations change. The exploration of outer space can be taken as opening up a whole new and exciting region in geography, one in which the earth itself is only a small part.

Whatever the features that give an area of the earth its unique identity, the geographer sees it basically in spatial and physical terms. He may indeed continue to describe its culture and its economy, but his primary awareness is of its physical characteristics, yet this awareness does not limit his approach. The study of geography fans out to include most aspects of human life; its purpose, in the words of Professor Helburn of Colorado, is to 'provide the student with some sense of his or her place in the world and how it works.'[85]

In order to describe the regions he perceives, the geographer makes use of certain concepts, theories, models and facts, some of these being exclusive to geography and some being shared by other disciplines. Tony Land, in an edition of the *Times Educational Supplement* specially devoted to describing recent developments in the teaching of geography, has given an amusing account of how these tools have changed in recent years.[86] On his first field trip as a boy he says, 'We measured nothing, counted nothing and bothered nobody.' The experience left him with a life-long love of woodland scenery and apparently very little else. As he himself remarks, he would not get away with that now; he would be measuring, counting and carrying out experiments. Gone are the days when children listened to cosy little stories about the Eskimos in a far off land; geography has undergone a revolution in its methods of investigation and has become quantitative and scientific in its approach, with, as this author and teacher puts it, 'the real world as a laboratory'.

This has led to a much more vigorous approach to the teaching of young children, the emphasis being on the scientific testing of hypotheses and on the quantitative assessment of data. It is rare to find a geography textbook today which does not include graphs of many kinds and probably some attempt at explaining elementary statistics. Although this approach has great value, it also has its dangers, particularly for the younger children. These dangers have already been noted by teachers. There is always the temptation to cut the coat according to the cloth, to omit those aspects of enquiry which do not lend themselves to quantitative assessment. As Tony Land points out somewhat drily, 'counting vehicles on the road is a much-favoured task in any environmental study involving geography, presumably because of the large amount of data that can be collected.' The children might just find it more rewarding to have a chat to one or two of the drivers, even if this does not result in an impressive graph that can be pinned up on the wall. It is true, also, that the tendency to turn geography into a branch of mathematics has created difficulties for many young children. The reasons throw light on the real significance of the environmental study. The truth is that numbers by themselves mean very little. What gives meaning to the number of petals in a flower is when these are seen in the context of the structure of the plant, and of its life-cycle; in the same way, the vehicles counted by the children in the street mean not a thing unless they are related to the pattern of work and human life that underlie them. Objective data need human and intellectual terms of reference.

The 'New Geography', as it has sometimes been called, has not been insensitive to the nature of young children. Although, on the one hand, there has been this move towards making geography an intellectually more vigorous and defined subject, on the other hand there has been an increasing awareness of children's needs and the way in which they learn. Research has been greatly concerned with the perceptual difficulties experienced by children with regard to maps and their interpretation; there has also been considerable interest in the use of games and simulation as a means of enabling children to explore real-life situations on their own terms; the ways in which children develop geographical concepts have come under scrutiny. Geography has, at the same time, become both more adult and more child-centred as an intellectual discipline.

Geography is about making maps; its very name reveals the heart of the subject and tells us that it is concerned with depicting the surface of the earth. Maps are the shorthand of the geographer. If we consider the nature of a map we can see some of the skills required in its making and understanding. A map implies the recognition of the points of the compass, north, south, east and west; if it is held upside down it does not make sense. The essence of a map is that it reduces a large space to a small and manageable one, while keeping the relationship between features like villages, railways and rivers constant. A grasp of the concepts of scale and ratio is essential for its interpretation. A look at any map reveals that its features are depicted in symbols; a squiggly blue line denotes a river, a cross marks a church, and the letters PH on the ordnance survey reveals the existence of a public house. In order to take in the significance of this language a young child has to equate the waving blue line with the happy muddy place where he (she) goes tadpole fishing with his friends, and PH with the place where his parents go for a pint in the evenings. In other words, he has actually to reject his immediate sensory perception of the environment. To cap it all, a map leaves out a great deal, being just a skeleton, yet it cannot be properly understood unless what it has left out is tacitly recognised. It is not enough to be able to see where the rivers and towns are, we also have to infer the influence of the river pattern and deduce what has led to the growth of the towns. This assumes quite a degree of social sophistication on the part of the map-reader, and often a knowledge of history. The language of a map can be read like words, but its full significance is missed unless the information it supplies is interpreted inferentially. Even this is not the end of the story, for a map has to be seen as a whole, in every sense of the word. This can only be done when the individual has a *Gestalt*-like perception of the whole environment. The making and interpretation of maps, then, demand mental abilities of a high order.

By means of inherited skills, through maturation and with constant and varied practice, young children soon develop a map-making ability. Ordering their environment spatially is one of their earliest tasks. Even the baby who is just able to crawl knows her (his) way round the play-pen; by the time she is three she will be able to remember where she has left her teddy-bear and go off to fetch it, or at least to search purposefully for it. She has, in other words, the ability to manipulate her own cognitive map. However, we must note the characteristics of the three-year-old's map, because they have important implications both for teaching and for what comes later. Firstly, it is her map and no one else's, made for her own purposes; she does not yet find it easy to interpret someone else's. Then it is a map based on a highly localised area which she knows very well; in fact, research has shown that young children find it easiest to construct cognitive maps of those areas with which they are most familiar, such as their own homes and classrooms. Lastly, this little girl's map is of a disintegrated nature, consisting of thread-like routes. She is not yet able to perceive her locality as a whole or to relate one area to others; she cannot conceptualise her surroundings objectively.

How has this three-year-old managed to order her environment geographically in this way? On what inner resources has she drawn? Some studies indicate that young children use themselves, their own bodies, as a reference scale, and this is borne out by general observation.[15] The nursery school children described in Chapter One continually journeyed backwards and forwards at varying speeds, sometimes walking, sometimes tearing past, and sometimes wandering aimlessly. In this way they built up an idea of distance, of the various landmarks in their environment and the relationships between them and, above all, of the time it would take them to reach their destination. The perception of time is closely linked to the perception of distance in early map-making.

When we talk about mapping ability in young children, we are really referring to two distinct abilities, although these have elements and skills in common. On the one hand, we mean that ability by which a child structures his daily environment in spatial terms; on the other, we are referring to his ability to interpret prepared maps. Both these abilities evolve with maturity, but the latter is more difficult and takes longer. S. J. Catling, himself a primary school teacher, has written a very good account of this evolution, demonstrating that map-work is quite possible even for very young children.[87] Here are some of the points he makes.

Even at three years of age, some children can find items in a room with the aid of a simple drawing. Until they are seven, they find it difficult to follow a specific route in order to uncover a 'hidden treasure' but are successful in a 'free search' situation. As for drawing maps, a six-year-old is unable to replicate size and distance correctly, finding it easier to construct a model. These very young children can understand symbols in maps, but have not yet grasped the conventions of map contruction.

The thinking of children of various ages is typified by certain characteristics; to the extent that these characteristics frequently appear together and are consistent with each other, it is appropriate to speak of stages.

Before the age of six a child is at the stage of egocentric spatial understanding. He, or she, can produce representations of his familiar world, making use of self-objects, such as his own home. The kind of mapping he embarks upon will resemble that of the three-year-old hunting for a toy.

When he is about seven years old, a child enters what Catling refers to as the stage of objective spatial understanding. He will be able to structure some of the relationships of his spatial environment, but he will be unable to integrate them into a structured whole. Typically, girls and boys of seven will be capable of mapping parts of their own neighbourhood accurately, but will have little understanding of the general configuration of their locality.

At the age of about ten, rarely before, a child reaches the age of abstract spatial understanding. He is now aware that all the parts are parts of a whole, he can extrapolate routes within the general structure, he can reverse mental operations. He can, in fact, draw a true map.

When it comes to interpreting prepared maps, here also the ability of children evolves slowly. Six-, seven- and eight-year-olds will use pictorial symbols when drawing their own maps; a grasp of the symbols of atlas maps comes very much later, sometimes not until adolescence. Their problem seems to lie in recognising that the symbol truly does represent something real. The points of the compass can cause confusion, even after eight years of age, particularly in the direction of east-west. In spite of this, junior school children are well able to use a map in simple creation exercises.

These children also understand the grid system used in mapping, the seven- to eight-year-olds finding simple letter grids manageable, while the ten- and eleven-year olds can cope with all-figure numbering. Perhaps the most difficult concept for children to grasp in map-reading is that of scale. At eight years of age, a child can appreciate relative sizes, but is often unable to measure to scale. Drawing in proportion and reading off distance in a conventional map is a difficult exercise even for a ten- or eleven-year-old.

S. J. Catling's valuable article, and his review of the relevant research, has many implications for teachers of geography. We will note some of them at this point. Young children do not, at first, possess the ability to work abstractly. They think with their own bodies. They need plenty of opportunity to run and move about in familiar surroundings in order to develop mapping ability. Secondly, and this is a very important point, it is implied by Catling and has been shown by other research, that the higher the degree of familiarity an individual possesses with the material on which he is working, the greater the sophistication he can develop along the dimensions of differentiation, complexity and abstraction. It has actually been demonstrated that, in Piagetian terms, one who produces a formal operational map of his own well-known locality will produce a map of pre-operational standard for an area he does not know at all.[88] This reveals once more the significance of the environmental study and what it can do for the mental development of young children. Children know their own locality well. Working through the familiar actually pushes them forward towards the formation of more abstract and sophisticated concepts, towards higher modes of thinking.

What follows are some suggestions as to how young children can be helped in map-making, that is, in ordering their environment in spatial, symbolic terms. A number of these have been thought out by ingenious teachers.

With the under-fives, plenty of free physical activity is the prerequisite for accurate and truly understood map-work later. These young children can also play simple 'finding' games. They can begin by hunting for a sweet or a small treasure, helped by spoken clues as they search. This helps them to form their own inner cognitive maps. From this, they can progress to using a simple map in diagram form in order to find something; even three- to five-year olds are able to do this. Overleaf is a diagram of a part of a nursery school classroom:

A map-diagram of a nursery classroom

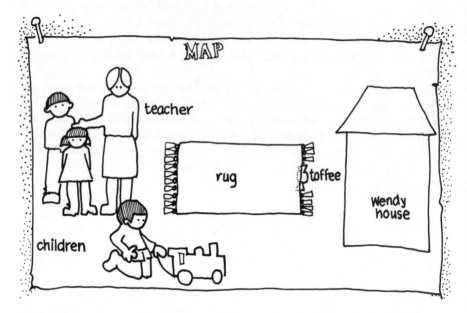

The children have to hold the map the right way up in order to make sense of it – this therefore gives them a rudimentary introduction to the use of the compass. The Wendy house, rug, teacher and children are stylised, so that the children are using representations of real objects, which leads them on to map symbols later.

A little later, perhaps between the ages of five and seven, they can draw their own maps, and also try using those drawn by each other. There may well be a great deal of heated argument, misunderstanding and disagreement, but these are the stepping stones to insight. A map must be written in a language that can be understood by everybody; further, it has to be accurate, and if distances and proportions are not scaled down and properly reproduced, the map is incomprehensible. This kind of realisation comes slowly to young children, not in days or weeks but over a period of years. Games like these need to be played often and with many variations.

As time goes on, it may dawn on the children that their maps would be easier to use if they all adopted the same terms of reference, or a grid system. Seven-year-olds upwards can try this, beginning in their own classroom, as illustrated opposite.

In this classroom, in which the numbers of pupils are greatly reduced for reasons of convenience, Tracy can be found in 1C, Percy in 2B, and so on. Games can be played using this grid system and the children should grow accustomed to reading their maps both from the front of the classroom, facing the other children, and from their own seats. In this way, they will realise that a map, and co-ordinates, can be read from any

Co-ordinates using the classroom

	1	2	3
A	John	Mary	Betty
B	Eleanor	Percy	Peter
C	Tracy	Jenifer	Tim

vantage-point. Betty (3A), can be asked to fetch a pencil from 1A's desk (John), and Eleanor (1B) can be asked to tell 3B (Peter) to stop nattering and listen to what is being said. Interesting objects suggested by the children themselves should be included in the classroom map. They might well leave the blackboard out, but the radiator where they warm their hands and feet in the winter will go in, so will the floorboard that creaks when they stand on it.

Such explorations need not be confined to the classroom. There are many mapping themes suitable for young children outside school, and some excellent accounts, written by teachers themselves, as to how they have helped their children to perceive their environment in geographical terms, and had great fun in doing so. Anne Bauers took her infants on a walk round their village in Suffolk. They looked carefully at all the buildings, comparing their sizes and discussing what they were used for.[89] When they returned to school, the children set about making a model of their village. Then they looked at a large-scale map and saw that the roads made the same shapes on the map as they did on the model. On the map they stuck pictures of their own houses and the village buildings. Working in this way, inspired by their natural interest in houses and buildings, they were guided from making representations in models through to an understanding of the symbols on a map. Incidentally, children need to be allowed to stick their own pictures on maps because, from their point of view, a map may well leave out what is most interesting, like the cars on the road, all the shops, and the bustling people.

Pillar-boxes are a popular mapping theme with older children, conveying as they do exciting thoughts of letters plopping through the letter-box. Not only can all the pillar-boxes in a locality be mapped, hypotheses about them can be postulated and tested. Old-age-pensioners post more letters than young people; women post more letters than men. Are these statements true, and how can they be verified? Are the pillar-boxes distributed evenly in the locality? If they are not, is there a correlation between numbers of pillar-boxes and the number of houses or businesses in the area? Another mapping approach is to chart, for a given area, all the signs of services that keep the community running. There will be road signs, fire-hydrants, litter-bins and lamp-posts and, farther afield, the police station, fire station and hospital.

'Coming to school' is an obvious theme. Children can either concentrate on the roads and streets along which they travel, or they can map features of interest. Kevin Watson asked his junior school children to count all the bridges they crossed on the way to school, to note the obstacles they encountered, and to see how many types of bridges there were.[90] Then the study broadened into a consideration of how bridges are constructed and their history. John Moles encouraged his class to consider the problems involved by himself trying to cross over a piece of plaster board placed between two desks. He crashed down to the floor.[91] This enjoyable demonstration was followed by allowing the children to design their own bridges. They were given problems of engineering to solve, using Matchbox cars. At first, the designs were grandiose and elaborate, but, as the children continued to experiment, their ideas became simplified and effective.

There will come a time when the children begin to interpret other people's maps, not merely their own. At one end of the scale, map-reading is simply a matter of clear visual perception. Considering how important it is, this aspect of map-reading has been curiously overlooked in research, but one investigation written up by Liza Noyes in *Geography*, November 1979, suggests some interesting guidelines.[92] Although Ms Noyes's conclusions concerned adults' perception of features in maps, most of what she says applies equally well to children.

Words written with an initial capital and continued in lower-case typing are the easiest to perceive. 'Sand' is better than 'SAND'.

Words written horizontally, in a straight line and without a break are more legible than curved words, angled letters or split and hyphenated words. This means that diagram A is better than B.

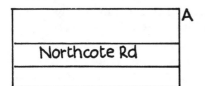 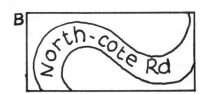

Words should be kept distinct from the surrounding material, making diagram C better than D.

A formalised representation is often easier for the reader to interpret than one which, although giving a more accurate picture of the terrain, is confusing. Thus diagram E is easier to read than F.

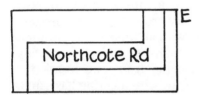
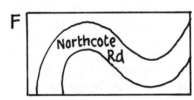

The reason why this is so is easy to see. What the reader needs is a clear indication of the general layout; the details do not matter, mose of these he has to find out for himself anyway.

The skilful use of colour greatly helps the map-reader. It can help him to discriminate, colours being more easily perceived than patterns. However, no more than eight colours should appear on any map, otherwise the reader is confused.

Colour can also help the reader to perceive height and contour, layer tints being more easily discernible than numbers.

These are all useful hints for any teacher preparing a map for young children to use.

Teachers themselves have found imaginative ways of helping young children through difficulties they might experience in interpreting maps. Steepness, gradient, depth and height are represented on maps by contour lines. It has been found that children come to appreciate this if they are allowed to model in plasticine. Given a lump of plasticine, they can model the contours themselves, either for an imaginary piece of land, or, if they have reached that stage, for a feature of their own neighbourhood. When they look down on their model, they can see the contour lines; when they are close together the gradient is steep; when they are far apart the slope is gentle, exactly as in the formal atlas map.

When children are studying the physical features of an area, such as the hills and rivers and the lie of the land, they enjoy spotting them on an aerial photograph and then pin-pointing them on a map. For children of seven onwards, it is helpful to pin up different scale maps of the same locality, such as those published by Ordnance Survey, and allow them to be studied. Slowly the children will realise that maps may vary in size and scale and give us different information, but that the locality remains the same. They are building up 'map-constancy'.

Children frequently find the concept of scale difficult to grasp. They are helped if they work in a small area familiar to them to begin with. Equipped with ice-lolly sticks as markers and pieces of string, they can make a scaled diagram of their own classroom or part of the school grounds. The children of today are familiar with scale in their everyday surroundings, after all, they play with model cars, dolls and soldiers which are often built accurately to scale. Some teachers have found it helpful to start with these, and encourage children to work out the scale on which a toy truck or infantryman has been built by comparing it with the real thing. Then they can apply the same reasoning to their map-work.

Interesting detail should never be allowed to obscure what is at the heart of map-reading: the ability to find one's way around. An exciting new approach has emerged in recent years, one with all kinds of implications for the teaching of geography to young children. It is orienteering. Orienteering involves the individual travelling from one location to another. Usually, he takes a compass with him. Orienteering has caught on as a hobby for adults in many parts of the country, but its appeal for children is enormous; so is its value in encouraging them to explore their environment geographically. Travelling across any kind of terrain is an adventure, tapping those age-old instincts that lie deep within us all, of finding a way round territory that may be difficult or dangerous, and of surviving. It is useful, even in today's so-called civilised society, to be able to negotiate dense forest, or open fields, or even a maze of streets. For children, orienteering can make a map spring to life. They learn of the great variety of phenomena concealed behind the symbols of the map, that there are all kinds of woods, tracks and streams. They learn that the features of the map have to be perceived differently according to the purpose of the observation. They have to orientate themselves in relation to the map, to read co-ordinates and use the grid system, to use the compass accurately and to take account of contour patterns. Eventually, they will be able to work out their own routes from point to point avoiding hazards and reaching their destination speedily and safely.

Orienteering encourages young children to order their environment spatially by those means natural for them, that is, through their own physical activities. As they run and jump and clamber over obstacles, they can match distances with their own ability to cover them, and check their perceptions of physical features with what they actually turn out to be. Moreover, this is a problem-solving activity, calling for resourcefulness and initiative.

There are several kinds of orienteering and each can be adapted and also be fun, even for very young children. The classroom and the playground can be turned into simple courses, with routes round obstacles and physical features like trees and mounds of earth, or desks and the Wendy house.

In cross-country orienteering, individuals leave the starting-point at fixed intervals of time and visit set control points in a prescribed sequence. The aim is to see who completes the route most quickly. Everyone carries a map, a compass and a whistle to use in case of emergency. Even if the children are only using the local recreation ground and are in sight most of the time, they should carry this equipment and know how and when to use it. They should also travel in pairs. In score orienteering, individuals start off at fixed intervals and visit as many control points as possible within a given time. Control points near the starting point carry a lower number of points than those farther away. In line orienteering, individuals follow a precise line with control points concealed along the route, having no information as to the number or exact location of these.

Orienteering does not have to be competitive and it can be adapted in all sorts of ways. Either relay or bicycle orienteering would appeal to eight- or nine-year-olds. Teachers can devise all kinds of routes according to how they wish to direct the attention of the children; there might be an architectural route through a town, while in the country the journey could take the children through terrain of various contours, or through areas where there is a variety of natural life. Back in the classroom, the children can recall what they have noticed.

Although in serious orienteering a compass is a necessity, younger children exploring smaller areas can manage without one. In fact, it is quite salutary to use one's eyes, knowledge of the locality, and common sense instead.

There are all sorts of natural compasses around us. The children should find a tree standing slightly apart from the others and examine it closely. The bark of the tree will be harder, light in colour and drier to the touch on the south than on the north side. On the north side of the roots, especially if the children are looking at an ash, oak or elm tree, there will usually be moss growing. Then the children can take a look at the leaves. Those facing north will be larger, a darker green and have lighter veins than those growing on the south side. Spiders will be living on the south side of the bark, because spiders like warmth.

However, it may be winter, with not a leaf to be seen anywhere. In that case, the children can search for the stump of a tree that has been cut down. The spaces between the rings will be wider on the south side and the heart of the ring will be nearer the north.

If there are no trees, the children can look at the stones, the hills and the vegetation. Stones and boulders often have moss growing on the north side. The grass growing on the northern side of a hill is usually greener than than on the south, and flowers and ferns will appear there later in the year.

Experience of their own neighbourhood will help children develop a sense of direction. In some coastal areas the wind has blown the trees so that they all lean over. There is usually a prevailing wind in any district, so that the children can work out the points of the compass by watching the clouds in the sky.

A tree-stump compass

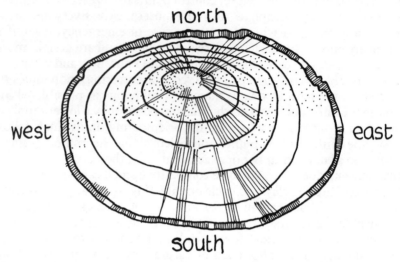

Orienteering has become quite a craze since the 1960s, only recently surpassed in popularity by jogging. In many districts there are orienteering clubs, and whole families go out together. Enthusiasts have not been slow to see the implications for teaching. One of them, Tony Merritt, has written a lively article in the periodical *Teaching Geography*,[93] in which he includes some good suggestions for teachers, as well as for background reading. The British Orienteering Federation publishes a book *Orienteering for the Young* by Peter Palmer. The address of the Federation, and incidentally there are regional clubs all over the country, is given in the Appendix (page 240).

Your way with Map and Compass (Blond Educational, 1971) has been written by J. Disley specially for teachers and school children; so has *The Use of Maps in School* by J. C. Bentley (Blackwell, 1975). These books can be found on most library shelves.

Orienteering is probably associated in the minds of most of us with negotiating hills, rivers and streams in the open country, but this does not have to be so. It can be just as exciting, and just as educational, in the towns. *Urban Walks and Trails* by B. Goody (Geographical Association, 1976) provides valuable information for teachers on how to prepare trails and gives a bibliography on trail-making. In the issue of the *Bulletin of Environmental Education* of November 1983, there are some interesting suggestions for the making of town trails.

A great deal of help can be obtained from the many excellent publications of enterprising local authorities and groups of teachers, especially in exploring possibilities in a particular area. Take, for example, Hammersmith and Fulham in inner London, deprived, built-up areas that are not renowned for their open spaces or the opportunities they provide for work out of doors by children. Yet the London Borough of Hammersmith and

Fulham, in conjunction with the Teachers' Centre, publish an excellent directory for teachers entitled *Roundabout*, full of material and suggestions for local and urban studies. Also helpful to teachers devising orienteering routes would be the suggested urban and nature trails and the educational packs used by the Sherbrooke Teachers' Centre on 'London Wildlife' and 'The Thames'.

On the general subject of interpretation of maps, an excellent article has been written specially for junior schools by an officer at the Ordnance Survey, R. Cameron.[94] It is called *Maps and Mapping*, and in it the author explains what maps do, what co-ordinates mean and how maps should be interpreted. For younger children, both Ladybird and Longman publish books that they can read themselves on the purpose of maps.

The children's activities in the classroom reinforce what they have learnt outside it. Playing games is a good way of doing this. The educational value of the game lies in the way it reduces what is complex to the bare essentials. It also draws on instincts and desires buried deep in human nature, like the will to win and a fondness for solving problems. It is exciting, because the issues are clear and stark and there are no half-colours. At its best, the game is a good example of child-centred teaching. The following game is aimed at helping young children to acquire two of the numerous skills necessary to interpret a map: remembering atlas symbols and using the points of the compass.

The game of 'Snap!' can be adapted as a teaching aid enabling children to equate symbols with the phenomena they represent. The children can make the cards themselves, and if they are covered with clear film they will last a long time.

If the game is played by two children, each starts with an even number of cards. Some of the cards have the symbols drawn on them, in this case those used by the Ordnance Survey Landranger Series, while others have the words, or it could be pictures, of the things they represent. The children take it in turns to place a card face upwards on the table so that the resulting piles are side by side. When two matching cards turn up, that is, when the symbol on one card matches the word or picture on the other, the child who shouts 'Snap!' first takes all the cards on the table. Then they continue the game. The winner is the boy or girl who ends up with the whole pack, both symbol and word cards. The game is illustrated overleaf.

Older children, such as the eight- and nine-year-olds, might well enjoy plotting imaginary journeys. They could take these from the adventures of favourite characters in books, in comics or on television. They can trace the journeys undertaken in *Herman and the Masters of the Universe* (ITV, 1984), or map the exploits of *Dangermouse* (ITV, 1984).

Geography is a discipline of many levels, even though these are encompassed within a regional perspective. The strategy of the child is not, therefore, confined to the ordering of his environment in spatial terms, but goes beyond it into human affairs. People, their homes and work and the

Symbol-snap

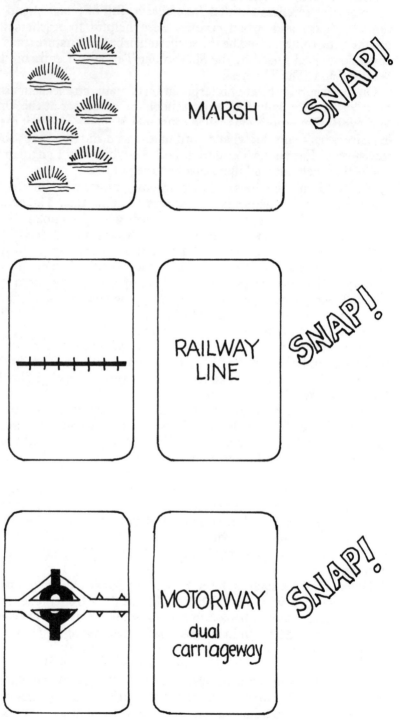

way in which they earn their living are all part of the environmental study in geography, simply because no environment consists merely of physical phenomena. Stanley Jex, a primary school teacher, expressed this very well when he stated, 'Every environment is formed by the relationships which exist between man and his surroundings, now and in the past.'[95] If their work is planned carefully, young children can come to understand the world in many geographical tones, in its animal life, geology and the ways in which human communities run themselves. Their own immediate surroundings and the lessons learned there are of inestimable help to them, because these are alive and familiar, but the environmental study in geography should not begin and end there. The models discovered in an exploration of their own village or town can carry children much further afield, to the other ends of the earth. A home is basically the same in England, the American jungle or near the north pole because it exists for the same purpose of providing shelter and a centre for life. Industry is organised in basically the same way, wherever it is found. Environmental is not synonymous with local. Be this as it may, most teachers of young children will place emphasis on the immediate surroundings in which they live, or at least those that can be reached easily. Apart from those advantages that have been frequently stated, this way of working gives children a heightened awareness of their world. One teacher, Derek Carter, took his class of eight-year-olds on a visit to the Kentish hop-gardens.[96] On their return to school, he asked them to write about what had impressed them most. They wrote about the sticky feel of the hops, the funny smell, the noise of the machinery. Allowed to perceive what was going on in their own way, the children 'felt' the environment. It came alive. This is an important but neglected dimension in children's learning, reinforcing as it does intellectual effort later.

When young children order their environment geographically, they are perceiving it in terms of region. Being able to map the features of their environment is one of the skills they need, but it is only the means to a deeper level of understanding. The teacher's task is to choose ways natural to children of bringing this about.

One way is to investigate a region's soil. All children have a natural affinity with mud, stones and the earth; they are enthusiastic and talented diggers with an eye for concrete detail. In other words, they are born geologists. If three- to five-year-olds are encouraged to dig a hole in the ground, they will notice several characteristics of the earth. Firstly, it is full of stones. If they collect these, they will see that they are of many different colours. They will also notice that the soil changes as they dig more deeply; it is layered and the layers, too, are of various colours, and may even feel different, the top-soil being of a more granuled consistency and being easier to rub between the fingers, while, deeper down, the clay forming part of the sub-soil will be light-coloured and sticky. There are great variations according to district; in some areas the top-soil is sandy, or there may be a thin layer of top-soil and then hard rock. All this can be noted and a collection made of the stones. The depth of the various layers can be measured by marking them off on strips of cardboard; small samples can be taken and a record kept in the classroom by spreading glue on pieces of card and sprinkling the soil on. Slightly older children will be able to carry out a survey of the soil in their gardens. Those who live on top of a hill, may find they are living on quite different ground from those living near a river. Simple experiments will prove to young children that soil is a mixture; those that follow have been suggested by Muriel Whittaker, herself a teacher.[97] If the children place a little soil in a glass jar, half fill it with water and shake it, they will see the constituents separate. Decaying plant and animal material, like leaves, will float to the top, the bigger grains like gravel will sink to the bottom, while fine particles of sand will be seen in the middle.

The children can then prove to themselves that soil contains water and air. They can probably feel the dampness in the earth with their fingers; it rarely dries out in Britain completely. If they weigh a sample, then allow it to dry out in the classroom, then weigh it again, they will realise that soil contains a high proportion of water. That it also contains air can be proved by plunging a flower-pot full of earth into water and watching the bubbles rise.

The children will be able to see the importance of soil to plant life. They can see, when they are digging, that plants grow in the top-soil, by noting how far down their roots go. The parents will be able to tell them, especially if they are gardeners, that plants have their own marked preferences. Some like peat, some like clay, some only thrive in loam. Some plants will only grow in soil that is almost water-logged, while others will happily grow in a few inches of sand. Older children can construct a soil map for their locality and link its features to the vegetation. Older children can read Helen Piers's book *The Soil* (Angus and Robertson, 1979).

Young children are always picking up stones, especially after the rain when they are polished and look like jewels. Not only are stones beautiful, they each have a name, a composition and tell the story of the earth itself. Several books have been written so that children can identify and read all about their finds for themselves. A really detailed account is given in *Rocks and Minerals* by H. S. Zim and P. R. Schaffer (Hamlyn, 1957). Although this book is, unfortunately, out of print, it is a mine of information. These authors have produced a dictionary of gems and rocks with 400 coloured illustrations, accompanied by explanations of how they were all formed, thousands of years ago.

It may be, if they are really lucky and live in the right areas, that the children will discover some fossils. These are the traces of plants and animals that lived long ago. There are numerous books on fossils and some have been written specially for children. *Prehistoric Life on Earth* by B. Záruba (Hamlyn, 1983) will help children to understand how bones, imprints and apparently dull pieces of stone, are actually the remains of plants and animals that lived on the earth thousands and even millions of years before their own time.

We have already seen how one teacher took buildings as a mapping theme for her class of infants, using it to great effect (page 189).[89] Here is how another teacher, Miriam Linke, used the same theme rather differently.[98] Ms Linke noticed that her infant children in Kent always wanted to play in the Wendy house, almost to the exclusion of everything else. She and the children therefore set out to build some houses in the classroom, a whole street in fact. They built the houses from boxes covered in paper. They had to estimate the number of sheets they would need and they made a graph of the children's estimates. The classroom street was given life because it was provided with visitors, people like the milkman and postman, who the children would see in their own streets every day.

All this led to an interest in real houses outside. A house brick was brought in and thought about. It was tested for porosity by standing it in water and placing blotting-paper on top of it. It was noticed that, in real houses, rows of bricks are arranged so that the joins alternate. The children understood why when they made their own constructions from Lego.

Then everybody thought about what kind of ground is best to build on. Objects were pushed into soft ground and the fact that they slowly sank was duly noted. The children also tried their hands at using real building materials. They made concrete bricks in plastic moulds, using one part of cement to two of sand and mixing this with water. The class discovered that they could measure out the constituents either by weight, or by volume. Finally, everyone became interested in the real-life process of building, so a building site was constructed in the classroom. Miriam Linke includes in her article instructions for making a simple, child-size crane that actually works.

The versatility of this approach hardly needs emphasising, neither does its imaginative response to the needs of young children. Their love of construction and their curiosity about the outside world was used to draw them into creativeness and adventure. The project was not confined to one kind of thinking, but encouraged the children to see the significance of buildings from several points of view.

Such a theme can be developed to suit the needs of older children. They can look carefully at the buildings in their own area, noting, for example, how many kinds there are. There will be homes, factories, shops, churches and civic centres. The children can consider why these buildings are found where they are and map them. Are factories and homes found jumbled together or are they in distinct and separate areas? The sites of farms and factories depend on several factors, such as the availability of good transport and the kind of soil there is. History will have played its part; in towns and cities that came into being at the time of the Industrial Revolution, hovels were flung up near the factories so that working people were near their work; in a New Town built in this century, town-planning will have ensured that factories and people's homes are kept far apart.

An analysis of the factory, the farm and the home will build up models in the children's minds which will take them far beyond the confines of their immediate geographical environment. What, for example, is the essence of a home? Why do we need one? Should everyone have a room of his own? Does every home need a garden? What were people's homes like in the past? All human beings, wherever they are, have homes of a kind, even the tramp who makes a temporary shelter from old newspapers at night. Animals have homes too. They seem basic to existence.

It comes naturally to very young children to centre their thinking on their own homes and families, and to work outwards from there. A bright, attractive series for infants is 'Going Places' by Renwick and Pick (Nelson, 1979). The authors, in Book One, start in the home and look at the family, continuing with the work each member does each day, to a consideration of where the food comes from and how much time the younger ones spend playing. A simple graph shows how many hours a day the imaginary Pickwick family spend in various pursuits, introducing children easily to a quantitative approach. The baby, of course, spends a lot of his time sleeping, though father and mother do not. Book Two expands to consider the world outside the home.

The May 1981 issue of *Child Education* is devoted to the theme of Buildings and gives a comprehensive list of sources of films, books and societies that will help the teacher. Of great assistance in suggesting ideas is the study pack 'Homes', produced for infant and junior school children by the Building Societies Association (the address can be found in the Appendix on page 241).

Most educational publishers produce books on homes and buildings for children to read themselves. The 'Instant Readers' published by Methuen (1984) are attractive little books for young children. They cover 'Homes', 'Traffic', 'People you Know', 'Travelling', 'Pets' and 'Around the House'.

The children can expand their thinking and begin to consider life outside their own homes. There are all sorts of services that are essential to their well-being but which they do not provide for themselves. If they go on a short walk with parent or teacher, noticing all the interesting objects that indicate the provision of a community service, this can begin as a mapping theme. On the list might be pillar-boxes, fire-hydrants, drains, road-signs, litter-bins and lamp-posts, all beloved by children. They can draw them and imagine the incidents that call upon these services; they will have already seen the postman and the dustmen; some might have seen firemen fighting a fire. Publishers produce a variety of books for children on the public services. Blackwell and Ladybird are but two. Classroom pictures are obtainable from a few educational publishers, and they are also frequently included in journals produced specially for teachers of young children, such as *Pictorial Education*, *Child Education* and *Junior Education*.

Sometimes the children might be able to go and see the headquarters of these services for themselves. In the borough of Hammersmith and Fulham, in London, the fire and police stations, the Post Office sorting depot, the bus garages and the United Daries are all glad to receive visits from parties of school children. They might even be willing to send some of their number into the classroom to talk to the children.

Certain societies have an interest in educating children about the public services and produce material suitable for the older ones. The Keep Britain Tidy Group publish a teaching pack, 'Look around the town', which suggests a number of themes to explore (see page 241 for the address).

Older children, too, can benefit from the use of films and filmstrips. Most local authorities run a free lending service for schools, and other material is produced commercially.

Projects on community services lead naturally on to the themes of work. Work is an invaluable environmental theme, introducing children imaginatively to the human environment. It provides an ever-changing and key commentary on the kind of society in which we live; one can see it as a kind of touchstone. It is the link between the individual and the community, and link between the child and the outside world.

The under-five-year-old will know one doughty worker very well indeed, his or her own mother. The housewife and mother brings a number of amazing skills to her work and these should be listed and discussed. She has to possess manual skills for work requiring dexterity, like sewing, mending and cooking. She must also develop considerable powers of organisation, or, to put it grandly, managerial ability that would not shame a board of directors. The children can consider how she organises the family so that they all get off to school, clean and fed, while she herself probably goes to work. How does she organise herself so that there is a meal for everyone when they come home in the evening, even if they arrive at different times? How does she manage to remember Brownie meetings and swimming classes and the cornflakes for breakfast? Most housewives develop a highly complex sense of time-scale of the kind described in the chapter on Sensory Perception, though they would not necessarily put it in those words. Mothers also possess considerable emotional skills, because their job calls for it. The children will probably agree that they are usually patient and understanding, comforting when it is necessary, and sometimes strict. This kind of skill is important and usually overlooked; it plays a part unexpectedly in many other kinds of work. Who would the children rather be served by, the shop assistant who smiles and admires their shiny new boots, or the one who frowns and tells them to get their hands off the counter? The children can continue to discuss all the abilities required in other kinds of work, the work of their dinner-ladies, of policemen, the gardeners in the park, or of their own mothers and fathers outside the home. They will learn a lot about the community.

Work is a two-sided mirror, reflecting both the nature of the individual and the nature of society. The needs of one are met by satisfying the needs of the other, although there are areas of conflict. The children will have learnt something of this duality already, because they will be aware of how they depend on other people. It does not take much imagination to see what would happen if the dustman didn't come, or mum didn't bother to get the evening meal. Older children can take a more perceptive look at the needs of the individual. It is true that the dinner-lady ensures that the children are fed, and by doing so earns money for herself and her family. There is more to it than that, though, because work gives people satisfaction and dignity. I remember a dinner-lady who appeared on television. She had lost her job, due to a cut-back in local expenditure, but she was continuing to work, at a much reduced salary, in a scheme run by the parents, just, as she put it, 'for the satisfaction.' The children themselves will know of grandparents and, sadly, others too who have no paid work but who still determinedly busy themselves.

Eight- and nine-year-olds can build up a library of tape recordings, allowing people to say what they feel about their work. In doing so, they will be building up an important investigative method in geography. Skills we have mentioned; satisfaction comes to people in sometimes unexpected ways. The money earned is important, but it is not the only thing that counts. I remember an interview with a man who spent his life washing up dirty dishes in a hamburger stall. He thought it very important work indeed, explaining that if he did not do it properly, many people would be ill. He was content. There was a story in a daily newspaper of a hospital porter, earning about half the average national wage. He felt he was underpaid, but he explained that he took most pride in cheering up elderly patients on their way in to the operating theatre. He had job satisfaction.

The children can investigate other aspects of people's working lives. What do they like best about their work and what do they dislike? They may be in for some surprises. One recent survey found that, for most people, the worst part of the day was actually getting to work, the travelling. On the other hand, some people enjoyed the journey, using it as a kind of no man's land between home and work, in which they could think their own thoughts and escape from both. Friends and colleagues are important at work; frequently the work itself is less important than the people one is working with; having 'good mates' matters. Some people find monotony, as at a factory bench, quite intolerable, while others cope with it easily. On one occasion I met a middle aged lady whose job it was to slip screws into holes in metal plates as they slid by on a conveyer belt. I thought it awful work, but she liked it, explaining that it left her mind free to plan her meals, her housework, her holidays and what she was giving everyone for Christmas.

Work provides a running commentary on the way in which society has evolved. As the needs of a community change, so old jobs disappear and new ones are created. What old jobs have disappeared from the children's own locality and what new ones have arrived? To take an example from a rural area, the ice-manufacturing industry of certain villages in Dartmoor died out at the turn of the century because other methods of preserving food were invented. Instead, townsfolk began to spend their holidays in Dartmoor, thus creating a new industry for the local people. On a national scale, the children will certainly have heard of the microchip and the computer. What skills are needed for this kind of work, and how will they affect people's lives?

Work also provides a commentary on the values of a community. The children can see this if they consider their own lives. They go to school by law, but in the eighteenth and nineteenth centuries children as young as four went to work, like adults, in the mines and factories. They still do in some parts of the world. In our society, we have removed children from such work for two reasons, firstly because work in an industrialised society is harmful to them, and, secondly, because some of it requires a high level of expertise. That is why the children are in school, both as protection from and as an apprenticeship to the adult world of work. They can find out all about the work children did in the past, ending their study by considering what they themselves aim to do in the future.

A more formal approach to work lies in the study of industry itself. Every industry, and this is taking it in the broadest sense of farming as well, has basically the same needs of a good site, capital, adequate transport, a reliable supply of labour and a market for its produce. Its success depends partly on geographical and partly on economic and human factors, so that, in considering an industry, the children will be exploring a region at many levels. As all industries, wherever they are, have the same requirements, the children will be building an inner geographical model that will take them beyond the confines of their own neighbourhood into the world at large.

A popular approach with children could be by means of games. Illustrated on page 204 is a diagram of a game, Industrial Ludo, which gives a vivid account of the trials and errors experienced by a firm (we will call it Riscie Ltd) as it struggles to set up a toy factory. The children can play the game in small groups. Another game could illustrate the ups and downs of Riscie Ltd in its first year of life, emphasising the importance of adequate capital, a labour supply and a market for its goods.

Homes and buildings, work and industry, the life of the community and the earth itself are all aspects of geography in the environment. In exploring them, the young child builds up environmental skills. He or she learns to perceive the environment in physical and spatial terms and to appreciate its many levels of existence. He does not necessarily have to go far afield in order to build up geographical concepts, for the school itself is a spatial area, a mini-environment, and a working community in its own right. Bill Pick, himself a teacher, has pointed out all the ways in which the children's own school can be used as a geographical resource.[99]

It is possible, for example, to carry out a traffic survey in school, examining the layout of corridors, halls and classrooms and ascertaining

Industrial Ludo

FACTORY BUILT!

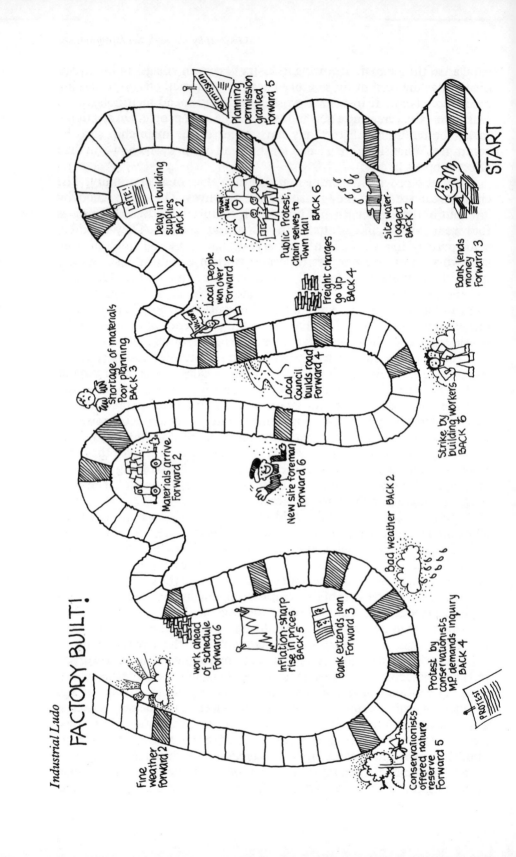

START

Bank lends money
Forward 3

Site water-logged
BACK 2

Public Protest; chain selves to Town Hall
BACK 6

Planning permission granted
Forward 5

Delay in building supplies
BACK 2

Local people won over
Forward 2

Shortage of materials Poor planning
BACK 3

Freight charges go up
BACK 4

Local Council builds road
Forward 4

New site foreman
Forward 6

Strike by building workers
BACK 6

Materials arrive
Forward 2

Bad weather BACK 2

work ahead of schedule
Forward 6

Inflation-sharp rise in prices
BACK 5

Bank extends loan
Forward 3

Protest by conservationists M.P. demands inquiry
BACK 4

Fine weather
Forward 2

Conservationists offered nature reserve
Forward 5

which are the busiest points. Diffusion can also be studied and a plan drawn up showing how water, electricity, gas and the children's dinners reach the school. Every school possesses a complex system of communications, not just in terms of bells and assemblies, but in the way in which decisions are taken. This aspect of school life may not be easy to investigate, but the children can at least try. Who influences the Head? Do the parents, the staff, and even the children have a say? Perhaps the decision-makers could be interviewed, or maybe a mole in the staffroom will indicate to the children fruitful lines of inquiry.

Valuably, the school offers scope for the use of some of the new approaches to geography. There will be problems that call for solution, because problems exist in any community. Are there areas of dangerous congestion in the corridors? Can traffic flow be improved, not just by shouting teachers, but by better planning, such as staggering break-times? There are opportunities for hypothesis-testing. Bill Pick suggests, 'Litter is found in areas where teachers don't go.' Is this true? Here is a hypothesis from me, to be verified, or not, by careful observation. 'More boys have second helpings than girls at dinnertime.' Imaginary situations involving the school can lead the children into role-playing and the contemplation of consequences. A coal-mine or a supermarket might be about to be built in the school grounds, or news might come that there is a subsidence in the road outside.

For teachers using the school itself as a geographical resource, there are several helpful books, for example, *Using the School's Surroundings* by Stephen Scoffham (Ward Lock, 1980).

Much of the emphasis in geography today lies on the accurate recording of findings. The varieties of stones dug up by the enthusiastic three-year-old, the profits made by Riscie Ltd and the traffic problems in the children's own school, all need to be depicted clearly in quantitative terms. This makes them manageable. The rest of this chapter will be devoted to ways of helping children become 'New Geographers'.

In many schools, studying the weather first introduces young children to the accurate recording of data. There are excellent reasons for this. The weather is an intriguing topic for the environmental study, partly because of its complexity and the number of influences at work. It provides children with almost infinite opportunities for the testing of hypotheses. Do holly bushes have more berries if it is going to be a hard winter? Can dogs hear thunder before we do? Is Granny's rheumatism worse in wet weather? Added to this, many of the phenomena associated with the weather are of perennial interest to young children. One such is the wind, which can be felt and heard, but never seen. Finally, the weather is always with us, and, in Britain at least, a great variety of it too.

The first exercises can be simple. Under five-year-olds can record, in words, whether it is a windy day by noting the clouds scudding across the sky and the washing flapping on the clothes-line. They can stick coloured windmills, of the kind bought for a few pence, in an open patch in the school grounds and record whether they whirl round slowly, fast or not at all.

The behaviour of plants, animals and insects gives many clues as to the weather. The children can watch for these. Most of them will know where a spider lives. Spiders seem to know when turbulent weather is on the way; they can be seen scurrying round their webs, tightening up the strands like the guy-ropes of a tent. In hot, dry weather, when there is no wind to wreck their work, spiders spin extra long threads.

Nearly all children pass trees on their way to and from school. If these show the under-sides of their leaves and so look lighter in appearance, it is a sign of rain. There is a scientific reason for this: the higher moisture content of the air softens the stalks, so that the leaves turn over.

A simple weather-vane, such as the one illustrated, can be constructed and will tell the children from which direction the wind is coming.

A weather-vane

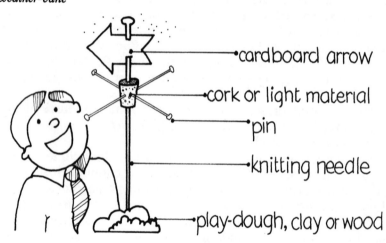

cardboard arrow

cork or light material

pin

knitting needle

play-dough, clay or wood

A wind is always named according to where it blows from; a south wind blows from the south, an east wind blows from the east, so the children will need to know the points of the compass. Either they can take out their weather-vanes and orientate them to point north, or the points of the compass can be indicated permanently in the school playground.

One Head of an infants' department has thought out a good way of enabling children to record the kind of weather associated with the various winds.[100] A strip of card is allocated to each point of the compass and every day the children note the direction of the wind and the kind of weather it has brought. Symbols denoting rain, sun, cloud, hail, or whatever is necessary are placed on the strips of card, so that, at the end of the week the children can see what kind of weather there has been, and how the wind and the weather are associated. They could continue their observations if they wanted a longterm picture. In the diagram opposite, the south wind brought the sun, while the west wind, blowing strongly, brought the rain.

There was also a rainbow, when, for a brief moment, the sun shone while it was still raining.

What kind of weather does the wind bring?

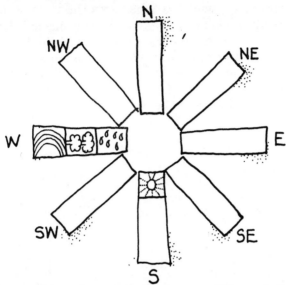

The south wind has brought the sun. The west wind has brought wind and rain.

As well as varying in direction winds vary in size. Some are many miles in breadth, while others measure only a few feet. Sometimes it is possible to measure the width of the wind. If it is blowing steadily, the children might be able to find a high vantage-point like the top of a hill or the top floor of the school, and notice that, although the leaves of a nearby tree are moving vigorously, those further off are quite still. The width of a small wind such as one that blows round a street corner or a large tree, might be

Measuring the width of the wind

measurable. Strips of tissue paper can be tied at regular intervals along a cane, which should then be held out into the wind. The points where the strips of paper are still, mark the boundary of the wind.

The children will be aware that the wind varies in its force. Sometimes it hardly moves anything, while on other days the washing flaps on the clothes-line, dust-bin lids bowl along the pavements and the family cat races madly about with his tail crooked. Young children can collect evidence of this. Children of about seven onwards are able to measure the force of the wind quite accurately. Julie Fitzpatrick, writing in *Child Education*, has devised a simple machine for this purpose, made from a cardboard box.[100] It is illustrated below.

Measuring the force of the wind

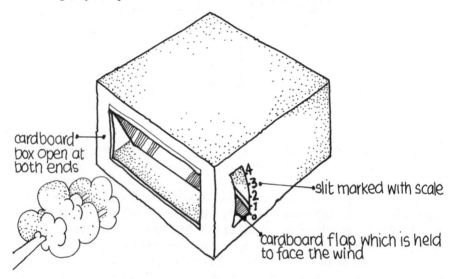

The hollow box is held up to face the wind. As the wind blows through it, the flap lifts to a point on the scale.

Alternatively, the force of the wind can be measured by making a windmill and counting the number of revolutions per minute as the wind blows. If the arms of the windmill are painted in different colours they are easier to count. The two experiments described above have the advantage of serving as an introduction to the Beaufort Scale.

Clouds, rain and thunderstorms are just as interesting as the wind, indeed, young children have a natural love of the rain. The first step is for them to measure the amount of rain that falls in any given period, by means of a rain gauge, as is illustrated opposite.

For accurate measurement, the area of the top of the funnel must be the same as that of the bottom of the bottle, and the bottom of the bottle must be flat. Older children can use the information they collect in order to construct a block graph, showing rainfall day by day.

A rain gauge

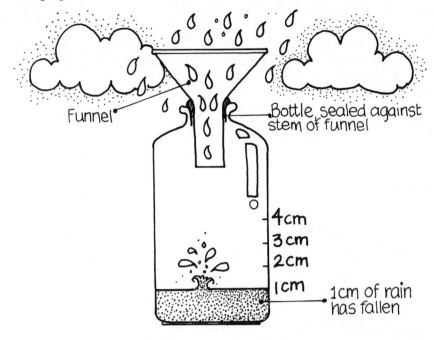

Funnel

Bottle sealed against stem of funnel

4cm
3cm
2cm
1cm

1cm of rain has fallen

We have all heard the ominous words 'An area of low pressure is moving over Britain'. We know that low pressure systems bring rain and often wind. Air pressure is measured by the barometer, in millibars; although some barometers are complicated, it is possible for the children to make a simple one for the classroom. The following suggestion is adapted from an idea by Rose Wyler (*The First Book of Weather*, Watts, 1960). A piece of balloon rubber is stretched tightly over the mouth of an empty jar, the bigger the better. This should be done on an average kind of day, when it is neither very wet nor gloriously sunny. A plastic straw, or a sliver of one, is then glued to the centre of the rubber. The jar may look empty, but the children should be reminded that it has air trapped inside it. When the air outside the jar becomes heavier than that inside, having less water vapour, it will press down on to the rubber, causing the straw to rise, indicating fine weather. If, on the other hand, the air outside the jar becomes lighter due to the pressure of water vapour, the rubber will rise slightly, causing the straw to drop down. This will indicate rain.

A card can be fixed behind the bottle, recording the varying positions of the straw and, as Rose Tyler suggests, if a thermometer is fixed nearby, its reading may be taken in conjunction with those of the barometer in order to forecast the weather. A reading of below 32°F or 0°C, coupled with a straw bending downwards, may herald snow. In the illustration (page 210), the straw has risen and the thermometer is 21°C, so good weather is on the way.

A simple barometer

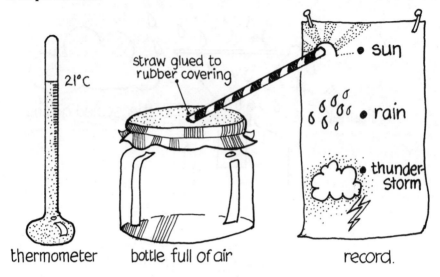

21°C

straw glued to
rubber covering

• sun

• rain

• thunder-
storm

thermometer   bottle full of air   record.

There are all kinds of natural barometers around us and young children will enjoy using these. They actually possess their own personal ones, in the form of their own heads of hair. Those of us who put our hair in curlers know, to our regret, that we soon lose our curls in damp weather. This is because humid conditions cause hair to stretch. Long, fair hair is the best indicator, because fair hair is finer than dark or red, so some children will need to borrow a strand or two from a blonde classmate to measure them under differing conditions. Other barometers can be searched for out of school. Seaweed and fircones show typical responses to humidity; the seaweed loses its hard, crackly texture and becomes soft and damp, while the fircone closes. The scarlet pimpernel is easy to find in both urban and rural areas. It opens its flowers when sunny weather is on the way and closes them in the rain. Animals and insects react as well. Cows huddle together in preparation for bad weather and stand with their tails to the wind; it is said that when the missel-thrush sings into the night from the top of a tree, it is a sign of rough winds and rain to come. Not for nothing is it known as the 'storm thrush'. Gnats perform their giddy dance in fine weather, while if there are no bees or wasps about in summer it is a sign of a storm. They have all sought shelter. Newts, tadpoles and fish will drop to the bottom of their pond if they sense bad weather on the way; when it is fine they swim near the surface. The children can make a list of these natural barometers and note their reliability. They can also try out some of the ancient sayings about the probability of rain. Two are: 'Red sky at night, shepherd's delight', and 'Rain before seven, fine before eleven'. In *Junior Education*, April 1980, Brian Philips,[101] who is a forecaster with the Meteorological Office, explains exactly why we sometimes see a red sky at night so loved by shepherds, and also how snow and hail are formed.

Sunshine is as much a part of the weather as wind and rain, but it receives much less attention in schools, probably because it is not so easy to measure and quantify. The under-fives can begin by considering what would happen if the sun disappeared. With some glee they might say that they would not be able to see without the electric lights on (and wouldn't be able to come to school). They might feel cold. It might dawn on some of the more far-sighted children that eventually there would be no food.

The sun is a source of heat and light, and this can be demonstrated to children. They will already know that they wear fewer clothes on sunny days and that in winter when there is less sun, the radiators are turned on in school. They can be shown that the nearer they are to a source of heat, the warmer they are and that the further away they are, the colder they will be. They can prove this by holding their hands an inch from the electric bulb of a switched-on table-lamp, then six inches away, then a foot. The lesson is that the nearer we are to the sun, whether this is because of the time of the day or the time of the year, the more warmth there is.

The children can see for themselves, by means of a few simple experiments, how the heat of the sun melts ice, helps to create winds and causes water to evaporate and so form the clouds that bring rain.

Once convinced of all this, a class of infants can see how it applies out of doors. If they take the temperature of the air in sunny and shady spots on a fine day, they will find that it is warmer in the sun. This finding needs to be discussed and expressed clearly in a simple sentence, 'It is warmer in the sun than in the shade', with some accompanying pictures. If the children take their observations further, by carrying them out at various times during the day, they will also notice that the temperature readings are higher in the middle of the day than at either end. They might even notice that these differences coincide with variations in the length of the shadows and with the position of the sun in the sky. It is warmest when the shadows are shortest and the sun is nearest to overhead. The children can record this by drawing pictures.

It is just possible that a child will ask *why* there is more warmth in the middle of the day and less in the morning and evening, and why the shadows change in length. The reason is that the earth revolves on its axis once every twenty-four hours; when our part of the earth faces the sun it is daytime; when it faces away from the sun it is night. Throughout the twenty-four hours the earth is turning, so that at dawn it is just coming round to the sun and at dusk it is turning away.

The older children can demonstrate this for themselves, by marking on something that is globe-shaped, like an orange or a tennis ball, an ink-spot which is called 'home'. If all the children take it in turns to revolve their tennis balls slowly in front of a lighted electric bulb, they will see that the sides facing the 'sun' are bathed in light. This represents daytime. As they turn their 'globes' round, the spot 'home' will move away from the sun until it is in darkness. This represents night. As the little globe continues to revolve, however, it comes round to face the sun again, so that, once more, it is daytime. The children can note that when it is 'night' on some parts of their tennis balls it is 'day' on others. They will be asleep when people in other parts of the world are awake. Many diaries provide charts giving the time of day in the capitals of the world when it is noon in Greenwich, London, and the children will enjoy looking these up.

There are some interesting points to consider here. The explanation must take children far beyond their own immediate personal experience, for, the persistent and intelligent ones might argue, they do not feel that they are spinning round and round, they are quite clearly standing still. The reason why they do not feel the earth revolving is that they have no means of perceiving it. In order to perceive movement, we must have some visual cues, and in this instance we do not possess them. The children may have experienced odd sensations when travelling by rail or motorway, on occasions when other vehicles have passed theirs and, for a moment, they were unable to tell whether they were moving or not. Momentarily, they lost their visual cues. We have none to tell us that we are revolving with the earth.

This is one reason why the environmental study is so valuable. It encourages children not merely to observe phenomena, but to think about them as well. It is safe to say that when children ask a question, they have already acquired enough insight to benefit from an honest explanation, even though full understanding comes later. Children will be interested to know that scientists have not always known about the movements of the earth. In medieval times, philosophers believed that the earth was the static centre of the universe and that the sun moved round it. That is why we still describe what happens in out-moded terms, referring to the rising and the setting of the sun when it is the earth that moves.

In carrying out their observations of the sun as a source of heat, the children will use the thermometer. They need plenty of opportunity to examine thermometers for themselves, holding them in in their hands and watching the mercury climb. It can be explained to them that some things are more responsive to heat than others, mercury being one, which is why it is used to indicate temperature. We have to have an instrument to record temperature because our own senses are inaccurate and can mislead us. The children can prove this to themselves by warming their hands on the radiator and then touching the window-sill. It will feel cold. Then they can hold their hands under the cold water tap and touch the window-sill again. This time it will feel warm.

From the age of about seven, children should be able to understand that there is nothing absolute about the thermometer and that there can be more than one scale. The two scales commonly used, Fahrenheit and Celsius (centigrade), are based on different zero points. (There is another, more recent scale, used only by scientists and named after the English physicist Kelvin. Its zero is the point at which all motion ceases and all atoms and molecules rest. It is written as OK and the zero point is equivalent to $-273°$ Celsius.)

Let us imagine now that the children, whether they be five or nine, are embarking on topics that will take them out of school. Even the youngest will need to measure tree trunks, bricks and buildings and all kinds of distances. Here are some suggestions.

Children under five, indeed all those who cannot yet handle a tape measure or read a map, can make use of their own bodies for small measurements. The length of a finger from its tip to its first joint is useful; it can help estimate the width of a flower or a footprint. The length of one finger or the span of a small hand is roughly the width of a brick and, when multiplied, can give an estimate of the height of a building. The width of outstretched arms, repeated along a wall, can measure its length. Useful for judging distance along the ground are the length of a foot and the number of strides it takes to cover the route. The children will probably arrive at slightly different estimates from each other. This is a good thing, for it will convince them of the need for an objective measurement and serve as an introduction to the tape measure and the ruler.

Older children can be more accurate. They can work out the length of their stride by averaging. To do this, they walk any distance, then divide that distance by the number of strides they have taken. This method is useful if the children cannot each have a tape measure, or if they are covering large areas.

Chris Puttick, a teacher, has made some useful suggestions for helping children to map an area.[102] He suggests that the children draw a free-hand sketch of the area first, noting essential distances. They should then agree on a scale; 1:8, 1:24, 1:42 are possibilities. They will be acquainted with the idea of scale through a familiarity with scale models. Before taking the actual measurements and compiling their maps, the children can draw up a conversion table. A calculator would help. Then they are ready to measure actual distances and compile their map.

Sometimes the children will need to work out widths that cannot easily be assessed by tape measure. Such would be the case if they were surveying a stretch of river and measuring its width at various points. The following method is based on the properties of the triangle; the steps are as follows:

(1) Sight an object, such as a tree or a building, on the opposite side of the bank to the one where you are standing. Call this A.

(2) Place a stick in the ground on your side of the river in line with object A. Call this point B.

(3) Walk along the bank in a straight line, at right-angles to B for any distance, let us suppose 50 metres, and put in another stick, C.

(4) Then walk on from C, half the distance between B and C, which is 25 metres in our example. Put in stick D.

(5) Walk back from D at right angles to the river until you are in a straight line with stick C and object A. Call this point E.

The distance from D to E is half the width of the river.

Estimating the width of a river

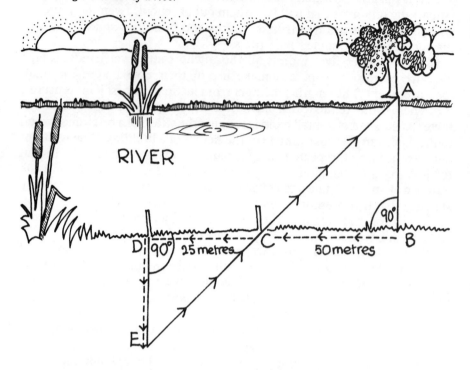

The height of a tall building or a tree can sometimes be measured on a sunny day by using the principle of ratio. A stick is planted in the ground and the shadow it casts is measured. Suppose the stick protrudes one metre above the ground and its shadow is two metres long. This gives a ration of 1 to 2, and it will be the same for lamp-posts, tower-blocks or oak trees, provided that their measurements are taken at the same time of day as those of the stick. Their heights, too, can then be calculated.

Another method of measuring the height of an inconvenient object is, like that of calculating the width of the river just mentioned, based on the properties of the triangle. This time we will imagine that the children are trying to work out the height of a tall building, as illustrated opposite. Metric measurements are given again, but it should be noted that children really need to master the old imperial system because it is still widely used. It is useful to know that one metre is equivalent to 39 inches.

(1) The top of the building is point A, while the bottom is point B.
(2) Walk from point B at right angles to the building in a straight line, for any distance, for example 9 metres. Put a stick in the ground, say 2 metres high, and call this point C.
(3) Walk on in the same straight line until, lying on the ground, you can see the top of the stick and the top of the building in a straight line, in this case 3 metres. Call this point E.

Measuring the height of a tall building

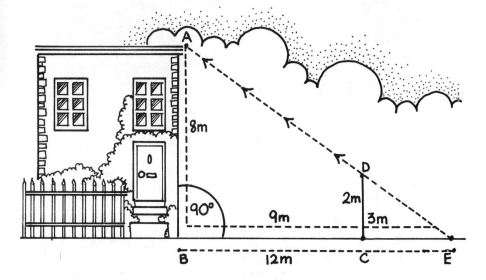

(4) The ratio of the sides of the small triangle, CD to CE, is the same as the ratio of the sides of the larger triangle, AB to BE.

CD is ⅔ of CE

∴ AB is ⅔ of BE

⅔ of 12 metres is 8 metres.

∴ The height of the building is 8 metres.

Often there is a simpler method, which the younger children can use. If they can calculate the height of one floor of the building, perhaps by measuring a brick and then counting how many rows there are to the first window-sill, they can then estimate the height of the whole block by means of easy multiplication.

When children are collecting data, they will find it much easier to think about if it is clearly portrayed. This is the essential aim of all charts, graphs and pictograms; they are thinking aids. In many cases, symbols are used to represent data because they clarify a situation. For example, if a group of five-year-olds have measured the height of everyone in the class, it is simplest to represent boys and girls by means of pictograms, as overleaf. Older boys and girls will be concerned with larger quantities. They may count the numbers of men and women engaged in various tasks in a factory, or the goods lorries along a stretch of road, or the age-groups posting letters in a pillar-box. They can save themselves a lot of counting by letting each pictogram represent 10 or 50 or 100 people. If cats and dogs were being studied and a whole pictogram represented 10 of either, five would be depicted as in the diagram.

A pie-chart is a popular way of portraying information, or data, graphically. Suppose a class of eight-year-olds is analysing all the kinds of

Pictograms

Boy   Five cats   Girl   Five dogs

shops that do business in the local High Street. They have drawn up the following list:

Shops	Numbers	
Bakers	3	
Butchers	3	
Supermarket	1	
Drapers	2	
Green grocers	4	
Fish-mongers	2	
Freezer centre	1	
Woolworth	1	
Boutique	1	
Take-aways	2	Total = 20

The full circle of 360° is to represent 20 shops in all, so in order to obtain the proportion of the pie each kind of shop should be allotted, the children have to make the relevant simple calculations, as below.

Shops			Proportion of the pie, or circle
Bakers	$\frac{3}{20} \times 360°$	=	54°
Butchers	$\frac{3}{20} \times 360°$	=	54°
Supermarket	$\frac{1}{20} \times 360°$	=	18°
Drapers	$\frac{2}{20} \times 360°$	=	36°

Shops			Proportion of the pie, or circle
Green grocers	$\frac{4}{20} \times 360°$	=	72°
Fish-mongers	$\frac{2}{20} \times 360°$	=	36°
Freezer centre	$\frac{1}{20} \times 360°$	=	18°
Woolworth	$\frac{1}{20} \times 360°$	=	18°
Boutique	$\frac{1}{20} \times 360°$	=	18°
Take-aways	$\frac{2}{20} \times 360°$	=	36°
		Total	360°

These proportions can then be portrayed on the chart, as below, which, as its name suggests, look just like a pie that has been divided up ready for eating.

The shops in the High Street

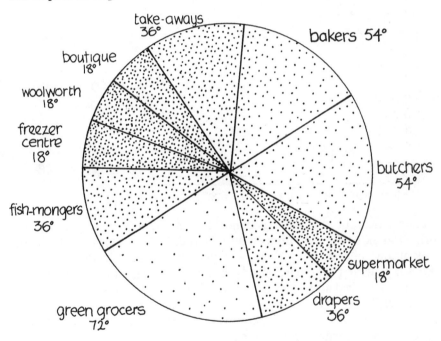

The drawing of the pie-chart should not be the end of the story. The interesting part comes in the interpretation. This High Street is plainly an amalgam of old and new, for it has shops of the old kind, like bakers and green grocers, and also some of the new, trendy shops, like boutiques, take-aways and a freezer centre. Why do the children think these have grown up? The reasons will be connected with the life-style of the community. There are also hints as to further lines of investigation that could be carried out. Counting the shops does not give a reliable indication of which commodities are most popular with shoppers, because certain shops sell the same kinds of goods. The bakers, Woolworth, the freezer centre and the supermarket all sell bread, for instance. If the children want to find out what the local people buy, can they think of a way of doing this?

Equally useful for recording and analysing data are charts and graphs. Charts and graphs have two axes; the vertical axis is used to denote the frequency of the data and so is sometimes referred to as ordinal. A bar-chart, block graph, is used to record quantities, like the respective weights of the carrots, cabbages and potatoes the green grocer sells each week, or the amount of food the children leave on their plates after school dinner. It is also a popular way of recording rainfall. Below is a bar-chart recording rainfall over the space of a week.

A bar-chart recording rainfall

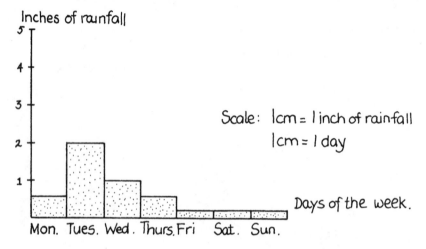

The vertical, or ordinal, axis denotes the amount of rain in inches; the horizontal axis tells the children on which day of the week it fell. In the week under observation, there was very heavy rain from Monday to Thursday, which was particularly bad on Tuesday, but after that the depression cleared and there were three fine days.

If the children were recording the temperature at various times during the day they would use a graph. Opposite is a graph depicting thermometer readings taken during a day in summer.

On this summer's day, it was warm but heavy cloud periodically obscured the sun. The temperature tended to rise steadily, though falling between 11 a.m. and 12 noon and between 2 p.m. and 3 p.m. It should be noted that a dotted line is used in this graph, because the rate of increase or decrease between consecutive readings is not constant. If the relationship between consecutive readings is constant, a continuous line is used. This would be the case if the children were plotting the time it would take for a lorry to cover a given distance at a steady speed, as was illustrated in the chapter on Mathematics.

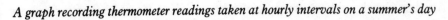

A graph recording thermometer readings taken at hourly intervals on a summer's day

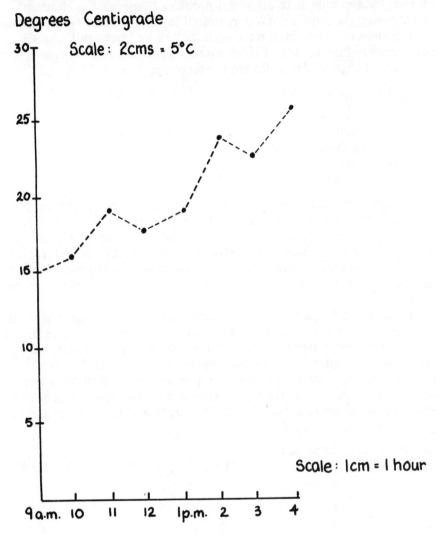

Degrees Centigrade

Scale: 2cms = 5°C

Scale: 1cm = 1 hour

Charts and graphs help the children to describe what they have observed accurately. A short step from this is to be able to analyse their observations carefully. They can be helped towards this by introducing them to the tools of very simple statistics. As far as I know, these are not taught at the moment to children in junior schools, but they should be, as they give great insight into the affairs of everyday life and are also fun to use. Statistics represent a way of thinking about the environment. As will be seen, this kind of thinking is well within the grasp of a nine-year-old.

One of the most versatile and easy statistics is Chi square, pronounced 'Kye square'. The symbol for it is χ^2, χ being a letter of the Greek alphabet. Most of the symbols and terms used in statistics are borrowed from the

Ancient Greeks, who were great mathematicians. How χ^2 works can best be seen by applying it to an actual problem. Suppose the children are investigating the number of letters posted in various pillar-boxes in their town between certain times on a weekday. As we know, pillar-boxes are popular with children. On a Friday afternoon two children were allotted to each pillar-box, and they collected the following data:

Location of pillar-boxes	Letters posted	
On outskirts of town	4	
Outside a factory	15	
In centre of shops and offices	18	
On a council estate	10	
At the side of a Common	3	Total = 50

The test of chi square investigates whether the differences observed in the numbers of letters posted in the various boxes are due to chance. It does this by assuming, as is reasonable, that all else being equal, we would expect all the pillar-boxes to receive the same number of letters. The expected frequencies, or numbers of letters posted in each box, would in this case be ten (the total divided by the number of pillar-boxes, which is five).

The expected frequencies, ten in each case, are then compared to the actual, or observed frequencies, represented by the columns headed E and O. The differences between the expected and observed frequencies are calculated and squared, in the columns headed $O - E$ and $(O - E)^2$. In squaring, it does not matter whether plus or minus quantities are involved. The resulting figures are then divided by the expected frequency, ten, as in the column headed $(O - E)^2/E$. The total of this column gives us χ^2. We can set it out as below.

Observed frequencies O	Expected frequencies E	$O - E$	$(O - E)^2$	$(O - E)^2/E$
4	10	−6	36	3.6
15	10	5	25	2.5
18	10	8	64	6.4
10	10	0	0	0.0
3	10	−7	49	4.9
				$\chi^2 = \underline{17.4}$

In order to find out whether the differences in the frequencies are due to chance or not, that is, whether χ^2 is statistically significant, we have to consult some tables. Opposite is reproduced the distribution of χ^2 which is given on page 123 of A. C. Crocker's book *Statistics for the Teacher* (1968, 1981). The significance levels, given in italic figures at the top of the columns, are those of 0.05 and 0.01. If a χ^2 is significant at the 0.05

level, it means that there are five possibilities in a hundred of that particular result being due to chance; if the χ^2 is significant at the 0.01 level, it means that there is only one possibility in a hundred of the result being due to chance. These possibilities, although they exist, are so remote that it is generally accepted that the results obtained must be due to other factors and that these must be sought.

Distribution of χ^2
(Abridged from KELLAWAY, F. W. (ed.) (1968) *Penguin-Honeywell Book of Tables*. Harmondsworth: Penguin.)

Degrees of freedom	0.05	0.01	Degrees of freedom	0.05	0.01
1	3.84	6.63	16	26.30	32.00
2	5.99	9.21	17	27.59	33.41
3	7.81	11.34	18	28.87	34.81
4	9.49	13.28	19	30.14	36.19
5	11.07	15.09	20	31.41	37.57
6	12.59	16.81	21	32.67	38.93
7	14.07	18.48	22	33.92	40.29
8	15.5	20.09	23	35.17	41.64
9	16.9	21.67	24	36.42	42.98
10	18.31	23.21	25	37.65	44.31
11	19.68	24.72	26	38.89	45.64
12	21.03	26.22	27	40.11	46.96
13	22.36	27.69	28	41.34	48.28
14	23.68	29.14	29	42.56	49.59
15	25.00	30.58	30	43.77	50.89

One or two observations are worth considering. The first is that the tables denote *statistical* significance. They are worked out by mathematicians and give us a much tighter definition of significance than that which may exist in our own minds. To us, at first sight, a result may look highly significant, but when it is subjected to a statistical test it may turn out not to be. The reverse can also be true. This means that when a teacher, or the children, use a simple statistical analysis they have a powerful and accurate tool for exploring the environment.

Another thing to remember is that there is nothing magic about levels of significance. The 0.05 and 0.01 levels are accepted as useful in most research, but in other areas, particularly in medical research, much lower levels are often accepted. Even if there are ten possibilities in a hundred that a result indicating that a substance can cause cancer in human beings is due to chance, it is still worth investigating further.

The column on the extreme left of the table is headed 'degrees of freedom'. Degrees of freedom denote the least number of expected values we must have before we deduce the remaining one. In the observations of the pillar-boxes, five frequencies have been collected, 4, 15, 18, 10 and 3. Keeping the total of 50, if we know the first four numbers we can deduce the fifth. To put it another way, the first four numbers can be any but the fifth is restricted. We therefore have four degrees of freedom. When χ^2 is used in this way, the degrees of freedom always equal the number of categories minus one. If six pillar-boxes had been observed, there would have been five degrees of freedom, if there had been eight, degrees of freedom would have numbered seven.

Returning to the table, we can now see whether our χ^2 of 17.4 is statistically significant or not. Looking along the values for four degrees of freedom (df), we find that the χ^2 *exceeds* the value under the 0.01 column. It therefore is significant at the 0.01 level, there being only one chance in a hundred that this result is due to chance. A result is accepted as significant if the χ^2 equals or exceeds the value given in the appropriate column. Our result can be written:

With $df = 4$, $\chi^2 = 17.4$, $p < 0.01$.

$<$ means 'less than'; $>$ denotes 'greater than'.

The children have therefore discovered that there are significant differences between the numbers of letters posted on a Friday afternoon in the various pillar-boxes. Then they come to the really interesting bit, trying to explain why. Could the larger number of letters posted in the box near the shops and offices be due to the clerical staff sending off business letters? Is the low number of letters posted in the box near the Common due to the fact that there are not many houses there? Who posted the letters on the housing estate? Was it old age pensioners or mums who are in all day? There are many possibilities and the findings open up new avenues of exploration.

Chi square is well within the abilities of most nine-year-olds; it provides them with an accurate, clear method of assessing phenomena in the environment, and it is very versatile. The children could use it to explore their own school. They could count the numbers of people using the various corridors and discover whether some are significantly more crowded than others. If so, there may be a pressing need for re-arranging the classrooms, or staggering playtimes. Going farther afield, the data collected could refer to the types of farms in the locality, or the kinds of trees growing there, or the favourite haunts of squirrels. Are there significantly more fir trees found on sandy soil than on heavy clay? Do the hungry squirrels favour one particular garden or site?

Simple statistics can be applied by the children in most subject areas. There are obvious uses in the field of mathematics; in history, chi square could also be used in a topic like the study of a graveyard. It could, for example, reveal which age-groups were most vulnerable to death in the past, or whether women tended to live longer than men. The children can also analyse their own tastes, preferences and life-styles, exploring such areas as the most popular television programmes, the times everybody goes to bed and their favourite shops. Once they are in possession of such a tool, a new dimension is added to their exploration of the environment.

Some methods of statistical analysis are very simple, like chi square, while others are highly complex, but behind them all lies a way of thinking. This way of thinking is logical, explorative and surprisingly new, dating, at the earliest, from the last couple of hundred years. It is based on certain assumptions and discoveries made about the universe, about the laws which govern our earth and the design of life within it. One of the most important discoveries was that many distributions, where they vary about a mean, or average, all follow a similar pattern. A good example is that of the heights of the children in a class. If they measure themselves, some will be short, most will be average, and a few will be very tall. The distribution falls into what is known as the normal curve; a diagram of it is reproduced opposite, again from A. C. Crocker's book.

The normal curve

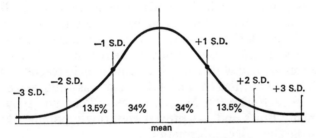

The same is true of all sorts of other phenomena. If the class records the number of seconds it takes each of them to run round the school playground, or the size of their feet, they will find that these distributions, too, fall into a normal curve. Statistical analysis is based on this; it reflects a fact of life that most of us accept without pondering over unduly, that most of us are average while a few of us are exceptional.

As they work farther afield, the children will have to consider one or two problems. One concerns sampling. Suppose they intend, for some purpose, to examine all the farms in their county. It may well be impossible to visit every single one, so what will they do in order to obtain a representative sample? There are various possibilities. They can draw up a list and take, say, every fourth farm to study (regular sampling); they might decide that the farms fall into various types and take so many from each (stratified sampling); or they may choose random sampling, in which case they will give each farm a number, mix all the numbers in a hat and draw so many out. They can decide for themselves on the best method, after discussion.

A source of perennial and fruitful discussion is that of the relationship between cause and effect. It is particularly valuable for children to start thinking about this, because it is round about eight years of age that they come naturally to consider causation in the world at large. The point is that when things go together they do not necessarily cause each other, or, to put it another way, correlation does not denote causation. There is a good example of this, once more, in the study of the gravestones the children might have carried out as part of their environmental history. Again it concerns the fact that women, on average, have always tended to live longer than men, a matter that has exercised doctors, statisticians and sociologists for years. It has often been assumed that the difference in life-span is sex-based. Yet very recently, one line of research has indicated that women may live longer simply because they are smaller. Studies of both men and women suggest that sheer size militates against long life. The difference in life-span may be, at least in part, not sex-based but size-based. Sometimes a correlation may be seen to exist but has no rational explanation at all. Such is the one between the number of apples imported into Great Britain and the number of divorces over the years.[103] Eating imported apples does not make one more prone to divorce.

Statistical analysis is a new area both for young children and for most of their teachers, but it is worthwhile and interesting. It is not all that difficult either, provided that one refuses to be put off by the mathematical formulae and abstract terminology. A. C. Crocker's invaluable book, *Statistics for the Teacher*, has already been recommended; it is written simply, engagingly and with a genuine desire to help teachers who are not mathematicians. The third edition of this book was published by NFER in 1981. *Facts from Figures* by M. J. Moroney (Penguin, 1969) has been reprinted many times and has proved enduringly popular. His book is witty, readable and full of information.

The environmental study in geography is not limited to any locality, or to any one region. It is basically, like all the disciplines, about thinking. Most of the phenomena observed in the immediate environment cannot be understood without reference to what lies far beyond them. To refer once more to the remark made at the beginning of this chapter by Tony Land, the mere counting of vehicles on the road tells us very little about them. The exercise can, however, help children to build up a theoretical model of how transport operates, as the observation of their own homes and communities can help them build up a model of homes as they exist in human communities throughout the world, and as a study of the local factory invokes a paradigm of the industrial process wherever it is found.

Moreover, because it is possible to conceptualise any region in numerous diverse ways, from the soil that the children delve in to the weather that prevails, from the houses in which people live to the work that they do, the environmental study can lead them to some understanding of the complexities of human life.

8
Creativity through the Environment

At first sight, creativity would seem to be the quality of the human mind that is the least accessible to environmental influences, being highly personal, and unseen as to the way in which it operates. Nothing, though, is further from the truth. Creativity is like the rainbow, reflecting all the colours of human activity and adding a new dimension to life.

On the one hand, all the qualities of the personality are environmental, although they have rarely been considered in this light. Intelligence, being intrinsically the quality with which we cope with the problems that the environment presents to us, solves those problems and at the same time modifies our surroundings to suit ourselves. At the other end of the scale, the length of our legs and the keenness of our eyes are very much environmental qualities, dictating the extent and moulding the sensory characteristics of our world. Further, all the states of mind that we experience, and all our traits of character, our feelings of self-confidence, inner conflict, happiness or gloom, create our environment for us.

On the other hand, every aspect of the environment exerts an influence on the personality. Some of these aspects have been identified, particularly those social influences affecting childhood, such as size of family, order of birth and social class. Teaching and schools exert a powerful influence on children. Other aspects have received very little attention, especially those which act on inner mental qualities, of which creativity is the most important and the most ignored. Interest in creativity was only awakened in the 1960s and most of the relevant studies have been based in America.

A consideration of creativity demonstrates the very delicate interaction that continually operates between the individual and the environment in which he or she lives; as such it is vital to our study. The basic question to ask, as teachers, is by what means creativity in young children can be encouraged. One thing is certain; creativity cannot form part of an environmental study in the same way that mathematics, history and geography can. The subject disciplines select certain aspects of the environment only for investigation, whereas creativity acts on them all. It is, therefore, a matter of evolving general, rather than particular, teaching strategies. It is necessary to consider some of the characteristics of creativity first.

What is creativity? There are two methods of definition. Creativity can be defined as a concept, which is at present vague and ill-defined, or it can be described operationally, which involves identifying creative individuals by means of their performances on various tasks and thus building up a working definition. Psychologists have adopted the latter method for the last twenty years. From our point of view, it is important to consider the concept first, in order to avoid the danger of defining creativity too narrowly and so omitting vital areas, the kind we are concerned with, from our thinking.

Creativity implies the making of something new and unique, that is, a transformation of the environment. More often than not, it is the intellectual and emotional dimensions of the environment that are transformed. It may be that a new word has been found, or a new way of looking at familiar surroundings. This uniqueness needs to be carefully examined, because it is rare indeed that anything entirely new is created. Victor Lee, in his contribution to the excellent account of creativity published by the Open University, gives an interesting example of a child's original thinking.[104] He quotes the words of a four-year-old who described his bath water as 'devil deep'. This is a striking and original description, of a freshness not unusual in young children. The words, however, are built from known associations; devils live deep under the earth, and maybe the unease with which we think about them was associated in the mind of this little boy with the momentary insecurity of stepping into his bathwater. So he built up a new idea from what he knew already. This is an important point, because it implies that the creative act may consist, in part, of forging new combinations of what is already known. It also indicates something of the relationship between environmental influences and creativity. Sheer richness and abundance of experience must be important, as well as the freedom and self-confidence to make good use of them. That little boy plainly had both, as well as a cultural background that had made him familiar with the power of words. There are implications for the teacher here.

Another characteristic of the uniqueness of the creative art is that it may result in the discovery of a new perspective. The outcome can be dramatic, sometimes shattering. Such an event occurred when Freud decided to accept the apparently meaningless statements of his patients as rational and significant, to them at any rate. As a result, he built up an entirely new philosophy of the human psyche. On a more concrete level, but no less stupendous in its repercussions, Richard Arkwright 'invented' the spinning-jenny by realising that the spinning-wheel could be made to work more efficiently if it were turned over on its side. Here again, one can note how intimate familiarity with the material that was to be transformed played a part. Freud listened to his patients; Arkwright watched his wife spin for many hours before their respective solutions finally dawned on them. One can note also the importance of certain mental qualities in the creative act. There is an awareness of all the possibilities inherent in a situation and perhaps an unconscious analysis of them, though this is often intuitive. The creative individual must certainly have the kind of mind that is uncluttered by the pre-conceived notions that generally impede insight. Such was the clarity of Alexander Fleming, when he did not dismiss the green mould left on the plate in his laboratory as the annoying outcome of his laboratory boy's careless washing up, but recognised it as something new. It proved to be penicillin. Perhaps the moral for the teacher is that he or she should not teach too authoritatively, too forcefully or too dogmatically. There should always be room left for doubt, for argument and the consideration of new possibilities.

However novel and unique the creative art may be, it is always rooted firmly in reality. It usually enlarges and expands that reality. The creative person is usually the one who opens the eyes of the rest of us, but once she (he) has done so, we know perfectly well what she means, and often feel rather surprised that we have not seen it all before. Novel the results of her endeavours might be, but they are rooted in what is relevant and real, and her thinking operates within the broad perspective of human rationality. I had a neighbour who decided to go without shoes, but to polish her feet with shoe polish instead. Those living near her certainly found this a novel idea, though oddly disturbing. Thinking it over, it is possible to see that she, like the little boy quoted by Victor Lee, was building up a new concept from what she knew already, like the connection between shoe-polish and shoes. Sadly, though, her idea opened up no vision, uncovered no deeper meaning for the rest of us, because it bore no relation to rational human experience. The thinking of the four-year-old, as well as that of Sigmund Freud, Richard Arkwright and Alexander Fleming, was relevant to the whole human world; my neighbour's thinking began and ended with her own feet.

It is characteristic of creativity that it imparts new meaning to the environment. This, of course, has a significance for teaching strategy. It is incumbent upon the teacher of young children to teach well, because it is largely through good teaching, whatever the subject or approach, that the nature of rational thought is brought home to them.

The creative act is unique, the result of a very delicate interaction between the individual and the environment. Creativity is not the possession of certain supremely gifted individuals, but is in all of us. The simplest everyday activity requires its exercise. Reading, for example, is a highly creative activity, quite meaningless unless the reader mentally transforms the written word. Even going for a walk does not consist merely of repetitively placing one foot in front of another, it means going out carrying in our own minds a vision of the whole exercise. Unless we can form and sustain such a vision there is no point in leaving the house in the first place. Exactly the same process applies to more complex activities, like writing a story, building a house, or setting up a new business. Creativity is not a one-off activity, it is a vital human endowment, bound up with intelligence and our strategies for everyday living.

This general characteristic, which permeates the ordinary lives of both children and adults, is sometimes heightened into what is recognised by others as a creative act. This occurs when an individual solves a problem.

It may be an artistic problem, one that he has deliberately posed for himself, involving the putting together of many elements in order to say something new; it may concern mechanics or engineering, as with those nineteenth century shipbuilders who decided, in the face of all common sense, that iron ships were possible; it may be a problem of business organisation. Whatever it is, the problem is always there and the solution of it is intrinsic to the creative process. From this follows another characteristic of the creative act. It always imposes order on the environment. That is why it is so pleasing to the rest of us: unity has been forged from diversity, and conscious design can be seen shining through what has hitherto been meaningless.

It is characteristic of the creative act that it is recognised as such by others. Although unique and highly personal to the individual, it requires social recognition and this indicates the existence of subtle and complex lines of communication between the creative person and his, or her, cultural milieu. Sometimes it happens that an inventive genius labours unrecognised for years, because the lines of communication are not there. He can be acclaimed, somewhat to his surprise, some time later, when society is ready for him. Countless original ideas must have been lost in the past. The creative act would not be performed were the creative person not the creature of his own culture; he might wear a long beard and live a dissolute life in the imagination of the rest of us, but he is in touch with society where it really matters.

We can note also that our society places more value on certain kinds of creative act than it does on others, which is sad. If asked to describe a creative person, most people would think of a poet or a painter; few would mention a mechanic. Teachers should avoid this mental strait-jacket.

Creativity takes many forms, and it may well be the case that the creativity of children differs from that of adults. Adults, for example, place a heavy emphasis on verbal creativeness, yet the imaginations of young children may operate differently. Their creativity can involve physical movement, handling things and games. They are endlessly inventive in games. I once watched an intriguing game being played between a girl of four and a boy of seven. Basically it consisted of taking it in turns to arrange little piles of bricks, which had been placed in long rows, into patterns. The patterns were three-dimensional and the rows could be moved along, so the game was complicated. After a time I enquired who had won. I was told, 'Nobody wins; you just do it as well as you can.' I was rightly rebuked. Their game, with its emphasis on design and excellence and its absence of competitiveness, was much more interesting than the kind adults continually invent (and sell), for them.

Often also, children choose unexpected mediums for their creativity. All teachers are aware of this. A class of four year olds were recently equipped in their classroom for painting. Dressed in a waterproof apron in front of his carefully arranged easel, one young boy was working away with extreme concentration. He was painting his paint brush. Not far away were two of his classmates, similarly prepared by a conscientious teacher and also faced with blank sheets of paper. They were painting each other.

Bearing in mind the characteristics of creativity and the milieu in which it operates, it is possible to perceive the kind of teaching strategy needed to encourage its development in young children. Young children need to be introduced to as rich and varied an environment as possible, because the outside world presents them with an unmatched abundance of materials, possibilities and problems, all of which are essential to the creative process. They are essential as models; for example, the intricacies of design and structure in flowers, insects and snowflakes are far beyond anything that could be devised by a single human mind. Many artists and scientists have drawn inspiration from such phenomena. These materials also provide the means of expression that creativity must seek for itself. Then the problems of the human environment, such as shopping, travelling and sheer living, call for creative solutions to which children readily respond. Apart from being a powerful stimulus to thinking and providing an urgent incentive to seek new perspectives, the everyday environment has the advantage of being familiar. It is surely true that the unique is not created out of the blue, but emerges step by step from what is already known. Originality and courage may be facets of the creative mind, but so also is a deep and intuitive knowledge of the material to hand. This knowledge is only won through continual activity and experiment. Children therefore need the opportunity to explore and to think in ways congenial and natural to them, and the time and freedom to do so. Their self-confidence should be encouraged, which, in practice, means that the harassed teacher surrounded by forty children should resist the impulse to brush aside the stumblingly expressed and apparently irrelevant idea put forward by a six-year-old.

Creativity is set in the general context of human rationality, human culture and human society. All these are reflected in the academic disciplines which underlie our culture. It follows, as has already been pointed out, that sheer good teaching encourages creativity, because young children are first introduced to this understanding through their parents and teachers.

A general teaching strategy for encouraging creativity in young children is to introduce them to every aspect of the environment, to teach well and coherently but open-endedly, leaving plenty of time for the children's own experimenting, and bolstering up of their self-confidence.

We come now to consider operational definitions of creativity. This is a different area from the considerations of creativity as a concept tentatively discussed above, because operational definitions aim simply at identifying those individuals who are thought to be creative. This is achieved by describing their characteristics. This kind of research does not, at the moment, throw much light on the broad aspects mentioned so far, but it is interesting, and it has a relevance to the kind of situations teachers face in the classroom. Moreover, it indicates that environmental influences on creativity in the child are so broad and at the same time, so subtle, as to suggest the need for a new conceptualisation of the environment.

Tests of creativity have their limitations. They rely heavily, for example, on verbal ability, which means that other forms of creativity, particularly those which one suspects exist in young children, are omitted. In fact, most studies are concerned with children over ten. Another point is that, when dealing with such a broad aspect of the personality, it is very difficult to distinguish cause and effect. E. Paul Torrance, one of the pioneers in this field, investigated the personality characteristics of 150 creative children in the USA.[105] Many of these children were over-active, annoying, absent-minded and 'loners', the kind of children it must be said, that one dreads to meet in the classroom. However, were these personality traits the necessary conditions for creativity, were they the result of an overwhelming absorption in one kind of activity, or were they completely irrelevant? It is impossible to tell. Most of us know people who are all these things but who are not creative.

Investigations suggest that all kinds of environmental factors exert a potent influence on creativity in the individual. Anne Roe, enquiring into the personalities of a number of creative scientists, found that a high percentage of them were first-born children, a significant proportion had lost a parent before the age of ten or at adolescence, and many of them were both non-church-goers and were rebellious of family ties.[106] This hints that emotional trauma may play a part in creativity. There seems also a possibility, from the work of other psychologists, that the creative person has had a particular relationship with his or her parent, usually the mother.

There is considerable disagreement as to how far creativity and intelligence in children go hand in hand. This is an important matter for teachers, who would like to know whether, in creating conditions that maximise intelligence in their children, they are at the same time encouraging them to be creative. Some research, as for example by Getzels and Jackson, indicates that creativity and research are not separable characteristics in children,[107] while other work, such as that by Wallach, Kogan who used new tests of creativity, has demonstrated that there is a quite clear separation.[108] Significantly, both studies were concerned with children over ten. It may be that, while a certain level of intelligence is required, beyond that, creativity and intelligence are separate qualities of the personality in a child. With children of average and below average intelligence, there seems to be no such distinction. With very young children there is no firm answer, but it is fairly safe to assume that what stimulates their intelligence will also encourage creativity.

A good deal of interesting research leads us to believe that creativity in children is a complex quality. J. P. Guilford has suggested that flexibility, that is, freedom from rigidity of thinking, and originality are significant characteristics of the creative mind. He has devised tests for these children and also for fluency and the ability to elaborate.[109]

E. Paul Torrance, whose pioneering work has already been mentioned, has listed twenty-one typical behaviours of creative children, after analysing descriptions given of these children by their parents. Many of them were poorly adjusted in school; they tended to show an annoying curiosity; they were absent-minded; humorous and inclined to day-dream. Often they were thought rather peculiar by the other children and tended to work by themselves. Frequently, they showed an early inclination to specialise in a particular field, such as science and music.

Other psychologists have described the creative personality as high in self-confidence and self-approval and also, if male, in femininity. Interestingly, the same qualities were seen as characteristics of both creative children and creative adults, so it may be that some aspects of creativity at least, manifest themselves early in life and persist throughout.

The exact significance of personality traits associated with the creative individual remain unclear. Determination, noted by Anne Roe, might be a pre-condition for the development of an originality that might otherwise remain quiescent; so might self-confidence. A child might be rebellious because he (she) can see new ways of doing things, or rebellious by nature anyway and so pushed into divergent thinking.

Although research is still in its infancy, most teachers will recognise what has been described above. We have met the young girl who persists in reading by herself on a subject nobody else is interested in, at a time when she should be doing something else; we are acquainted with the boy who tries to interest his classmates in weird and complex games of his own invention, fails to do so and henceforth retires into a shell. Sometimes intuition tells us that these children have a precious quality that transcends the normal. What can we do to help them? What kind of classroom environment do they need?

Their needs go beyond those of other children. Their creativity is already present; in any case the influences that have brought it about lie way beyond the control of the teacher, or of anyone else for that matter. Nobody would conceivably want to orphan a child, or make it lonely, or enhance the femininity of a young boy, in order to encourage him to be creative. Nor is it easy to 'channel' traits of personality, as some psychologists have suggested. One cannot channel absent-mindedness, or individual peculiarities, or rudeness. What the teacher can do is to make the lives of these children easier.

Creative children need considerable tolerance. If possible they should be allowed to work by themselves when they want to, they should be provided with a wealth of materials in the classroom. Like the little girl who, when asked by her teacher what she had been doing, replied that she had been 'very busy doing nothing', creative children need time and opportunity for their own pursuits. At the same time, they also need to be encouraged to stay within the mainstream of classroom activities; they should not be allowed to become anti-social. Often the creative and gifted child is lonely; needing sympathy and human companionship more, if anything, than others. A sensitive teacher can sometimes tactfully engineer a friendship. Above all, she can be a friend herself.

Appendix of Useful Addresses

For Chapter 2   Perception and the Environment

The following firms provide excellent materials for use in the classroom and are pleased to send out catalogues on request.

E. J. Arnold Ltd
Butterley Street
Leeds
LS10 1AX
Tel: Leeds (0532) 442944
(Particularly good for materials for the nursery school.)

Philip and Tacey Ltd
North Way
Andover
Hants
SP10 5BA
Tel: Andover (0264) 61171

Galt Ltd
Brookfield Road
Cheadle
Cheshire
Tel: 061 428 8511

ESA Creative Learning Ltd
Esavian Works
Fairview Road
Stevenage
Herts
SG1 2NX
Tel: Stevenage (0438) 726383

For Chapter 3   Language and the Environment

Many teachers' journals provide pictures with the purpose of stimulating language in young children. *Child Education* can be obtained from:

Scholastic Publications (Magazines) Ltd
9 Parade
Leamington Spa
Warwickshire
CV32 4DQ
Tel: Southam (092 681) 3910

Junior Education is available from:
Subscriptions Department
Scholastic Publications (Magazines) Ltd
Westfield Road
Southam
Warwickshire
CV33 0JH

For teachers wishing to make their own books for use in the classroom, or wishing to help children make theirs, Xeroxing is the quickest method of reproducing both the written word and pictures. Write to:
Rank Xerox (UK) Ltd
Bridge House
Oxford Road
Uxbridge
Midlesex
UB8 1HS
Tel: Uxbridge (0895) 38230

There are Reading Centres all over the country. One is attached to the University of Reading. It is open throughout the year and the Tutor-in-Charge will give advice by letter or telephone, or when a teacher visits, on matters such as suitable reading material for children, and on reading problems. Write to:

The Tutor-in-Charge
Centre for the Teaching of Reading
University of Reading, School of Education
29 Eastern Avenue
Reading
RG1 5RU
Tel: Reading (0734) 62662/3

For Chapter 4   Mathematics through the Environment

The materials of Francis Evans can be obtained from:

PAVIC Publications
Sheffield City Polytechnic
Collegiate Crescent
Sheffield
Yorkshire

For ideas on mathematics trails, write to:
Town Teacher
25 Queen Street
Quayside
Newcastle-on-Tyne
NE1 3UG

Teachers will find many practical suggestions in teachers' journals. One of the most useful is *Mathematics in School*, the journal of the Mathematical Association. It is obtainable from:

Longman Group Ltd
Subscriptions (Journals) Department
Fourth Avenue
Harlow
Essex
CM19 5AA

Philograph Publications produce, among other things, colourful templates in various shapes; products are distributed by Philip and Tacey Ltd (see page 233).

For Chapter 5   History through the Environment

The Local Historian is published by the National Council for Voluntary Organisations. The address is:
National Council for Voluntary Organisations
26 Bedford Square
London
WC1B 3HU

Teaching History can be obtained from:
The Historical Association
59A Kennington Park Road
London
SE11 4JH
This Association also offers all kinds of help and advice to teachers.

The English Place-Name Society is centred at:
University College
Gower Street
London
WC1E 6BT
Write to the Honorary Secretary.

Enjoying History can be obtained from:
The Editor
Teesside Polytechnic
Flatts Lane
Normanby
Middlesbrough
Cleveland

Victorian Ordnance Survey Maps can be obtained from:
David and Charles (Holdings) Ltd
Brunel House
Newton Abbot
Devon
TQ12 4PU

For Chapter 6   Science through the Environment

The address of the Resources Centre of the Learning through Science Team is:
Resources Centre
25 Albury Street
Deptford
London
SE8 3PT

The address of Audio-Visual Productions Ltd is:
Audio-Visual Productions Ltd
Hocke Hill House
Chepstow
Gwent
NP6 5ER

For projects on pets, the following two organisations are helpful:

(i)   Pedigree Petfoods Education Centre
      Waltham on the Wolds
      Melton Mowbray
      Leicestershire
      Tel: Melton Mowbray (0664) 64171

(ii) The Universities Federation for Animal Welfare (UFAW) publishes books and proceedings of its symposia/workshops on a wide range of animal welfare topics and has inexpensive information leaflets for teachers on the care of animals (for example, cat, guinea pig, dog and so on). For a list of its publications, write to:

The Secretary
UFAW
8 Hamilton Close
South Mimms
Potters Bar
Herts
EN6 3QD

The British Butterfly Conservation Society willingly gives advice on the rearing of butterflies. Write to:

British Butterfly Conservation Society
Tudor House
Quorn
Leicestershire
LE12 8AD
Tel: Quorn (0509) 412870

The London Butterfly House not only has a display of live British butterflies, but will let members of the public have surplus stocks from time to time. Their address is:

The London Butterfly House
Syon Park
Brentford
Middlesex
Tel: 01 560 7272

For help with natural history projects, write to the Secretary of the School Natural Science Society.

Mr Williams
22 Chada Avenue
Gillingham
Kent

The Society also runs an Advisory Service for Teachers, to help with special problems and particular needs. Write to:

The Secretary
6 Pollyhawgh
Eynesford
Dartford
Kent
DA4 0HF

The RSPCA have produced a city wildlife pack, containing a number of information and worksheets, teachers' notes and ideas for projects. The address is:

RSPCA
Causeway
Horsham
West Sussex
RH12 1HG

The Royal Society for Nature Conservation markets books for children on natural history, and will also help a school set up a WATCH group in order to study all aspects of the environment. The Society is at:

The Green
Nettleham
Lincoln
LN2 2NR

The Publications Department of the Natural History Museum is an excellent source of superb, accurate colour postcards and also leaflets on many of our native animals. Materials can be ordered from the department at:

British Museum (Natural History)
Cromwell Road
London
SW7 5BD

The National Audio-Visual Aids Library hires out films on all aspects of wildlife in Britain. For example, there is a film on British carnivores and one on animals in Autumn. The address is:

NAVA Library
Paxton Place
Gipsy Road
London
SE27 9SR

Oxford Scientific Films have films on a variety of subjects. Details can be obtained from:

Oxford Scientific Films
Lower Road
Long Hanborough
Oxon
OX7 2LB
Tel: Freeland (0993) 881881

The Forestry Commission produces an enormous amount of material for schools on trees. To obtain free leaflets, such as 'A brief guide to Britain's principal trees', and inexpensive colour posters, write to:

The Forestry Commission
Information Branch (Schools)
231 Corstorphine Road
Edinburgh
EH12 7AT
Tel: Edinburgh (031) 334 0303

For free packets of seeds, and young trees for planting, enquire at the local Forestry Commission Conservancy Office.

For booklets on the creatures that depend on trees, such as birds, insects and toadstools, write to the Forestry Commission at:

Box C17
Alice Holt Lodge
Wrecclesham
Farmham
Surrey
GU10 4LH
Tel: Bentley (0420) 22255

The Royal Society for the Protection of Birds will help children set up bird study groups in and out of the classroom; it also has a film service for schools and produces leaflets and a newsletter, and runs courses for teachers.
   Write to:

The Education Officer
RSPB
The Lodge
Sandy
Bedfordshire
SG19 2DL
Tel: Sandy (0767) 80551
The Society has many regional offices, the addresses of which can be obtained by telephoning the above number.

Local rambling societies and the Countryside Commission can give guidance on nature trails. The Ramblers' Association can advise on footpaths. Its address is:

The Ramblers' Association
1–5 Wandsworth Road
London
SW8 2LJ
Tel: 01 582 6826

The Countryside Commission produces a free leaflet on the long paths of England and Wales, obtainable from:

Countryside Commission
Publications Department
19–23 Albert Street
Manchester
M19 2EQ

Of great help to teachers are the journals, *School Science Review* and *Natural Science in Schools*. The former is published by the Association for Science Education, whose address is:

Association for Science Education
College Lane
Hatfield
Herts
AL10 9AA
Tel: Hatfield (070 72) 67411

Teaching Science is published by the School Natural Science Society, and can be obtained from:

The Secretary
8 Sandy Lane
Sevenoaks
Kent

For Chapter 7   Geography through the Environment

The address of the British Orienteering Federation is:

BOF
41 Dale Road
Matlock
Derbyshire
DE4 3LT
Tel: Matlock (0629) 3661

'Maps and Mapping' and other articles are available from:

Ordnance Survey Information Branch
Ordnance Survey
Romsey Road
Maybush
Southampton

Materials for projects on homes and local communities are obtainable from:

The 'Keep Britain Tidy Group'
Bostel House
37 West Road
Brighton
West Sussex
BN1 2RE
Tel: Brighton (0273) 23585

The study pack 'Homes' is available from:

The Building Societies Association
14 Park Street
London W1
Tel: 01 629 0515

Films and Filmstrips can be hired from:

The Central Film Library
(Central Office of Information)
Government Building
Branyard Avenue
Acton
London W3

On the subject of weather, films, and filmstrips and educational materials can be obtained from the address below, as well as from the suppliers mentioned in connection with Chapter 2.

Educational Products Ltd
Bradford Road
East Ardsley
Wakefield
Yorkshire

The journal of the Geographical Association, *Teaching Geography*, is full of ideas for teachers. It is published for the Association by the Longman Group (see page 235).

Geographical Association
343 Fulwood Road
Sheffield
S10 3BP

Appendix

The *Bulletin of Environmental Education* is a valuable teaching resource for geography and science, giving advice on projects and making town trails. It can be obtained from:

'Streetwork', BEE Subscriptions
c/o Notting Dale Urban Studies Centre
189 Freston Road
London
W10 6TH

References

1 AGGERNAUS, A. and HAUGSTED, R. (1976) 'Experienced reality in three to six year old children: a study of direct reality testing', *Journal of Child Psychology*, October.

2 HM GOVERNMENT (1977) *General Household Survey*. London: HMSO.

3 OFFER, R. (1969–70) *The outdoor leisure activities of some ten-year-old children in Putney*. Academic Diploma in Education, Maria Grey College, London.

4 HESLOP, E. J. (1975) 'An investigation into the leisure pursuits of children 8–13 years', University of London Diploma in Education of Children up to Thirteen Years. Maria Grey College, London.

5 SLADE, M. E. (1965) 'An investigation into the leisure-time activities of children aged 10–11 years', University of London Diploma in Education of Children in the Junior School. Maria Grey College, London.

6 MCGRATH, K. (1975) 'Children in their own time', *Where?* August.

7 CARPENTER, G. C. *et al.* (1970) 'Differential visual behavior to human and humanoid faces in early infancy', *Merrill-Palmer Quarterly of Behavior and Development*, 16, (1).

8 TURKEWITZ, G. *et al.* (1972) 'Responsiveness to simple and complex auditory stimuli in the human new-born', *Developmental Psychology*, 5.

9 BIRNS, B. *et al.* (1965) 'Behavioral inhibition in neonates produced by auditory stimuli', *Child Development*, September.

10 TURNER, C. (1971) 'Response to voice by babies in the first year', *Developmental Psychology*, March.

11 DIRKS, J. and GIBSON, E. (1977) 'Infants' perception of similarity between live people and their photographs', *Child Development*, March.

12 DAEHLER, M. V., PELUTTER, M. and MYERS, N. A. (1976) 'Equivalence of pictures and objects for very young children', *Child Development*, March.

13 LYONS-RUTH, K. (1977) 'Bi-modal perception in infancy: response to auditory-visual incongruity', *Child Development*, September.

14 GOTTFRIED, A. W., ROSE, S. A. and BRIDGER, W. H. (1977) 'Cross-model transfer in human infants', *Child Development*, March.

15 GENTNER, D. (1977) 'Children's performance in a spatial analogies task', *Child Development*, September.

16 JOHNSON, E. G. (1977) 'The development of color knowledge in pre-school children', *Child Development*, March.

17 KELTON, J. J., HOLMES, S. K. and POLLACK, R. M. (1977) 'Visual acuity for single lines as a function of hue and age', *Child Development*, March.

18 BISHOP, A. (1979) 'Visualising and mathematics in a pre-technological culture', *Educational Studies in Mathematics*, May.

19 FRIEDMAN, W. J. and SEELY, P. B. (1976) 'The child's acquisition of spatial and temporal word meanings', *Child Development*, December.

20 SIEGEL, A. W. and SCHADLER, M. (1977) 'The development of young children's spatial representations in their classrooms', *Child Development*, June.

21 COHEN, R., BALDWIN, L. M. and SHERMAN, R. C. (1978) 'Cognitive maps of a naturalistic setting', *Child Development*, December.

22 HAZEN, N. L., LOCKMAN, H. L. and PICK, Jnr, H. L. (1978) 'The development of children's representations of large-scale environments', *Child Development*, September.

23 JAHODA, G. (1963) 'Children's concepts of time and history', *Educational Review*, 15, February.

24 LEVIN, I. (1977) 'The development of time concepts in young children: reasoning about duration', *Child Development*, September.

25 UMIKER-SEBECK, D. J. (1979) 'Pre-school children's intraconversational narratives', *Journal of Child Language*, February.

26 RODGON, M. M. (1979) 'Knowing what to say and wanting to say it: some communicative and structural aspects of single-word responses to questions', *Journal of Child Language*, February.

27 RATNER, N. and BRUNER, J. (1978) 'Games, social exchange and acquisition of language', *Journal of Child Language*, October.

28 EILERS, R. E., WILSON, W. R. and MOORE, J. M. (1979) 'Speech discrimination in the language-innocent and language-wise: a study in the perception of voice onset time', *Journal of Child Language*, February.

29 DONALDSON, M. (1979) *Children's Minds*. London: Collins/Fontana.

30 JORDAN, T. E. (1979) 'Influences on vocabulary attainment: a five-year prospective study', *Child Development*, December.

31 SCHLESINGER, I. M. (1977) 'The role of cognitive development and linguistic input in language acquisition', *Journal of Child Language*, June.

32 SHIBAMOTO, J. S. and OLMSTED, D. L. (1978) 'Lexical and syllabic patterns in phonological acquisition', *Journal of Child Language*, October.

33 ROGERS, S. (1978) 'Self-initiated corrections in the speech of infant school children', *Journal of Child Language*, June.

34 HART, N. W. M., WALKER, R. F. and GRAY, B. (1977) *The Language of Children: A Key to Literacy*. Reading, Mass.: Addison-Wesley.

35 TYACK, D. and INGRAM, D. (1977) 'Children's production and comprehension of questions', *Journal of Child Language*, June.

36 LOCKHART, K. L., ABRAHAMS, B. and OSHERSON, D. N. (1977) 'Children's understanding of uniformity in the environment', *Child Development*, December.

37 COIE, J. D. and PENNINGTON, B. F. (1976) 'Children's perceptions of deviance and disorder', *Child Development*, June.

38 COSGROVE, J. M. and PATTERSON, C. J. (1978) 'Generalisation of training for children's listener skills', *Child Development*, June.

39 UDELSON, T. A. M. (1975) Unpublished PhD thesis, Northwestern University, in ROGERS, S. (1978) 'Self-initiated corrections in the speech of infant school children', *Journal of Child Language*, June.

40 MEYER, J. S. (1978) 'Visual and verbal processes involved in the development of picture-recognition skills', *Child Development*, March.

41 CARR, T. H., BACHARACH, V. R. and MEHNER, D. S. (1977) 'Preparing children to look at pictures: advance descriptions direct attention and facilitate active processing', *Child Development*, March.

42 WOLF, T. (1977) 'Reading reconsidered', *Harvard Educational Review*, August.
43 MOON, C. and WELLS, G. (1979) 'The influences of home on learning to read', *Journal of Research in Reading*, February.
44 GROFF, P. (1977) 'Oral language and reading', *Reading World*, October.
45 JAMES, D. (1978) 'Promoting voluntary reading', *School Librarian*, June.
46 BURKE, E. (1976) 'A developmental study of children's reading strategies', *Educational Review*, November.
47 TURNER, K. (1979) 'Rhyme and reading', *Child Education*, November.
48 BRIGGS, E. (1979) 'The gifted are deprived', *Junior Education*, November.
49 VERGNAUD, G. (1979) 'The acquisition of arithmetical concepts', *Educational Studies in Mathematics*, May.
50 LIGHT, P. (1979) 'Can children stand outside themselves?', *New Society*, May.
51 BISHOP, A. (1979) 'Visualising and mathematics in a pre-technological culture', *Educational Studies in Mathematics*, May.
52 WARD, M. (1979) In 'Back to the basics in mathematics', *Education*, March.
53 ASSESSMENT OF PERFORMANCE UNIT (1980).
54 GREEN, B. and LAXTON, V. (1979) 'Stacking cups and nesting dolls', *Where?* April.
55 COWAN, R. (1979) 'Performance in number conservation tasks as a function of number of items', *British Journal of Psychology*, February.
56 SIMMONS, R. (1978) 'Colloquial mathematics', *Mathematics in School*, November.
57 LAMBERT-BRITTAIN, W. (1976) 'The effect of background shape on the ability of children to copy geometric forms', *Child Development*, December.
58 MATTHEWS, J. (1979) 'Maths from a fair', *Child Education Special*, 6.
59 COLLINGWOOD, R. (1946) *The Idea of History*. Oxford: Oxford University Press.
60 GILLIS, C. (1977) 'The English classroom 1977: a report on the English Journal readership survey', *The English Journal*, September.
61 JAHODA, G. (1963) 'Children's concepts of time and history', *Educational Review*, 15, February.
62 COLTHAM, J. B. (1960) 'Junior school children's understanding of some terms commonly used in the teaching of history', unpublished PhD thesis, in BURSTON, W. H. and THOMPSON, D. (eds) (1967) *Studies in the Nature and Teaching of History*. London: Routledge and Kegan Paul.
63 ROBERTS, M. (1972) 'History – a waste of time?', *Special Education*, December.
64 HALLAM, R. (1972) 'Thinking and learning in history', *Teaching History*, November.
65 LE FEVRE, M. (1969) 'Introducing history to young children', *Teaching History*, November.
66 COLLICOTT, S. (1979) 'Bring back the past', *Child Education*, November.
67 WINTON, M. (1973) 'History is all around us', *The Teacher*, March.
68 HENSTOCK, A. (1980) 'Town houses and Society in Georgian country towns', *The Local Historian*, May.
69 PEMBERTON, W. A. (1979) 'A parson's account book', *The Local Historian*, August.

70 BRIERLEY, V. (1976) 'James Woodforde, a Norfolk rector from 1776–1803', *Teaching History*, 1976.

71 HENDERSON, J. L. (1958) 'Jung and the living past', *British Journal of Educational Studies*, May.

72 WOODS, J. (1979) 'The concept of crime in the first half of the nineteenth century, with special reference to the organisation and administration of the two Houses of Correction in Middlesex', special study for University of London BA degree.

73 WILLOUGHBY, J., (1979) 'Public amenities of Chiswick, 1875–1911', special study for University of London BA degree.

74 TSCHIRGI, J. E. (1980) 'Sensible reasoning: a hypothesis about hypotheses', *Child Development*, March.

75 GELMAN, R., BULLOCK, M. and MEEK, E. (1980) 'Pre-schoolers' understanding of simple object transformations', *Child Development*, September.

76 HORTON, M. and MARKHAM, E. (1980) 'Developmental differences in the acquisition of basic and superordinate categories', *Child Development*, September.

77 KISTER, M. C. and PATTERSON, C. J. (1980) 'Children's concepts of the causes of illness: understanding of contagion and of immanent justice', *Child Development*, September.

78 WARD, A. (1980) 'Physics concepts from a bubble', *Natural Science in Schools*, Autumn.

79 ISENBERG, C. (1976) 'Problem solving with soap films', *School Science Review*, September.

80 MORRIS, L. (1980) 'Waves on the shore', *Natural Science in Schools*, Summer.

81 DIAMOND, D. (1979) 'Edible science', *Junior Education*, December.

82 EVANS, T. (1980) 'Switch on to science', *Junior Education*, May.

83 LOVELL, K. (1974) 'Intellectual growth and understanding science', *Studies in Science Education*, 1.

84 LAVENDER, S. (1980) 'The educational value of a derelict landscape', *Natural Science in Schools*, Summer.

85 HELBURN, N. (1979) 'An American perception of British geography', *Geography*, 64, November.

86 LAND, T. (1980) 'Late thoughts of a field-work addict', *Times Educational Supplement*, 10 October.

87 CATLING, S. J. (1979) 'Maps and cognitive maps: the young child's perception', *Geography*, November.

88 POCOCK, D. C. (1979) 'The contribution of mental maps in perception studies', *Geography*, November.

89 BAUERS, A. (1981) 'A village where old meets new', *Child Education*, May.

90 WATSON, K. (1981) 'Bridgebuilders' arts and skills', *Junior Education*, July.

91 MOLES, J. (1981) 'Classroom engineers', *Junior Education*, July.

92 NOYES, L. (1979) 'Are some maps better than others?', *Geography*, November.

93 MERRITT, T. (1980) 'Orienteering: an essential geographical pursuit', *Teaching Geography*, 3, January.

94 CAMERON, R. (1981) 'Maps and Mapping', *Pictorial Education Special*, 15.

95 JEX, S. (1980) 'Seeing what is there', *Times Educational Supplement*, 10 October.

96   CARTER, D. (1980) 'In Kentish hop-gardens: junior pupils' perceptions', *Teaching Geography*, 3, January.

97   WHITTAKER, M. (1981) 'Down to earth', *Junior Education*, May.

98   LINKE, M. (1981) 'Firm foundations', *Child Education*, May.

99   PICK, B. (1979) 'The school itself as a geographical resource', *Teaching Geography*, 1, July.

100   FITZPATRICK, J. (1979) 'Weather report', *Child Education*, September.

101   PHILIPS, B. (1980) 'The language of the sky', *Junior Education*, April.

102   PUTTICK, C. (1980) 'According to plan', *Junior Education*, June.

103   MAXWELL, A. E. (1980) *Basic Statistics in Behavioural Research*. Harmondsworth: Penguin.

104   THE OPEN UNIVERSITY (1972) Educational Studies: A Second Level Course. Personality and Learning Units 3 and 4: 'Creativity (prepared by Lee, V. and Williams, P.). Milton Keynes: Open University Press.

105   GOWAN, C. J., REMOS, G. D. and TORRANCE, E. P. (eds) (1967) 'Non-test ways of identifying the creatively gifted', in *Creativity: Its Educational Implications*. Chichester: John Wiley.

106   ROE, A. (1951) 'A psychological study of eminent biologists', *Psychological Monographs*, 65, 68 (Whole No. 331).

107   GETZELS, J. W. and JACKSON, P. W. (1962) *Creativity and Intelligence*. Chichester: John Wiley.

108   WALLACH, M. and KOGAN, N. (1965) *Modes of Thinking in Young children*. Eastbourne: Holt, Rinehart and Winston.

109   In BANKS, C. (ed.) (1965) 'Implications of research on creativity', in *Stephanos*. London: University of London Press Ltd.

Index